JACK CHRISTIE

52
BEST DAY TRIPS

from VANCOUVER

NEW EDITION

GREYSTONE BOOKS

D&M Publishers Inc.

Vancouver/Toronto/Berkeley

For Louise

Greystone Books
An imprint of D&M Publishers Inc.
2323 Quebec Street, Suite 201
Vancouver BC Canada V5T 4S7
www.greystonebooks.com

Cataloguing data available from Library and Archives Canada
ISBN 978-1-55365-597-8 (pbk.)
ISBN 978-1-55365-598-5 (ebook)

Editing by Iva Cheung
Cover design by Jessica Sullivan and Naomi MacDougall
Interior design by Peter Cocking, Jessica Sullivan and Naomi MacDougall
Cover photograph © Darrell Gulin/CORBIS
Photos by Louise Christie
Maps by Kelly Alm and David Lewis
Printed and bound in Canada by Friesens
Text printed on acid-free, 100% post-consumer paper
Distributed in the U.S. by Publishers Group West

Every attempt has been made to ensure that the information in this book
is accurate and up to date; however, the authors and publisher assume no
liability for any loss, damage, inconvenience or injury that may occur to
anyone using this book. All outdoor activities involve an element of the
unknown and thus an element of risk, and you are solely responsible for your
own safety and health at all times. Always check local conditions, know
your own limitations and consult a map.

We gratefully acknowledge the financial support of the Canada Council
for the Arts, the British Columbia Arts Council, the Province of British
Columbia through the Book Publishing Tax Credit and the Government
of Canada through the Canada Book Fund for our publishing activities.

Contents

. . . . .

LIST OF MAPS

Preface

. . . . .

WHEN THE first edition of *Day Trips from Vancouver* appeared two decades ago, it helped steer Lower Mainlanders in search of quick access to the neighbouring outdoors. What we've set out to accomplish with this edition of *52 Best Day Trips from Vancouver* is to further refine the manner in which information on a variety of activities, including new details on dog walking, is presented. Key data to assist both spur-of-the moment and long-range decision making appear at the outset of each chapter. This format helps readers quickly determine which destination best suits the amount of time at their disposal and the activities they most enjoy on a season-to-season basis. New to this edition is an activities index found at the back of the book, including wheelchair access.

In the past 40 years, the number of both local parks and recreational interests has soared; the amount of leisure time many of us have to enjoy the outdoors has not kept pace. Thus it's more important than ever that this time-honoured guide help readers become better organized and informed. With this aim in mind, distances to destinations appear at the opening of each chapter. These are calculated from the bridges that link Vancouver with the North Shore and Richmond, or from the city's eastern boundary with Burnaby.

Readers will also be able to tell at a glance which activities are best suited to each destination. Since *Day Trips from Vancouver* first appeared, in-line skating, mountain biking, kayaking and snowboarding have grown steadily in popularity, as have the more gentle pastimes of walking, birding and nature observation. Our purpose with this current edition is to provide readers with the most detailed descriptions of trails and pathways suited to each of these pursuits. For car-free city dwellers, detailed transit information, including telephone numbers and Web sites, is listed. Wherever suitable, wheelchair access is also noted with a wheelchair icon (&) at the beginning of each chapter.

Choosing which destinations to include was a difficult assignment. After all, there are hundreds of trails—such as the ambitious Sea to Sky Trail to which we devote a new chapter—plus that number again of lakes and picnic sites scattered throughout the Lower Mainland. The inventory of provincial, regional and municipal parks continues to grow; we reflect that trend with the inclusion of Coquitlam's Colony Farm Regional Park (see chapter 15) for the first time in this edition. 52 *Best Day Trips from Vancouver* isn't intended to be the most exhaustive guide to our region. It does aim to be the most comprehensive look at 19 provincial parks, 18 regional parks, 29 municipal parks and recreation trails, five conservation regions, two BC Hydro recreation sites, two Parks Canada national historic sites, three B.C. Forest Service interpretive forests, plus one outstanding county park in nearby Washington State for good measure. How did we decide? Simple. These are the places we return to time after time, season after season, and that reward us with new approaches and fresh prospects year after year.

ACKNOWLEDGEMENTS

Rob Sanders, publisher of Greystone Books, is chiefly responsible for this new endeavour. He gathered the team to make it happen, principally editor Iva Cheung, managing editor Susan Rana and designer Naomi MacDougall. Louise Christie took and organized the photographs, and David Lewis fine-tuned the maps.

Encouragement came from many quarters, including Charlie Smith, Martin Dunphy, Amanda Growe, Janet McDonald, Dan and Matt McLeod and Yolanda Stepien at the *Georgia Straight*; Mark Forsythe at CBC Radio One's *B.C. Almanac*; Jim Reis, Rob Kowalchuk, Johanna Ward and Erin Shaw at Shaw TV's *The Express*; Christina Moore, Tabetha Boot, Amber Turnau and Ryan Proctor at Whistler-Blackcomb; Janice Greenwood-Fraser, Mika Ryan, Carla Mont and Cindy Burr at the Ministry of Tourism, Culture and the Arts. Valuable assistance was provided by Bonnie Blue, Wendy DeDalt, Doug Petersen and Frieda Schade at Metro Vancouver Parks; Tiina Mack at Surrey Parks; and Katharine Steig and Alex Wallace with the Friends of Cypress Provincial Park. Special thanks to Jon Strocel of upNext Media, webmaster for jackchristie.com.

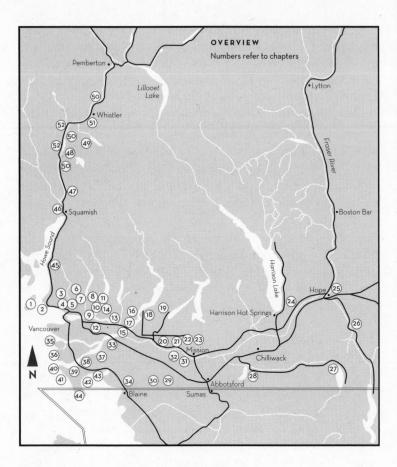

OVERVIEW
Numbers refer to chapters

LEGEND

—— Road	▲	Campground with picnic facilities	卉 Picnic site
------- Trail	(i)	Information	⋀ Mountain peak
—— Railroad	(V)	View	⊪ Dike/Dam
-·-·- Park boundary	(P)	Parking	⩔ Marsh
═══ Canada-U.S. border	(99)	Highway	⋈ Bridge
•—•—• Gate			

BOWEN ISLAND

WEST VANCOUVER

NORTH VANCOUVER

CRIPPEN REGIONAL PARK &

Bowen Island

. . . . .

> DISTANCE: 20 km (12.4 mi.) to Horseshoe Bay, northwest of Vancouver via Highway 1/99

> ACTIVITIES: Birding, dog walking, hiking, historic site, nature observation, paddling, picnicking, swimming, viewpoints, walking

> ACCESS: Drive the Upper Levels Highway (Highway 1/99) to the BC Ferries Horseshoe Bay terminal. Round-trip passenger tickets for the *Queen of Capilano* cost about $10 per person (slightly less during off-peak periods) with reduced fares for children aged 5 to 11; children younger than 5 travel free. There is an extra charge of $2 for bicycles. Call 1-888-223-3779 for sailing information or visit bcferries.com. *Note:* Allow at least 10 minutes to walk aboard from the BC Ferries ticket office. By car, the round-trip fee is $36, lower in the off-season.

Alternatively, travel to Horseshoe Bay by bus. Call West Vancouver Transit at 604-985-7777 or visit westvancouver.ca for schedule information.

For information on Crippen Regional Park, visit www.metro vancouver.org/services/parks_lscr/regionalparks/Pages/Crippen.aspx. *Note:* There are no off-leash zones in the park.

ISLANDS DEFINE British Columbia's coast. It's probably easier to guess the number of molecules of salt in a bucket of seawater than to try to add up how many islands there are along our coastline. Each island adds its own distinct note to the composition that plays out between the gulfs of Georgia and Alaska. And what an intricate tune it is.

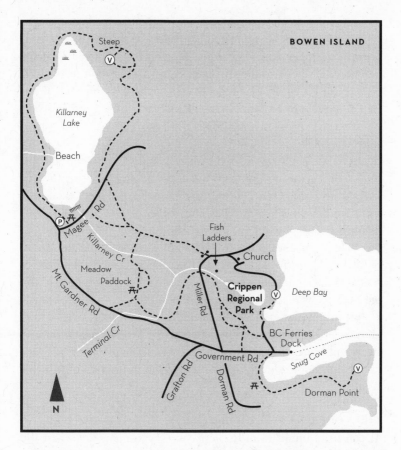

Steep

Killarney
Lake

Beach

Magee Rd

Killarney Cr

Mt Gardner Rd

Meadow
Paddock

Fish
Ladders

Church

Crippen
Regional
Park

Deep Bay

Miller Rd

Terminal Cr

BC Ferries
Dock

Grafton Rd

Government Rd

Snug Cove

Dorman Rd

Dorman Point

N

Come the sunny season, almost everyone in Vancouver contem-
plates an island adventure. If you want to sail over the bounding
main on a quick day trip, try Bowen Island. The *Queen of Capilano*
has a sheltered outdoor area for foot passengers where you can enjoy
the scenery even on a stormy day. The view of the Howe Sound
Crest mountains from the ferry's deck is one of the best reasons for
making this journey. The Lions (Two Sisters) stand out in bold relief.

Unlike most other islands served by BC Ferries, Bowen features a park as soon as you disembark. Crippen Regional Park
includes not only green spaces but also kayak rentals (visit
bowenislandkayaking.com), bakeries, curiosity shops, cafés, pubs
and the restored Union Steamship Company store, all clustered

3

around the dock. Head for a large map of the island situated on the store's lawn to orient yourself. The decision you'll face upon your arrival in Crippen Park will be how much of it to explore. For many people, the 1-hour round-trip ferry ride is an adventure in itself. *Note*: Bowen is a hilly island; count on a challenging bike ride if you want to explore more than Crippen Park.

> ## SNUG COVE

Before provincially owned BC Ferries assumed command in 1960, the Union Steamship Company was a going concern during the first half of the 20th century, bringing thousands of visitors each summer to its Bowen Island resort at Snug Cove and Deep Bay. Spacious picnic grounds for company outings and games, a lighted waterfront promenade, beaches, a dance hall, a hotel, cottages and the Union Steamship Company store made it as complete a recreation destination as Whistler is today, though on a more modest scale. Stop by the old store—now renovated as an information centre—to learn more.

Just minutes away from the ferry dock on the west side of Snug Cove are a wide beach and the open fields of the picnic grounds. A steep trail leads up the hill on the far side of the picnic area to Dorman Point. Look down from here for a vivid illustration of why this is called Snug Cove.

> ## KILLARNEY LAKE TRAIL

As you head uphill from the ferry on Government Road past the Union Steamship store, a trail marked with a green Metro Vancouver Regional Parks signpost leads off to the right to Killarney

> ## BIDE-A-WEE

. . . .

IF YOU follow past the Union Steamship Co. Marina along Lady Alexandra Promenade, you will pass two diminutive cabins, a floating guest cottage and Doc Morgan's Inn that remain from the Union Steamship days. If you become enchanted with Bowen, you can arrange an overnight stay. Call 604-947-0707 for rates or visit www.ussc.ca.

Snug Cove, Bowen Island

Lake. Allow 45 minutes to walk one way, half that by bike. Secondary growth closes in overhead, but the path is wide and welcoming. Within several minutes the trail passes Terminal Creek, which falls down a sharp embankment and into a lagoon beside Deep Bay. Two fish ladders climb the rocky canyon beside the creek. There is a small hatchery on the west side of Miller Road from which the returning salmon were originally released. Coho and possibly cutthroat trout may be seen running the fish ladders in October and November.

The fish ladders themselves have a pleasingly uniform design, and it's not hard to imagine the salmon jostling for position to leap from step to step. In winter, with snow outlining the ladders and daylight filtering through leafless trees, this is a photographer's playground. A narrow lagoon opens into the ocean at the bottom of the canyon. Walk down over the rocks to look out at groups of ducks and geese feeding in this backwater.

The trail continues for a short distance beyond the fish ladders, leading up to Miller Road. A yellow gate marks the entrance to the Killarney Lake Trail, just before the road passes Saint Gerard's Church. Killarney Lake is a 30-minute walk from here, half that by bike. The first third of the trail is on level ground, then it begins to rise gently through second-growth forest. Huge stumps are everywhere.

At the halfway point to Killarney Lake, Meadow Trail leads off to the left and across a small bridge over Terminal Creek. If you take this path, you'll discover that a short way along, meadows open up one after another. In one is an exercise paddock for horses. Just beyond the paddock, the trail links up with Mount Gardner Road, which leads back left to the ferry or right to the lake. Island residents often gather around the paddock. A picnic table stands under spreading trees nearby.

The main trail continues from the halfway point towards the lake, linking with Magee Road just before it reaches the shoreline. Bear left at this junction. Follow Magee as it drops down to the lake, and watch for the sign indicating the start of the lake trail. Almost immediately you will see the concrete dam that controls the water level of the lake. There is a small swimming area here and, a short distance beyond, picnic tables in the cool shelter of a fir tree grove.

The going is easy around the north side of the lake, where the ground is level. A short walk or ride leads to a developed gravel beach where a small creek flows into the lake. In summer the waters of Killarney Lake are warm enough for swimming. If you've come to Bowen by car with a canoe or kayak, this is a good place to launch. There is parking beside the picnic area. From here, trail access is restricted to those on foot.

Past the beach the trail begins to climb slightly, then joins a boardwalk that crosses the marsh at the far end of the lake. The steepest and roughest parts of the trail are here where the hillside rises, providing several good viewpoints of the lake and Mount Gardner, Bowen Island's highest point (760 m/2,500 ft.). Rustic benches, hewn from some of the old stumps at trailside, line the way until the trail links up once more with Magee Road. Allow an hour to circle the lake.

Bowen's population swells in summer, but in the off-season months, Metro Vancouver's 240-ha (593-acre) Crippen Park is a quiet haven. Although the park is irregularly shaped, all of the trails around Snug Cove, including those leading to and around Killarney Lake, are part of the park. Walk the trails while leaves float gently down and crunch underfoot in autumn. Enjoy the winter wonderland feeling after a snowfall. Catch the first hint of spring as skunk cabbage blooms in a forest where views are not yet obstructed by the foliage of a new season.

Although you don't need to take a car to Bowen, if you drive to Horseshoe Bay, you will have to find a place to park within walking distance of the ferry. If there are two adults in your party and you have much baggage, such as a stroller, consider dropping off one adult with the youngsters at the BC Ferries foot passenger entrance on Bay Street. Pay parking is usually available near the ferry terminal, except on long weekends, when it may be necessary to find space uphill under the Highway 99 overpass on Marine Drive, across from Gleneagles Golf Course. On long weekends, a local service group rents out spots immediately under the off-ramp to Horseshoe Bay on Marine Drive. Otherwise, there is free parking farther south on Marine in a large cleared area.

LIGHTHOUSE AND
WHYTECLIFF PARKS

. . . . .

> **DISTANCE:** 20 km (12.4 mi.) northwest of Vancouver, in West Vancouver

> **ACTIVITIES:** Dog walking, hiking, picnicking, playground, rock scrambling, scuba diving, swimming, viewpoints, walking

> **ACCESS:** Take the Upper Levels Highway (Highway 1/99) through West Vancouver to Horseshoe Bay Village. Alternately, follow Marine Drive. Lighthouse Park is located just south of Marine Drive a short distance east of Horseshoe Bay. The turnoff is prominently marked by a wooden sign. Turn south on Beacon Lane to reach the parking lot. A wooden bus shelter is also located here. After a short stroll or drive through a residential neighbourhood, you reach the parking lot. There is regular bus service from Park Royal Shopping Centre to Horseshoe Bay and Lighthouse Park; take the #250 Horseshoe Bay. Call West Vancouver Transit at 604-985-7777 for schedule information or visit westvancouver.ca.

The way to Whytecliff Marine Park, at the western end of Marine Drive, is well marked at all major intersections.

> **LIGHTHOUSE PARK**

Lighthouse Park's towering Douglas-fir trees are the sort of treat that somehow you don't expect to find this close to the city. They represent one of the last stands of unlogged forest in the Lower Mainland (aside from the local watersheds). The reason for their protected status is directly related to the lighthouse, strategically perched atop the rocky outcropping of Point Atkinson at the northern entrance to

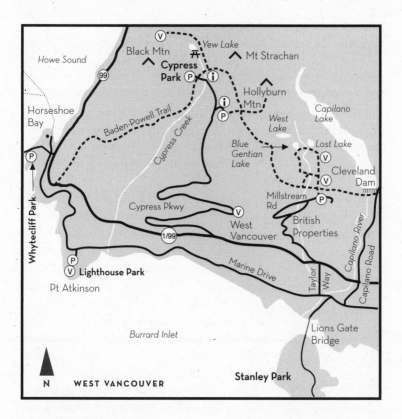

Burrard Inlet; the forest was preserved as a dark background to contrast with the lighthouse's beacon.

At the park's entrance at the south end of Beacon Lane, next to a yellow gate and a bicycle rack, an interpretive sign offers a large map of the park as well as some natural-history notes. A concise map of park trails is also available here for visitors to carry with them. Dogs are permitted off leash in Lighthouse Park provided they are under voice control.

Walk past the yellow gate and downhill along the paved service road or forest trail to the lighthouse. You'll be there in an easy 10 minutes. Along the way, the dimensions of the forest rapidly change. Suddenly, there are trees large enough to build an entire house out of—and occasionally they'll be leaning your way just enough to make you say a prayer of deliverance should you find yourself here in a windstorm. If you want to see nature in a state of high arousal, venture through here then, but be wary.

Phyl Munday House and a collection of cabins once used to house conscripts during World War II appear just before the lighthouse. Munday and her husband, Don, were ardent alpinists who explored the unknown wilderness of the Coast Mountains between 1920 and 1949. Munday was one of the first to scale 4 044-m-high (13,260-ft.-high) Mount Waddington, B.C.'s loftiest peak. West Vancouver Girl Guides tend Munday House, which is open on Sundays from 2 P.M. to 4 P.M.

There are good viewpoints over Burrard Inlet on either side of the lighthouse. A well-worn rocky trail winds its way above the shoreline in the trees, leading to East and West beaches. East Beach is the more sheltered of the two. West Beach is a great place to stretch out on the smooth rock face that slopes gently down to the often-agitated waters off Point Atkinson. There's protected swimming in a narrow bay. The lighthouse rises dramatically on the rocks beside the bay, and you get glimpses of freighters and the outer harbour beyond.

Point Atkinson boasts one of the oldest lighthouses on the West Coast; the first keeper took up residence here in the late 1880s. The lighthouse was automated in the 1990s.

The lighthouse stands in solitary splendour on a rocky promontory, just beyond the dense virgin forest with its thick undergrowth of ferns and berry bushes. The arches of the UBC Museum of Anthropology are visible above the cliffs of Point Grey across Burrard Inlet to the south. Scramble out onto the most seaward perch and look back at Burrard Bridge and False Creek, English Bay and Stanley Park. All that civilized expanse was, until relatively recent times, clothed in forest like that here in Lighthouse Park.

On calm summer days, the waters around the point become more tranquil, making it a quiet place to take in a sunset. A constant parade of boats of all shapes, sizes and speeds streams into Burrard Inlet from Howe Sound and Bowen Island. Walk west towards Jackpine Point, taking care on the rocks that line the undulating trail as it makes its way through the forest. Views of the nearby ocean can be distracting. After a long summer day, the warm rocks or a sturdy arbutus tree trunk make perfect backrests for watching the sun drop behind Bowen, with Lasqueti Island in the far distance. At other seasons, this can be a powerfully dramatic theatre for storm watching.

Circle back towards the parking lot from Jackpine Point. Small wooden benches with tables fashioned from old stumps sit beside the trail in places. Some substantial trees grow along here, particularly in one section where the trail climbs through a grove of amabilis fir, past rock walls and boulders covered with moss and licorice ferns. Plan on taking at least an hour to walk the circuit from the parking lot to the lighthouse, out to Jackpine Point and back to your car or the nearby bus shelter.

Other trails crisscross through the woods. Several of the trails that begin to the left of the yellow gate at the south end of the parking lot quickly lead to the park's high point, a knoll whose open summit offers a bird's-eye view of the majesty of the Douglas-fir forest. For a detailed map of park trails, visit westvancouver.ca/uploaded Files/Parks_and_Environment/Parks/LHP_Hiking_Trail_Map.pdf.

> **WHYTECLIFF MARINE PARK**

Whytecliff Marine Park is ideal for a quick visit to the rugged ocean shore. With its easy access to the water, you can find an hour or two's exploration when you're in need of a quick getaway under, on or near the water. If you're in no hurry, enjoy the scenic route by taking Marine Drive all the way to the park from the Lions Gate Bridge, rather than taking the Upper Levels Highway. As you make your way along the pebble beach in Whytecliff Marine Park, you may see scuba divers who have come to experience a little weightlessness in the netherworld just offshore, where the year-round cold temperatures matter little, provided you dress appropriately.

Very little of the true nature of the park is revealed when you first arrive. It all looks rather sedate and well ordered: rolling lawns beneath spreading limbs of cedar and oak, a children's playground and a covered picnic area just inside the park entrance. *Note:* Although dogs are welcome in Whytecliff, they are allowed off leash only on the trails on the east side of Marine Drive.

Although not as large as nearby Lighthouse Park, Whytecliff is surprisingly big and certainly has enough room for visitors to find a secluded spot in which to relax most times of the year. Come summer, the crowds increase noticeably.

In 1993, Whytecliff Park was designated as Canada's first Salt Water Marine Protected Area. This means that nothing in this West Vancouver municipal park may be disturbed: there is to be no harvesting of any marine life beneath the waters of the park. Although B.C. has created dozens of marine parks, there is very limited protection for the marine life within them. In effect, what has been created at Whytecliff is an underwater sanctuary, which conservationists hope will inspire extended protection in other marine parks, as happened recently in Gwaii Haanas National Park in Haida Gwaii (Queen Charlotte Islands).

Upwards of 200 animal species call these waters home and Whytecliff Park has become a magnet for local divers over the years. If you don't try diving, you see only half of what's on offer, particularly at night, when the ocean comes alive. That's when divers get to examine shy octopi and rock fish caught in their lantern beams. The good news is that there's nothing dangerous or even aggressive in local waters: sea lions are big and frisky, but that's as risky as the depths get. Care to see for yourself? Popular dive groups include the UBC Aqua Society, whose membership is open to the general public as well as students (604-822-3329; diveubc.com) and Rowand's Reef Scuba Shop (604-669-3483; rowandsreef.com).

For those who like to experience the extremes exhibited by nature at stormy times of year, Whytecliff provides exposure to the elements in a safe environment. On windy days, pull up your hood and walk down to the narrow cove, where a bench awaits. Stretch your legs along the wide expanse of beach. A rocky bar lies exposed at low tide, leading out to Whyte Islet. Clambering up its steep slopes is harder than it appears from shore. Far easier is to scramble around on the cliffs from which the park takes its name and find a sheltered spot beneath a lone shore pine. There you can find repose without having to constantly check the progress of the tide, which might otherwise cut off your escape route from the island.

Follow one of the rough but well-trodden trails that run along the

Burrard Inlet from Lighthouse Park

top of the cliffs. Small sets of rock stairways lead here and there. In various places signs have been installed, explaining the variety of marine life to be found beneath the waves. Although you have to take most of it on faith, occasional life forms do bob to the surface, such as the head of a curious seal or river otter.

> 3

CYPRESS PROVINCIAL PARK &

. . . . .

> DISTANCE: 17 km (10.5 mi.) from the Lions Gate Bridge, in West Vancouver

> ACTIVITIES: Dog walking, hiking, mountain biking, nature observation, picnicking, snow sports, viewpoints, walking

> ACCESS: Take Cypress Bowl Road (Cypress Parkway) from the Upper Levels Highway (Highway 1/99) at Exit 8, via an 8-km (5-mi.) paved highway. See West Vancouver map, page 9. In winter, Cypress Mountain runs a shuttle bus from Park Royal Shopping Centre. Call 604-926-5612 or visit cypressmountain.com for details. *Note:* There are no off-leash dog areas in the park, and dogs are not permitted on backcountry trails.

With OVER a million visitors a year, Cypress Park in West Vancouver is the most popular provincial park in B.C. Stop on the drive to or from the 3 012-ha (7,443-acre) park to admire the views of the Lower Mainland and Washington State from both the Highview viewpoint and the nearby Quarry picnic grounds. These vistas, along with the park's proximity to the city and its easily accessible trails, account for Cypress's attraction with the public.

Although most visitors ride up on four wheels, others make do with two, sometimes with a pair of skis strapped to the bicycle frame. On the way to the top, there are four major switchbacks. You'll usually see cars parked near each one. The Highview viewpoint is at the second of the switchbacks. There is ample parking here, an interpretive sign that identifies the geographical landmarks laid out before your eyes, and six picnic tables.

The Lions (Two Sisters) from Black Mountain

Just above the third switchback are two rough entrances to trails on the lower slopes of Hollyburn Mountain. The well-marked turnoff to the Hollyburn cross-country and toboggan centre and its parking lot is located farther uphill. The Cypress Bowl downhill area is just a short drive past the Hollyburn turnoff. Since 1985, commercial operations in the park have been run by a private company, Cypress Bowl Recreation Limited, which leases a fifth of the park's total area, including the alpine runs on Black Mountain and Mount Strachan, plus the Nordic and toboggan trails on Hollyburn. (In recent years, Cypress Bowl management has confusingly rebranded itself as Cypress Mountain, despite the fact that a mountain bearing the same name lies north of Squamish.) As the site of the Vancouver 2010 Winter Games' freestyle skiing and snowboarding events, Cypress Park benefited from the construction of the new three-storey timber-framed Cypress Creek Lodge, which houses all services in on building with ski-in/ski-out chairlift access.

Long before chairlifts came to Cypress, alpine skiers, ski jump-ers and cross-country skiers enjoyed the terrain on adjacent Holly-burn Mountain. In the 1920s and '30s, as many skiers trekked out around West Lake as do today. Hollyburn is the only one of the three mountains within Cypress Park that has not been extensively logged. Hence, one of Hollyburn's unique features is that it has the last accessible stand of old-growth western hemlock in the Lower Mainland between Garibaldi Park and Chilliwack. Add to this the fact that upper reaches of the mountains have not been touched by forest fires in the past one to four millennia, and you have an ecolog-ical area that many people passionately wish to preserve. Rings on a stump atop Mount Strachan indicated that the tree was nearly 1,200 years old when cut in 1988 as part of a previous expansion.

> **HOLLYBURN RIDGE**

Hollyburn Mountain is best known for its popular cross-country ski trails; however, Nordic activities take up at most half the calendar. The rest of the year, hiking boots make their mark on the trails that crisscross the slopes below the mountain's 1 325-m (4,350-ft.) peak. Hollyburn's companions, Mount Strachan to the north and Black Mountain to the west, stand at 1 454 m (4,770 ft.) and 1 217 m (3,993 ft.), respectively. Hollyburn's unlogged summit allows unimpeded views of the mountain ranges to the north, for the most part not vis-ible from Vancouver. You can hike to the summit in less than 2 hours.

A kiosk at the trailhead on the east side of the parking lot features a detailed diagram of trails on Hollyburn. It also lays out a sensible approach to exploring all wilderness settings: dress warmly, always let someone know where you're going and when you can reason-ably be expected back and never hike the mountains alone. *Note:* At almost any time of the year, you'll find water running in the rocky creekbeds that double as trails on the mountain. Waterproof foot-wear is advisable but not absolutely necessary.

From the cross-country parking lot, head uphill underneath the hydro lines to the warming hut beside Third Lake. Watch for the open ski runs through the forest, with their names—Burfield, Sitzmark, Telemark, Wells Gray—posted high in the trees. A trail marker beside the warming hut, announcing the approach to

Hollyburn Mountain, bears a map of the area and a summary of distances and times. Once you set out, you'll find that the trail divides after about 15 minutes, with the Hollyburn Trail heading straight ahead and the Baden-Powell Trail branching off west towards the parking lot at Cypress Bowl, a 40-minute journey. The hike to the top of Hollyburn from this divide takes another 50 minutes. Signs of summer manicuring are typically evident in places along upper parts of the trail, wider portions of which are brushed out to ensure that telemark skiers and snowshoers don't have to wait long to get going once winter arrives. Until the snow flies, the trail, which offers breathtaking views of the Lions from Hollyburn's peak, welcomes hikers. Although the route is boggy in places, a few mud holes hardly present much of a challenge. In fact, it might even encourage people to wear hiking boots instead of runners when going into the mountains and thus prevent accidents such as broken ankles.

Aside from a series of small lakes, the forest shields almost everything else from view, allowing you to concentrate on your footing. As on many of the trails on Hollyburn, much of the route is over exposed roots around the base of the sturdy firs. (On the way down, you'll be treated to views galore out over the Fraser estuary as far south as Boundary Bay.) Along the trail, you'll frequently catch sight of Hollyburn's beckoning summit, surmounted by a dense crown of old growth. Late in the summer, berry bushes line the way. Stretch out your hand with a piece of energy bar, and almost immediately you'll have a grey jay, or whiskey jack, eating out of your palm.

Just before the final ascent, where the going does get tricky in several places owing to rocks made slippery by running water or ice, a charming viewpoint appears, with a rustic bench. It's well situated for catching your breath—and the geographical display. The sides of Hollyburn drop away into the Capilano Valley, hidden below. Rising vertically to the north and east are the walls of Grouse Mountain and its companions; in the distance are the peaks and ridges of Coliseum and Seymour mountains. Although the view from the top is more panoramic, it somehow can't match this setting. Must be the bench.

The actual peak of Hollyburn is open and rocky, an encouragement in the last 10 minutes of the hike when you can see the sky beginning to appear above you, no longer masked by trees. Steps and ropes offer assistance to ascend the last steep rock section before the top, which is only several footsteps beyond. It feels as good to have accomplished this climb as it would if you'd mastered any other significant peak, a reminder that everyone has her or his own Everest within. From the summit, you can look west to Mount Strachan, past Black Mountain to the waters of Howe Sound and over to Gibsons on the Sunshine Coast in the distance.

A rough, steep trail leads from the summit of Hollyburn to Mount Strachan. I recommend that, rather than attempt this traverse, you retrace your steps to the warming hut; if you've still got strength in your legs, walk down the Wells Gray Trail to First Lake or follow the Mobraaten Trail to its intersection with the Grand National Trail, and around on Grand National to West Lake. Both Wells Gray and Mobraaten start from the warming hut, and both intersect with Grand National. Part of an old chairlift can still be seen at the north end of West Lake.

To experience the flavour of the original development on Hollyburn begun in the 1920s, be sure to return to the parking lot on the Burfield Trail, which passes beside a nest of old cabins and the Hollyburn Ski Camp Lodge. In winter, trails around the Hollyburn Ski Camp Lodge are brightly lit at night and provide plenty of opportunity for a workout on skis or snowshoes long after dark. On Tuesday evenings, there's no more remarkable sight than colourfully clad cross-country skiers gathered for sprint races, their bodies steaming under the lights like race horses at Hastings Park.

> **CYPRESS BOWL**

Cypress Bowl presents an opportunity for visitors to make easy, moderate or extensive explorations of the park. A short, 1.5-km (0.9-mi.) interpretive trail leads from the parking lot to nearby Yew Lake. (Cypress Creek originates in the marshy wetland surrounding this lake.) This trail has been built with wheelchair access in mind. Yellow cypress trees, from which the park takes its name, ring the little lake. Most stunning of all here in the ancient "snow forest" are the amabilis fir, western and mountain hemlock and yellow-cedar on the Old Growth Loop Trail that leads from Yew Lake's north end into the surrounding forest.

Those with more time and energy to burn can hike trails that ascend Black Mountain to its summit, a 30-minute climb, or head north along the newly upgraded Howe Sound Crest Trail—another 2010 Winter Games legacy—towards the Lions and the provincial park at Porteau Cove (see chapter 45), a one- or two-day trek. Even if you don't intend to go all the way to the Lions (Two Sisters) on this trail, several viewpoints including the new Bowen Lookout lead up to St. Marks Summit, 5.5 km (3.4 mi.) from Cypress Bowl. Along the way, you'll be treated to a view of the Lions from Strachan Meadows (2.6 km/1.6 mi.) and then of Howe Sound at St. Marks Summit. Snow may cover parts of this trail, especially at higher elevations, well into July. North of St. Marks the trail deteriorates as it approaches aptly named Unnecessary Mountain.

Other trails to pursue in Cypress Park include the Black Mountain Plateau Trail, a moderately difficult, 2.5-km (1.6-mi.), 2-hour tour of the mountain's subalpine meadows and pocket lakes with a terrific viewpoint on top. The loop trail ties in with the Yew Lake Trail, both of which begin at the base of the Black Mountain chairlift.

A section of the Baden-Powell Trail leads from the parking lot at the top of the Cypress Parkway across Black Mountain to Horseshoe Bay. That's a long, challenging 12-km (7.5-mi.) haul, one you needn't contemplate if you just set your sights on staying within park

> ## LODGED IN MEMORIES

. . . .

IN 1926, when the Hollyburn Ski Club—Vancouver's oldest—first converted a former logging camp cookhouse into a warming lodge, the snowline almost reached Burrard Inlet. The following year, there was so little white stuff that horses were used to haul the Hollyburn Ski Camp Lodge to its present location at an elevation of 930 m (3,051 ft.) on Hollyburn Mountain. Ironically, snowfall the subsequent season was so deep that skiers had to dig their way down through the drifts to reach the lodge's entrance. At least the lodge had found a good home—one that has served skiers and snowshoers alike in the intervening eight decades.

Howe Sound from Mount Strachan

boundaries. Fold into the mix the prospect of a dip in one of several lakes that ring Black Mountain's twin summits, spice it up with several panoramic viewpoints, and you've got the makings of a great day-trip recipe. And if the thought of sweltering in the summer heat is just too daunting, consider that the best time to make this trip is later in the afternoon when most of the trail is cloaked in cool shade. Given the open and dusty nature of the first several kilometres of the route, that's a good thing indeed.

Before hitting the trail between April and October, it's important to take care of a piece of business—the parking fee: currently $1 for 1 hour, $5 for the entire day. Revenue collected from the parking fees goes directly into BC Parks coffers to maintain facilities and services.

With your head appropriately covered and plenty of water at hand, follow the well-marked Baden-Powell Trail as it leads uphill past the sites of the 2010 Winter Olympic freestyle skiing and snowboarding events.

Birdsongs and colourful wildflowers work wonders in distracting one's thoughts from the initial tedium of this hike. After three switchbacks, the Baden-Powell Trail none too soon veers into the forest adjacent the top of the Black Mountain chairlift where a fine prospect of the Lions (Two Sisters) presents itself. From this point a single-track, rock-and-roots trail leads downhill towards a series of sienna-hued lakes and tarns, the largest and most popular of which is Cabin Lake.

I prefer the privacy afforded by some of the smaller ponds, the shorelines of which are only fleetingly glimpsed from the trail. You'll find that access to some, such as the chain of Cougar Lakes, is easy. Even though a modicum of bushwhacking is involved, most of the ground cover is red- and white-blossomed mountain-heather, much smoother on the skin than first appears. In fact, walking barefoot across mountain-heather produces a skin-tingling sensation similar to a pumice treatment.

You're most likely to spot juncos, varied thrushes or even industrious woodpeckers while sitting quietly at the shoreline. Tops of old snags in the surrounding forest are the perches of choice for a goodly number of songbirds whose cheerful and melodic voices far outweigh their diminutive sizes. Closer at hand, the heather blossoms are the targets of bumblebees, moths and flies, though none of the stinging variety. Marsh marigolds floating on the surfaces of the lakes open their buttery blossoms to the sky. The warmer the day, the headier the aroma given off by the predominately evergreen forest. The oxygenated air it exudes tastes as rich and thick as cereal cream.

No trip to Black Mountain would be complete without standing atop at least one of its twin summits. Cabin Lake lies in the saddle between the two. Conveniently placed boardwalks lead around wetter sections of the trail. From the south summit, an even more startling view of the Lions (Two Sisters) appears than that glimpsed earlier on, just one part of a panorama that encompasses all of the geography on the south coast: the snow-capped Tantalus Range; Howe Sound and the Strait of Georgia; the southern Gulf and San Juan islands; Metro Vancouver and the Fraser Valley; and, most resplendent of all, Mount Baker. That's enough to inspire a song out of almost any viewer, avian or otherwise. Just as strikingly, it makes one wonder if it's possible to enjoy a more bird's-eye view of Vancouver, short of an out-of-body experience.

For more information and to view a detailed map of Cypress Park, visit www.env.gov.bc.ca/bcparks/explore/parkpgs/cypress.html. In addition, see the Friends of Cypress Provincial Park's Web site: cypresspark.bc.ca

> 4

BROTHERS CREEK TRAIL

. . . . .

> DISTANCE: 3 km (1.9 mi.) north of the Lions Gate Bridge, in West Vancouver

> ACTIVITIES: Dog walking, hiking, picnicking, swimming, viewpoints, walking

> ACCESS: From the Lions Gate Bridge via Marine Drive, go to the north end of Taylor Way, then west (left) on Southborough Road to Eyremount Drive in the British Properties neighbourhood. Follow Eyremount to Millstream Road, then turn east (right). The trailhead lies on the north (left) side of Millstream and is prominently marked by a large wooden signpost (see West Vancouver map, page 9). There is room in front of the yellow gate for several cars to park. Nearby is a bus stop. The #254 British Properties bus leaves from Park Royal Shopping Centre. Call West Vancouver Transit at 604-985-7777 or visit westvancouver.ca for schedule information.

THESE DAYS it seems there can't be much of the North Shore that hasn't been walked through at least once. At the beginning of the 20th century there was no such certainty: when the little settlement of Ambleside was hardly more than a few cabins in size, residents had to guess at the origins of several creeks that flowed into the Capilano River from on high.

By the 1920s, at least four creeks in the region came to be known as Sisters Creek. Speculation had it that each could trace its headwaters to the runoff from the Two Sisters, the twin peaks that the non-Native community calls the Lions. Finally, a provincial-park survey team determined that Sisters Creek ought to be the small, rather insignificant stream that flows into the north end of Capilano Lake

Brothers Creek Trail

(now off-limits to the public, as it is in the restricted Greater Vancouver Water District). The remaining streams were rechristened. One of the larger ones became Brothers Creek, which empties into the Capilano River (see next chapter).

An enthralling series of trails follows Brothers Creek on the mountainside above the British Properties. A reward in summer for overheated hikers are two small lakes near the creek's origins.

Depending on your time and hiking companions, a visit to Brothers Creek can last anywhere from an hour to half a day. With the network of trails around the creek, it's possible to tailor a visit here to fit any circumstance and any age group.

A rocky old fire road serves as the beginning of the 5-km (3-mi.) Brothers Creek Trail, no matter which circuit you attempt. In a matter of minutes, tall trees close in around you, shutting out all signs of the city until your return. Soon, only an occasional sound will float up from the world you've left behind. Almost immediately, the past will rise to greet you. Thick wooden planks used in the construction

Lost Lake, West Vancouver

of skid roads are still evident in places. They are studded with heavy spikes and act as reminders, along with some enormous cedar stumps sprinkled throughout the forest, of the logging activity here 85 years ago.

A choice of routes soon presents itself, including remaining on the fire road that leads up the east side of Brothers Creek. Three bridges cross Brothers Creek, approximately 20 minutes' walk apart. If your time is limited, follow the soft and mostly level Baden-Powell Trail west to the first of these. The trail parallels a power line and crosses several small boardwalks. Watch for a tall snag that stands out above the forest just as the trail begins its descent to quaint First Bridge. The round trip to this point is 1 hour.

From First Bridge, Brothers Creek Trail climbs beside the creek's west bank, with staircases built into the slope to assist you. A number of sheltering western red cedars of astonishing girth stand on the west side of the creek, silent testimony that some of the largest trees on the West Coast grow in the nearby Capilano and Seymour watersheds, restricted areas since the 1920s.

If you circle back over Second Bridge, rejoining the fire road, you will have had a brief but stimulating 2-hour introduction to the area. Along the way between Second Bridge and the fire road is a stand of old-growth fir trees. These escaped the saw blade because they were too tall for early loggers to handle. Though not as dramatic as the fir and cedar higher up the slope near Third Bridge, they are still mighty impressive.

If you have another hour or two at your disposal, there's a most rewarding adventure in store. After climbing up the fire road or the trail beside Brothers creek to Third Bridge, follow the trail markers to Blue Gentian Lake. This small lake lies on the west side of the creek, a half-hour above Third Bridge. Lily pads dot its surface and, in truth, it more closely resembles a pond than a lake. Small Stoney Creek can be heard nearby.

To complete a circle trip, follow an older trail that cuts east across both Stoney and Brothers creeks to Lost Lake. Somewhat larger and more inviting, it takes 20 minutes of up-and-downing to reach. If it's a warm day, have a swim in the fresh water under the open sky. A shorter approach to Lost Lake runs from Third Bridge: simply follow the trail on the east side of Brothers Creek, about 15 minutes one way. One of the rewards of hiking the circle route to both lakes is the view of the upper falls on Brothers Creek that appears only between the two.

Across the fire road below Third Bridge are the tallest stands of trees on the entire journey. Some of the firs and cedars measure 2.4 m (8 ft.) in diameter. Many have had their tops snapped off, but green life persists in the remaining branches.

Brothers Creek is a perfect spot to escape the heat of the day or the falling rain, so well does its canopy of trees shelter visitors. The forest swallows you up, and it's not until you return to the trailhead that the city intrudes on your consciousness once more.

The West Vancouver Historical Society, in cooperation with the District of West Vancouver and the West Vancouver Museum and Archives, publishes a detailed map and forestry heritage walking guide to Brothers Creek entitled "Shakes, Shinglebolts and Steampots." For a free copy, contact Parks and Community Services, 604-925-7200.

5

CAPILANO RIVER TRAILS &

. . . . .

> DISTANCE: 1 to 7.5 km (0.6 to 5 mi.) from the Lions Gate Bridge, depending on starting point, in West and North Vancouver

> ACTIVITIES: Dog walking, fishing, hiking, nature observation, picnicking, viewpoints, walking

> ACCESS: Almost all of the Capilano River's west bank and forest perimeter is included in a regional park, a length of over 7 km (4.3 mi.). The quickest approach to the river's west side is from several park trailheads in West Vancouver. Good places to begin are at the mouth of the Capilano River at the south end of Taylor Way on Clyde Road. Walk east to the river and the Capilano-Pacific Trail—the river's major route, which also connects with the Park Royal Shopping Centre and Ambleside Park.

The upper section of the Capilano-Pacific Trail begins north of the Upper Levels Highway (Highway 1/99). To find it, follow Keith Road east off Taylor Way and park on either side of the underpass beneath the Upper Levels Highway.

To reach Capilano River Regional Park by bus from downtown Vancouver, catch a West Vancouver Transit bus to Park Royal Shopping Centre and begin exploring on the Capilano-Pacific Trail nearby. A Grouse Mountain (#236) bus from North Vancouver's Lonsdale Quay will drop you at the parking lot and picnic area beside the Cleveland Dam on Capilano Road. Call TransLink, 604-953-3333, for bus numbers and schedules, or visit their Web site at translink.ca.

HUGGING THE Capilano River's banks are numerous well-marked trails. Much of this 26-km (16-mi.) network is concentrated on both sides of the river below the Cleveland Dam. That's a lot of ground to cover; be selective when planning a visit. Note: Dogs must be on leash at all times in this park.

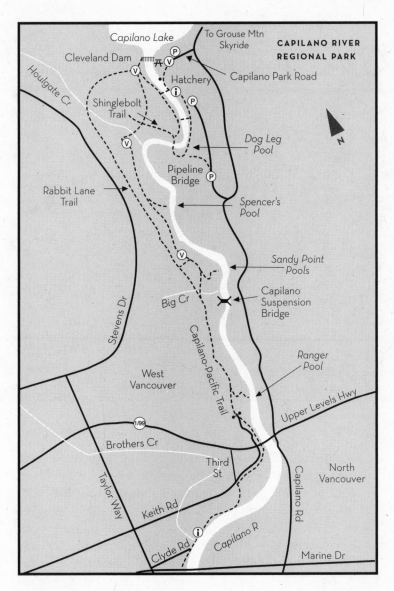

Capilano Lake

To Grouse Mtn Skyride

CAPILANO RIVER REGIONAL PARK

Cleveland Dam

Hatchery

Capilano Park Road

Shinglebolt Trail

Dog Leg Pool

Houlgate Cr

Pipeline Bridge

Rabbit Lane Trail

Spencer's Pool

Sandy Point Pools

Capilano Suspension Bridge

Big Cr

Stevens Dr

Capilano-Pacific Trail

Ranger Pool

West Vancouver

Upper Levels Hwy

1/99

Brothers Cr

Third St

North Vancouver

Taylor Way

Keith Rd

Capilano Rd

Clyde Rd

Capilano R

Marine Dr

N

> **CAPILANO-PACIFIC TRAIL**

The Capilano-Pacific Trail is Capilano River Regional Park's most popular route and runs 7.5 km (4.7 mi.) between the ocean and the Cleveland Dam. The trail is mostly level and takes about 3 hours to complete one way, and it offers many opportunities to explore the

Capilano-Pacific Trail

forest and some of the pools where the Capilano River narrows dramatically as it flows through a steep-sided canyon.

At its south end, the Capilano River is shallow and wide, with only slight banks on either side. The riverbed is a field of melon-sized stones. At low-water times, scramble down to walk on the smooth boulders exposed above the stream. From here, the trail leads away from the bank up to Keith Road as it nears the Upper Levels Highway bridge. Keith Road runs north to its terminus at the bridge, where a Metro Vancouver Parks signpost indicates the start of the next section of the Capilano-Pacific Trail. At this point, the trail is a charming old lane. Occasionally, you'll see signs of fainter branch trails. This was one of the first parks in the Vancouver region. Opened in

1926, the 160-ha (395-acre) park today receives more than a million visitors year round.

The first path that descends into the canyon off the Capilano-Pacific switchbacks to a section known as the Ranger Pool. Although the trail is moderately steep in places, it's worth the effort for the view of the canyon from the riverbed. A short distance beyond the Ranger Pool Trail, the Capilano-Pacific passes a wire fence surrounding the private property of the Capilano Suspension Bridge. The entrance to the bridge is on Capilano Road in North Vancouver, on the river's east side.

Just past the fenced area, the trail divides at a trail marker, with Rabbit Lane continuing in the open while the Capilano-Pacific heads into the forest. Throughout the year, the overstorey of tall evergreens perfumes the air with one great green essence. One of the joys of visiting here is the quiet that permeates the atmosphere. Even when it's raining, the branches of the forest are so sheltering that much of the precipitation never reaches the trail.

The Capilano-Pacific Trail begins to lead gently through a silent forest, above and slightly removed from the river sounds below. This is a good trail for people who enjoy exchanging hellos. There is almost always a pleasant stream of visitors, many accompanied by their dogs, to be met along the way. From one magnificent viewpoint, the canyon can be seen dropping away sharply to the river below. A bench beside some towering Douglas-firs welcomes hikers here. Just before this viewpoint, a path leads off to the Sandy Point Pools below.

From Houlgate Creek, the second of two major creeks north of the viewpoint, a branch of the main trail leads to the Shinglebolt Viewpoint, near the park's North Vancouver entrance. (A shinglebolt is a section of a cedar log from which shakes and shingles are cut.) The Shinglebolt Trail is best explored on clear days when the path isn't too muddy. This is the route used by the Capilano Timber Company railway from 1917 to 1933, which accounts for its gentle grade. A maze of trails runs through the woods here, past some beautiful old trees along the west bank. The easygoing Rabbit Lane Trail feeds into the Capilano-Pacific at several places around the Shinglebolt Viewpoint below Cleveland Dam.

There are several fine viewpoints of Capilano Canyon and the North Shore mountains—particularly the Lions (Two Sisters)—as well as picnic locations around the Cleveland Dam. At many times of the year, kayakers challenge the river in the region just below the dam, one of the best places in Vancouver to spot them in action or to get tumbled in the "washing machine" yourself.

An aquarium-like salmon hatchery sits at the north end of the river, below the Cleveland Dam. Wheelchair-accessible Palisades Trail connects the hatchery with a picnic area beside the dam at the corner of Capilano and Prospect roads. Explore farther south along the river on the Coho Loop Trail, which begins at the parking lot at the north end of well-marked Capilano Park Road, off Capilano Road below the Cleveland Dam. There's even more variety here, including two bridge crossings of the canyon and a descent to riverside at the Dog Leg Pool. Allow at least an hour to complete the loop, especially if you spend time beside the river, where your thoughts are likely to be caught up in the current as all else comes to a momentary standstill.

6

LYNN HEADWATERS
REGIONAL PARK &

. . . . .

> **DISTANCE:** 10 km (6.2 mi.) north of Highway 1/99, in North Vancouver

> **ACTIVITIES:** Cross-country skiing, dog walking, hiking, nature observation, picnicking, swimming, viewpoints, walking

> **ACCESS:** To reach the park entrance, follow Mountain Highway or Lynn Valley Road north off the Upper Levels Highway (Highway 1/99). Signs pointing to the park begin at the turnoff to popular Lynn Canyon Park (see next chapter). Stay on Lynn Canyon Road until it ends, then follow Intake Road for about 1 km (0.6 mi.) to the parking lot where the trail begins. (For busy months, there are two overflow parking lots on Intake Road close to the trailhead.) If you're travelling on foot, catch the #228 Lynn Valley bus from the SeaBus terminal at Lonsdale Quay. It drops you where Intake Road begins, the last stop on its route.

TUCKED IN behind Grouse Mountain and leading north for 15 km (9.3 mi.), Lynn Headwaters Regional Park opened to the public in 1985 after being off-limits for decades as part of the extensive North Shore watershed system. Stone, water and wood characterize much of the park's nature. Silence is another component. Turn the corner at the top of North Vancouver's Lynn Valley Road, and suddenly you leave behind the sounds of the city and enter another world. Even if the parking area is full, Lynn Headwaters is so large that it absorbs people quickly. You often feel as if you have the place to yourself.

Lynn Headwaters Park is a welcoming place where first-time visitors and those in wheelchairs may be content to picnic just inside the entrance beside the old flood-control bridge. Several tables and toilets, and a public telephone, are located here. Getting to the creek is easiest via a gentle approach just upstream on the east side of the bridge, where a visitor registration kiosk displays all you need to know about the park. Fires are not permitted; neither are bicycles, except on a connector road between Lynn Headwaters and the Lower Seymour Conservation Reserve (see chapter 8). *Note:* Dogs are welcome off leash on almost all park trails.

Roughly half the 74 km (46 mi.) of trails in Lynn Headwaters are fairly level and thus suitable for all. One arm of the Lynn Loop leads north to easygoing Cedar Mill, a creekside trail that runs through the folds of the valley for 4 km (2.5 mi.). Finding more challenging terrain is easy in this narrow-sided valley. Get to know it one bight at a time.

If you want to test yourself, try the Switchback Trail. Although the Switchback is only 0.7 km (0.4 mi.) in length, its ups and downs will get your heart rate up quickly. If you're here for the first time, try it from top to bottom. Ascend Lynn Loop Trail in a counterclockwise direction from the kiosk, then go down Switchback to meet the creekside trail in the valley. (Before making the descent, walk a short distance farther north on Headwaters Trail to see the old snag and viewpoint of the valley below.) The trail's switchbacks, staircases and serpentine layout provide a good way to gauge your fitness level. And don't let winter deter you: this part of the park is one of the most pleasantly sheltered environments in which to view a snowfall. The broad branches of hemlock trees catch much of the load, leaving the trail bare below.

> ## LYNN CREEK

Lynn Creek cuts through the valley over a wide bed of boulders. The mountains on either side rise so steeply that it is difficult to get a good perspective of them from Headwaters Trail. Only Mount Fromme is really prominent in the west. As you explore northwards along Lynn Creek beyond the debris torrent where Cedar Mill Loop Trail and Headwaters Trail link, a spiny ridge of peaks

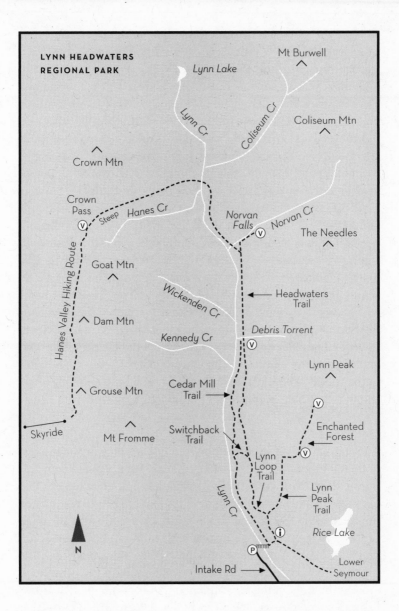

Lynn Lake

Mt Burwell

Coliseum Cr

Coliseum Mtn

Lynn Cr

Crown Mtn

Crown Pass

Steep Hanes Cr

Norvan Falls

Norvan Cr

The Needles

Hanes Valley Hiking Route

Goat Mtn

Wickenden Cr

Headwaters Trail

Dam Mtn

Kennedy Cr

Debris Torrent

Lynn Peak

Grouse Mtn

Cedar Mill Trail

Skyride

Mt Fromme

Switchback Trail

Enchanted Forest

Lynn Loop Trail

Lynn Peak Trail

Lynn Cr

Rice Lake

N

Intake Rd

Lower Seymour

known as the Needles comes into view to the east. Walking the trail is quicker and easier than boulder-hopping in the rough creek-bed. During spring months, the water in the creek rises and rushes

33

through the valley. As the unrepaired dam at the Headwaters trail-head suggests, North Vancouver gave up trying to control this as a watershed in the early 1980s.

For those who wish to really stretch their legs without much elevation gain, the 7-km (4.3-mi.) Headwaters Trail to Norvan Falls and the Cedar Mill Loop Trail are both ideal. (Consult the Metro Vancouver Parks trail guide, available at the park's visitor registration kiosk, for estimated round-trip times for a variety of destinations within the park.) Plan on a 2-hour journey to reach the debris torrent across from Kennedy Creek on the valley's west side. Headwaters Trail rises above the valley, whereas Cedar Mill Loop Trail travels along the creek bank. People of all ages use these easy trails, and in winter they're popular with cross-country skiers. In places along both trails, particularly at the "4.5 km" sign on Headwaters Trail, there is logging-camp debris—kettles, boot soles, logging equipment, bottle shards, saw blades—placed atop nurse logs or hung from branches.

The water in Lynn Creek is much colder than in the neighbouring Seymour River, and swimming spots are hard to come by. Some of the best pools lie between the debris chute, where the Cedar Mill and Headwaters trails converge, and Norvan Creek, 30 minutes farther north. The water is very soft. A cool breeze normally blows through the valley, keeping bugs down.

> **LYNN PEAK**

Looking for a more scenic though no less challenging alternative to the Grouse Grind? Seek out Lynn Peak. Hike several kilometres up the steep Lynn Peak Trail to a small grove of original trees that for some reason were left standing. This spot is appropriately named the Enchanted Forest. The trail to reach it is identified as the route to Lynn Peak on the large map at the trailhead. The forest is not marked as such but is located between two viewpoints near the summit. To find the turnoff from the main trail, follow Lynn Loop Trail to the right of the registration kiosk for 15 minutes. Near two lightning-blasted snags, one on each side of the trail, and three large stumps is a trail sign indicating the continuation of Lynn Loop Trail. A secondary trail that is signed as the Lynn Peak route branches off at right angles.

The sound of Lynn Creek begins to diminish as the trail climbs to the peak. A smaller stream becomes evident—one that often dries up for months once the spring runoff finishes. The trail follows the stream in places, and there may be some wet climbing over small rocks. Pack along something to drink, because the steep hiking trail increases in difficulty from this point.

Moving at a moderate pace, you will get to the first viewpoint about 35 minutes after leaving Lynn Loop Trail. From here, you look directly east to the Mount Seymour ski area and down into the Lower Seymour Conservation Reserve in the valley below.

The forest floor begins to dry out as you climb up the spine of Lynn Peak. The sound of wind high in the trees accompanies you. The trail is narrow but begins to open up for a short distance beyond a large blowdown over which you will have to clamber. You will sense your arrival in the Enchanted Forest by the hush that falls around you. The underbrush becomes much less dense. The sound of Lynn Creek rises and harmonizes with the wind. In the centre of the grove are fir trees that begin to put out branches at the 30-m (100-ft.) level and continue upwards from there. It takes four adults stretched fingertip to fingertip to encircle one of the smaller trees. Some are so old that their lower trunks have begun to crumble.

Upwards from here, the trail narrows and becomes rougher again as it climbs to its finish at the site of what was once a blimp tethering station, 10 minutes farther along. No effort was spared in logging Lynn Peak; 40 years ago, the blimp was used to lift logs off the mountain.

> **HANES VALLEY HIKING ROUTE**
Metro Vancouver Parks makes a distinction between hiking *trails* and hiking *routes* in Lynn Headwaters. The trails are well marked, and although you are guaranteed an energetic workout, they are also well maintained. In contrast, hiking routes in the park are much more of a challenge, particularly in adverse weather. The terrain is rockier, the paths much less distinct in places and the difficulties much more pronounced. Still, if you've explored other aspects of the park and are hungry for further adventure, prepare yourself for the long trek through the Hanes Valley. Total distance on this route is

more than 15 km (9.3 mi.) one way, a 7- to 8-hour trek from the park entrance to Grouse Mountain.

Getting to Grouse Mountain requires you to first cover the 7-km (4.3-mi.) Headwaters Trail to Norvan Falls. From the bridge over Norvan Creek, follow the trail west to Lynn Creek, then up a treacherous scree slope beside Hanes Creek. Allow 2 to 3 hours to cross the slope. Don't hesitate to turn back should the weather close in—this section is difficult even with good visibility. Snow patches may persist well into the summer in places shaded from the sun. One of the most satisfying stages of this route is at the top of Crown Pass, where you leave the scree behind and once more enter the forest. From this point on, the trail gently rises and falls as it makes its way towards the Grouse Mountain alpine area. For $10, ride the Skyride down to the parking lot at the foot of the gondola. Hardier souls could hike down the Grouse Grind. If you haven't arranged to be picked up here, you can catch the #236 bus back to Vancouver. Note: Dogs are not permitted on the Grouse Mountain Skyride.

> **VARLEY TRAIL**

As the palette of colours in local forests shifts with the seasons, bright pockets almost always persist. Such highlights lend an added poignancy for day trippers who walk the Varley Trail, which links Lynn Headwaters Regional Park with the Lower Seymour Conservation Reserve (see LSCR map, page 45). The trail commemorates Frederick Varley, considered the bohemian of the Canadian painters the Group of Seven. Between 1934 and 1937, Varley lived in a house that still stands on what is now Rice Lake Road. The gifted colourist who painted on the west bank of Lynn Creek included many scenes from the immediate surroundings in his work. Lynn Peak (which he dubbed "the Dumpling"), Mount Seymour and Grouse Mountain were all subjects in both his drawings and watercolours. And what an ideal location he had from which to view these landmarks.

Today, as one walks the trails that link an astounding amount of protected area on both the east and west banks of Lynn Creek—10.535 ha (26,033 acres) in total—one encounters the same sounds, sights and smells that Varley did. It's easy to see the influences that inform his work. In autumn, one of the most dazzling times of year,

Lynn Creek, North Vancouver

shafts of sunlight light up foregrounds of pumpkin-yellow alder groves against a backdrop of forest green. Lynn Creek rushes by at a faster clip than it has in months, as if celebrating its release from the summer drought. Its motion produces a constant melody that permeates the atmosphere. As the wind rises and falls, so too do the notes from the creek, like music from a concert hall orchestra. A heady, resinous odour emanates from millions of newly shed needles that carpet the forest floor.

This is the kind of trail that welcomes a variety of users, from walkers to equestrians, many of whom already make use of a profusion of other trails on both sides of Lynn Creek. In fact, portions of the Varley Trail cover sections of other trails to form a loop that leads through Metro Vancouver's Lower Seymour Conservation Reserve and Lynn Headwaters Regional Park, as well as Lynn Canyon Municipal Park. One stretch of Varley Trail runs for about 1 km (0.6 mi.) from the old Varley home at the north end of Rice Lake and Marion roads to the entrance of Lynn Headwaters Park.

Along much of the way, the trail parallels Lynn Creek's winding course. Boardwalks convey adventurers above some of the muddier parts. Signs warn that heavy rains may make the trail immediately adjacent to Lynn Creek "challenging" to pass. Be particularly careful if exploring the unstable riverbanks during periods of high water. Never underestimate the strength of the current, which flows faster at the shoreline than anywhere else in the creek's boulder-strewn channel.

For much of its length, Lynn Creek is easier to detect with ears than eyes. Its unseen cataract often carves through steep-sided granite gorges as it drops towards Burrard Inlet. Sounds of the creek are amplified by the canyon walls and the towering forest. However, as you walk the Varley Trail along the west side of Lynn Creek, flashes of its white water signal through the forest. It's easy to imagine that this relentless clamour must have provided Varley with a transcendent environment in which to create.

The Varley Trail is best approached from either of two locations: the Lower Seymour Conservation Reserve parking lot located at the north end of Lillooet Road (see chapter 8) or the entrance to Lynn Headwaters Regional Park at the north end of Lynn Valley Road. If you're travelling on foot from Vancouver, catch the #228 Lynn Valley bus from the SeaBus terminal at Lonsdale Quay to Intake Road. Walk a short distance north on Intake Road to Rice Lake Road. All the trails are well signed, including the rustic Baden-Powell Trail, which provides additional walking south of the Varley Trail through Lynn Canyon Park.

7

LYNN CANYON PARK

. . . . .

> DISTANCE: 7 km (4.3 mi.) north of Highway 1/99, in North Vancouver

> ACTIVITIES: Dog walking, mountain biking, nature observation, viewpoints, walking

> ACCESS: Take either Mountain Highway (Exit 21) or Lynn Valley Road (Exit 19) north from the Upper Levels Highway (Highway 1/99) in North Vancouver near the Ironworkers Memorial Crossing. Both roads intersect near the park (see North Vancouver map, page 57). From there, follow Lynn Valley Road north to Peters Road. Turn right (east) where a sign indicates Lynn Canyon Park. The suspension bridge, an interpretive centre and a restaurant are next to the parking lot at the end of Peters Road. If you're travelling on foot, catch the #228 Lynn Valley bus from the SeaBus terminal at Lonsdale Quay, which stops at Peters Road, several blocks west of the park entrance.

IN THESE days, when home life is so comfortable, it's important to occasionally expose yourself to the powerful forces of nature. North Vancouver's Lynn Canyon Park is a good place to do this. Younger children may find the canyon trail too steep for their little legs, but they will thrill at the sight of Lynn Creek as it carves its way through a narrow, granite-walled canyon. To heighten the excitement, there's a suspension bridge from which the hypnotic motion of the water can be observed. Although not as long as the Capilano Canyon suspension bridge, the one spanning Lynn Canyon will make just as big an impression, with the added advantage of being free of charge and just steps away from the parking lot.

Stop at the Lynn Canyon Ecology Centre to pick up a map of the park. Plan on spending some time in the centre as part of your visit. Younger children will especially enjoy the kids' "exploratorium corner," which features a puppet theatre. There's also a video room where you can choose from a catalogue of nature-related National Film Board shorts that are screened on request. The Ecology Centre's hours are 10 A.M. to 5 P.M. on weekdays, noon to 4 P.M. on weekends and holidays. Call 604-990-3755 for information on special seasonal programs, or visit dnv.org/ecology/index.htm.

Lynn Canyon Park is one of the oldest parks on the North Shore, having opened in 1912. Relatively modest in area, it's adjoined by two immense tracts of neighbouring wilderness: the Lower Seymour Conservation Reserve and Lynn Headwaters Regional Park. It's taken a while for them to become knitted together, but these days the three—totalling about 10 535 ha (26,033 acres)—are linked by a network of trails, bridges and old logging roads. You can spend an hour or a full day adventuring on foot or, where permitted, on bicycle or horseback without ever coming in sight of civilization.

Visiting Lynn Canyon Park is like attending a banquet where dessert is the first course served. Within a minute's walk of the parking lot, you reach the suspension bridge. Sturdy steel cables support the narrow walkway that is slung across the canyon. Enjoy the experience of standing high above a series of waterfalls cascading into Lynn Creek, 50 m (164 ft.) below. The walkway is ribbed like a gangplank for secure footing; its sides are encased in wire mesh for further safety. Below, white water comes to rest in placid emerald-green pools, then becomes white again in a flash; the pools reflect the thick conifer forest growing out of the canyon walls. On a quiet day, you can be mesmerized by the motion in the creek. At other times, when you share the bridge with other walkers and cyclists, there is just enough room for everyone to squeeze by when travelling in opposite directions.

A number of well-marked trails proceed from each end of the bridge. Tall fencing keeps visitors away from the most dangerous sections of the canyon. One of the fascinating aspects of this park is how quickly the landscape transforms the creek from a wide, meandering swath into a narrow funnel of surging energy. Within

Lynn Canyon Park suspension bridge

a 10-minute walk north of the bridge, you can be relaxing beside a gravel bar where the creek widens at a place named 30 Foot Pool. Water spills out of a narrow canyon into the pool. Nearby, a staircase leads up to the eastern rim of the canyon. On clear days, sunlight lances through the towering forest to brighten landings at several places on the staircase. In autumn, golden maple leaves spin and slice through the air. The sound of needles being shed by fir trees is like a shower of raindrops as they fall on the understorey of ferns.

From the top of the staircase, it's a short walk farther north to a wooden footbridge that leads west across Lynn Creek and connects with the Varley Trail, which in turn connects with Lynn Headwaters Park (see previous chapter and map page 33). An alternative route runs east from the footbridge and connects in minutes with the nearby Lower Seymour Conservation Reserve (see next chapter). Once you've experienced the proximity of one park to the other, you can understand their popularity with cyclists, who flit through the woods along the wide trails.

If you'd rather not retrace your steps, return to the suspension bridge using an alternative route, a section of the North Shore's extensive 48-km (29.8-mi) Baden-Powell Trail. This level pathway meanders along an old logging road on its way to the suspension bridge (see chapter 10). You can do the round trip from the suspension bridge to the footbridge in an easy hour, breaks included.

If you have time, take a 20-minute walk south of the suspension bridge on either side of the canyon to reach the Twin Falls bridge. The route offers a stunning view as water plummets over a tall waterfall into the canyon below. Once on the bridge, you stand much closer to the wildness of the creek than when on the suspension bridge: you're enveloped in mist and in one of nature's most profound sounds. The canyon walls are quite steep here, and towering Douglas-firs cut the amount of sunlight reaching the forest floor.

> **A TASTE FOR THE OUTDOORS**

FOR YEARS, visitors to Lynn Canyon Park lined up for take-out treats served up from a modest trailer beside the suspension bridge. In 2003, the district of North Vancouver opened the stunningly beautiful Lynn Canyon Café in its place. Designed by architect David Nairn, the vaulted wood-and-glass structure is a great place to reward little and big tummies alike. A stop here will confirm the age-old wisdom that food does indeed taste better outdoors. For more information call 604-984-9311, or visit www.lynnvalleycentre.ca/lynncanyoncafe.htm.

8

LOWER SEYMOUR
CONSERVATION RESERVE &

· · · · ·

> DISTANCE: 7 km (4.3 mi.) north of the Ironworkers Memorial (Second Narrows) Crossing, in North Vancouver

> ACTIVITIES: Cross-country skiing, cycling, dog walking, fishing, hiking, in-line skating, nature observation, picnicking, swimming, viewpoints, walking

> ACCESS: The main entrance to the Lower Seymour Conservation Reserve (LSCR) is at the north end of Lillooet Road, reached by taking the Mount Seymour Parkway (Exit 22) off Highway 1/99 in North Vancouver near the Ironworkers Memorial (Second Narrows) Crossing. A large green Metro Vancouver Parks sign at the intersection of the Parkway and Lillooet Road points straight ahead on Lillooet to the LSCR. Follow Lillooet past Capilano College, where it narrows. Beyond an entry gate and parking areas, the road becomes gravel for 4 km (2.5 mi.), to the main gate. The entry gate is locked towards dusk. There is a small parking area just outside this gate for those who wish to explore the reserve without fear of being locked in for the night.

An alternate approach to the LSCR begins at the north end of Riverside Drive via the Mount Seymour Parkway.

Note: Dogs are permitted only on a limited number of trails in the LSCR. For information, see www.metrovancouverorg/about/maps/Maps/lscrdogtrailsmap.pdf.

If you are travelling on foot from Vancouver, catch the #228 Lynn Valley bus from the SeaBus terminal at Lonsdale Quay to Intake Road. Walk a short distance north on Intake Road to Rice Lake Road, where the Varley Trail (see chapter 6) provides a link between the LSCR, Lynn Headwaters Regional Park and Lynn

Canyon Park. Lynn Headwaters and the LSCR are also linked by a kilometre-long stretch of old logging road.

F OR THE better part of the 20th century, the Seymour Valley watershed was designated off-limits to the public and held in reserve for future water supply. Stretching below the peaks of Mount Seymour, the watershed was a "look, but don't touch" jewel in our treasure trove of local wilderness areas. In 1987, the Greater Vancouver Regional District decided to open the lower valley south of the Seymour reservoir—an area 14 times the size of Stanley Park— after a study determined that the site would not be required until well into the 21st century, if at all. Known as the Seymour Demonstration Forest for the first 12 years, the recreation area operated by the Metro Vancouver's watershed management department underwent a name change in 1999 to the Lower Seymour Conservation Reserve, or LSCR.

A wide trail that begins just north of the LSCR's visitors' centre leads to Rice Lake and beyond to the entrance to nearby Lynn Headwaters Regional Park (see chapter 6).

> ### RICE LAKE

Only a short distance from the LSCR's entrance, Rice Lake is a small freshwater destination. Trails and broad boardwalks ring the lakeshore for easy access. All of the amenities here have been designed with wheelchairs in mind. Rice Lake's dock is an ideal place for young and old fry alike to try out their casting technique in hopes of landing one of the 5,000 rainbow trout with which the lake is stocked annually. Several picnic tables with views of the lake are located nearby. Look for salamanders in the small creek. If there are none in sight, check out the natural-history interpretive trail that loops through the shaded woods on the lake's west side. You're bound to learn something interesting.

> ### FISHERMAN'S TRAIL

Across from LSCR's main gate, the Twin Bridges Trail drops 2.2 km (1.4 mi.) to the lengthy Fisherman's Trail near an old iron bridge. Nearby, cement footings are all that remain of its twin. On foot this journey takes 30 minutes; by bike, 20 minutes. A third of the way

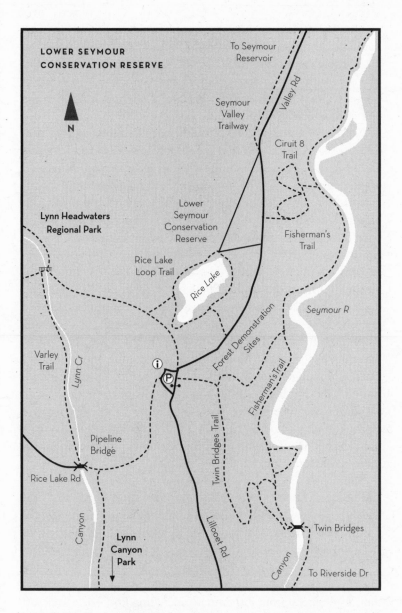

LOWER SEYMOUR
CONSERVATION RESERVE

N

To Seymour
Reservoir

Valley Rd

Seymour
Valley
Trailway

Ciruit 8
Trail

Lynn Headwaters
Regional Park

Lower
Seymour
Conservation
Reserve

Fisherman's
Trail

Rice Lake
Loop Trail

Rice Lake

Seymour R

Forest Demonstration Sites

Varley
Trail

Lynn Cr

ⓘ
Ⓟ

Fisherman's Trail

Pipeline
Bridge

Twin Bridges Trail

Rice Lake Rd

Canyon

Lynn
Canyon
Park

Lillooet Rd

Twin Bridges

Canyon

To Riverside Dr

to the bridge, an alternative pathway to the river appears. For walkers only, the Homestead Trail leads down into the river valley and meets the Fisherman's Trail 30 minutes upriver from the bridge. If you're headed upriver on foot, use this shortcut.

Over the millennia, the river has carved a deep channel through the wide Seymour Valley. Fisherman's Trail winds beside the Seymour River's west side from Twin Bridges north to its mid-valley junction with the Seymour Valley Trailway, a distance of about 7 km (4.3 mi.). South of Twin Bridges, Fisherman's leads to the LSCR's Riverside Drive entrance.

North of the bridge, wide, flat Fisherman's Trail follows the river past the site of an early-20th-century logging settlement. Watch for an old narrow-gauge rail tunnel on your left, partially concealed. Approximately 3 m (10 ft.) in diameter and 25 m (82 ft.) in length, it is one of the many remnants of the logging operations that cleared the valley of its original forest. Walking through its darkened interior is one of the highlights of a visit to the LSCR. Nearby, two paths branch off to the right a short distance apart and link up to form a semicircle at riverside. Bricks from an old chimney litter the ground at one point. The bank is generally steep heading down to the river, so watch for several easier approaches. On the opposite shore are many good locations for sunning and swimming where the afternoon light remains long after it leaves the western riverbank in the shade. Wading across is easy when the river is low. There are plunge pools galore, including one that's just the right size for you. Remember to wear an old pair of running shoes or sandals to negotiate the boulders, some of which are slippery with algae. You might find that you are sharing the river with the occasional group of anglers; however, the Seymour is wide enough that there is plenty of room for all.

South of Twin Bridges, the Seymour enters a narrow canyon and becomes almost impossible to glimpse from Fisherman's Trail, which now traverses the river's east bank to its junction with the Baden-Powell Trail at Riverside Drive. Allow 30 minutes by bike, an hour on foot.

Bike cruising doesn't get much sweeter than along this stretch. If you're in the mood for more vertical, a selection of cross-country trails feed off east from Fisherman's, including Bottle Top Trail just south of the bridge, as well as the multi-use Bridle Path at the halfway point.

On a hot summer day, it's a pleasant surprise to discover a soft breeze blowing through the Seymour Valley when there's hardly a whisper in the city. On the Seymour Valley Trailway to the Seymour Falls Dam, you'll find not only fresh air but comforting stretches of shade. As you cycle, in-line skate, jog or simply stroll along, cool green fragrances waft from the forest's interior.

The trailway runs for 10 km (6.2 mi.) between Rice Lake, one of the North Shore's original municipal watersheds, and the Greater Vancouver Water District's Seymour Falls Dam, which, since it opened in 1961, has controlled a third of the region's water supply.

That's a daunting round trip for small or inexperienced legs. When visiting with children or adults who may not have spent much time on a bike, make an easy-going loop by riding the first 2 km (1.2 mi.) to the forested Balloon Picnic Site, one of several strategically placed rest areas along the way. From there, make your way back past Rice Lake, and you'll have experienced arguably one of the finest urban wilderness outings on offer anywhere. What a thing of beauty this multi-use route is. In many places, the hillsides beside the trail have been brushed out, revealing the eerie spectre of enormous cedar stumps whose notched trunks leer down at passersby like jack-o'-lanterns. Backed by spindly second growth, the decaying stumps, whose massive upper trunks were felled a century ago, are suffused with a glistening red glow, particularly when illuminated by shafts of sunlight after a rainstorm.

Equally impressive are the arrangements of round boulders that have been skillfully positioned to assist stream drainage into culverts that run beneath the trail. These constructs are a stone mason's dream. Boulders are fitted together to mimic the steepness of the valley walls that rise on each side of the Seymour River.

All this is just eye candy, a momentary diversion from what really matters—the flowing band of blacktop that rolls beneath your wheels as you pedal or skate along. (*Note*: Novice skaters will find the trailway intimidating.) On your first outing north to the dam, you may find yourself holding back a little, thinking that tackling the hills on the return trip may be more of a test than your legs are ready for. Don't worry. The trailway has been cleverly designed to allow you to carry your speed around corners and uphill sections. In fact, the journey south to the LSCR entrance features several exhilarating downhill stretches. When you need to stop and rest, find one of the five picnic sites dotted along the way.

Just two caveats: as water is not available on the route, be sure to pack plenty along, particularly on hot summer days. Conversely, even in summer the air temperature in the heavily wooded LSCR can turn cold, especially during a downpour, so pack along an extra layer when skies are overcast.

When you finally arrive at the dam, you can peer through the high chainlink fence surrounding Seymour Lake, much longer than it is wide. Its blue surface stretches out of sight, running 20 km (12.4 mi.) to the Seymour River's headwaters. Rising above to the west is the full face of Coliseum Mountain, barely visible from Vancouver. In times of plenty, water spills over the top of the dam in thundering white torrents. In drier years, its voice is practically mute. A wooden viewing platform commands a good view of the dam's spillway and the river. For a close-up view of the river and recently expanded fish hatchery channels, cross the Bear Island pedestrian bridge at the foot of the falls.

The Hurry Creek salmon hatchery sits just south of the dam, a short distance downhill from the main road. Outdoor ponds are stocked with fingerling coho and steelhead, fattening up for their release in spring. Walk past the fence that surrounds the hatchery to find the Old Growth Trail, which leads south from here.

> **OLD GROWTH TRAIL**

During the 1990s, public attention was drawn to the significant stands of old growth that remain in local watersheds, particularly along the river valleys, where western red cedar, amabilis fir and Sitka spruce thrive in a moist environment ideally suited to promoting their growth. To allow public access to some of these giants, a gravel-surfaced loop trail has been constructed on the east side of Valley Road about 1 km (0.6 mi.) south of the Seymour dam. The Old Growth Trail's northern terminus is beside the Hurry Creek fish hatchery. It leads for almost 2 km (1.2 mi.) through the forest here. Much of the distance is over boardwalk above the rain forest floor,

Seymour River, Fisherman's Trail

with its tangle of devil's club and huckleberry and salmonberry bushes, as well as downed tree trunks coated with thick moss. To bushwhack through here would be no contest: this bush would whack the daylights out of you in short order.

Several strategically located viewing platforms along the Old Growth Trail allow visitors to observe this habitat. One special stop has been constructed beside the largest of the smooth-barked Sitka spruce on the trail. The tree rises like a pillar, casting a spell enhanced by the soothing, melodious gurgle of the river, passing unseen nearby.

Branches of the Seymour River channel through backwaters in which skunk cabbage thrives. Its leafy abundance, along with the imposing upper canopy of branches, lends this environment the air of a steamy Louisiana bayou. Although the gators won't git you, the skeeters might, so bring your bug spray.

After the close quarters of the forest, you might long for the release of the open sky above the river. Unfortunately, there's little more than a glimpse of the river at the end of a short side path that leads from the main trail to an eroding riverbank. Take care where you stand to view the water. The Old Growth Trail gives the river's main course a wide berth, and with good reason: it would be a shame to see the trail washed away by the flooding river. Over the centuries, the Seymour has dug itself a deep channel in the valley

> ## RICHARD JURYN

THE LATE Richard Juryn, who championed mountain biking on the North Shore, was known as a family guy who always spoke of creating a trail that would get the whole family out into nature. In late 2007, shortly after Juryn drowned while kayaking in Howe Sound, an outpouring of goodwill from family, friends and officials representing a quilt of North Shore jurisdictions resulted in instantaneous action to create a trail in his memory. Thanks to Juryn's encouragement, Metro Vancouver already had plans to develop a beginner- to intermediate-level mountain bike trail in the Lower Seymour Conservation Reserve.

floor. There are far safer places downstream to approach the water as you make your way back to the park's entrance. Meanwhile, just keep breathing in the rich forest air.

> ### RICHARD JURYN MEMORIAL TRAIL

In June 2008, hundreds of volunteers turned out to do what North Shore riders of all persuasions do best: build recreational trails of the highest standards, a skill so esteemed that it plays a central role in Capilano University's Mountain Bike Operations Certificate program. With the creation of the Richard Juryn Memorial Trail, there is now an opportunity to connect the LSCR with the waterfront Spirit Trail linking all the jurisdictions on the North Shore from Deep Cove to Horseshoe Bay and eventually from there north on the Sea to Sky Trail. Within the LSCR, operations foreman Heidi Hickey and her staff have worked to integrate the memorial trail into the larger framework of routes that spiral out across the mountainous and heavily forested domain, and thanks to their efforts, there's now a great loop that ties in with other routes, such as the Circuit 8 John Thompson Trail, which spirals off the Seymour Valley Trailway.

The Richard Juryn Memorial Trail enters the LSCR beside a yellow gate and small parking area, beyond which the road leads 4 km (2.5 mi.) to the main gate and the start of the Seymour Valley Trailway. For information on the LSCR, including detailed trail maps, visit www.metrovancouver.org/services/parks_lscr/lscr/Pages/default.aspx. The trail may also be accessed at the District of North Vancouver's Inter-River Park at the junction of Lillooet Road and Premier Street beside Lynn Creek. A map of the Richard Juryn Memorial Trail is posted at www.richardjuryntrails.com, as well as at its entrances in Inter-River Park and the LSCR.

9

MAPLEWOOD FLATS
CONSERVATION AREA &

. . . . .

> DISTANCE: 2 km (1.2 mi.) east of the Ironworkers Memorial (Second Narrows) Crossing, in North Vancouver

> ACTIVITIES: Birding, nature observation, picnicking, walking

> ACCESS: Follow the Dollarton Highway exit (#23) east of the Ironworkers Memorial Crossing towards Deep Cove (see North Vancouver map, page 57). Next to the Pacific Environmental Science Centre at 2645 Dollarton Highway is the Maplewood Flats Conservation Area. A road sign displaying the BC Wildlife Watch logo of a pair of binoculars indicates where to pull in. Bus service on Dollarton Highway (#212 Deep Cove) originates from the Phibbs Exchange at the north end of the Ironworkers Memorial Crossing. Call TransLink for schedule information, 604-953-3333, or visit their Web site at translink.ca.

FOR A PANORAMIC VIEW of the natural world that abounds on the mud flats of Burrard Inlet, head along the Dollarton Highway in North Vancouver, an easy 20-minute drive from Vancouver. Turn in at the Maplewood Flats Conservation Area, which made its debut in 1999. Make your first stop the Wild Bird Trust of B.C.'s Nature House, open daily and staffed by savvy volunteers. Pick up a self-guided viewing pamphlet of over 230 species of birds, with more being added to the list each year. One of the best ways to gain insight on both resident and seasonal species is to join one of the guided bird surveys offered on the first Saturday of each month (start time 8 A.M.) and nature walks on the second Saturday of each month (start time 10 A.M.). Special theme walks are led by wildlife doyens Al and Jude Grass, who have well-deserved reputations as leaders among provincial naturalists. The Grass duo shares their wide-ranging knowledge of the natural world on extended rambles along an extensive network of wheelchair- and stroller-friendly trails.

Even on overcast winter days, sweet birdsongs greet visitors here beneath forested Mount Seymour. It's as if the birds sense that this is *their* drop-in centre. Once you've checked the latest postings on bird sightings, make your way past the adjoining plant nursery and head for the ocean. Almost immediately, you're faced with a choice of either following a trail that loops west across a stately wooden footbridge or heading east beside the mud flats. Although helpful, rubber boots aren't essential to exploring the shoreline. Binoculars, however, are mandatory. Within minutes in either direction, you'll find yourself at a viewpoint overlooking Burrard Inlet.

Unlike eagles, which fly low over the waves and use their talons to snatch prey from the surface, ospreys hover above the water before plunging in feet first for their catch.

Begin your visit by searching for signs of an osprey nest. Ospreys were once a fairly common sight around Burrard Inlet. As the waterfront was developed during the past 60 years, the keen-eyed raptors were crowded out. So aggressive has infilling of the mud flats been that this 126-ha (311-acre) sanctuary is almost all that remains of what was once a 2 600-ha (6,425-acre) habitat.

Since 1999, when a pair of ospreys reared two chicks at Maplewood Flats, the first such occurrence in living memory, the osprey population has grown to four breeding pairs. Typically, ospreys build a spacious home atop a sturdy piling or "dolphin." Bundles of twigs indicate that a family of ospreys are in residence. However, in winter you'll have a harder time sighting the birds, as their nests are vacant: ospreys spend the season in California. (Many birders would agree that such behaviour betrays their Canadian roots.)

With binoculars, scan a line of evenly spaced pilings that march south into deep water. Atop the farthest ones are the piles of twigs that constitute the ospreys' nest. Lucky visitors are rewarded with a

Burrard Inlet, Maplewood Flats

close-up look at the adult birds, who often swoop low overhead as they scout the inlet for fish. During berry season, a less likely encounter will be with one of the black bears that frequent the reserve in autumn. Signs are posted when a bear is known to be in the area.

A sturdy footbridge allows visitors access to both sides of an old barge channel that cuts through the middle of the sanctuary. A stand of alder is starting to add forest cover to the marshland above the mud flats. Sanctuary staff have begun to augment the existing groundcover with plantings from their native-plant nursery. Carefully examine the broadleaf maple and red alder trees that border the hard-packed trail. Tiny Pacific tree frogs may be sitting motionless at the centre of the larger leaves. The trick is spotting the green or iridescent-coloured amphibians in the first place. Once you know what to look for, you'll find them everywhere.

For more information on Maplewood Flats and the Wild Bird Trust of B.C., call 604-922-2872 or visit www.wildbirdtrust.org.

MOUNT SEYMOUR
PROVINCIAL PARK

. . . . .

> DISTANCE: 8 km (5 mi.) northeast of the Ironworkers Memorial (Second Narrows) Crossing, in North Vancouver

> ACTIVITIES: Dog walking, hiking, mountain biking, picnicking, snow sports, viewpoints, walking

> ACCESS: Take Exit 22 from the Upper Levels Highway (Highway 1/99) just north of the Ironworkers Memorial Crossing, and follow Mount Seymour Parkway east to Mount Seymour Road. Turn left and drive a short distance north to the park's entrance. The #211 Seymour bus stops at the intersection of Mount Seymour Parkway and Mount Seymour Road, south of the provincial park's entrance. In winter, a private shuttle bus transports skiers and snowboarders from this intersection to the winter sport facilities.

VANCOUVER'S NORTH SHORE is blessed with a trio of provincial parks: Cypress, Mount Seymour and Indian Arm. Even before bridges spanned Burrard Inlet, day trippers made their way to West and North Vancouver to explore the mysteries of Hollyburn Mountain (in what is now Cypress Park) and Mount Seymour (which achieved provincial-park status in 1936). Not surprisingly, most of the trails in these parks have felt the impact of countless bootprints. Winter recreation was just as much a draw then as now and became increasingly so as rope tows and chairlifts were installed in the 1960s and '70s.

The day lodge and rental facilities at Mount Seymour (www. mountseymour.com) have retained a classic "old school" feel. Most

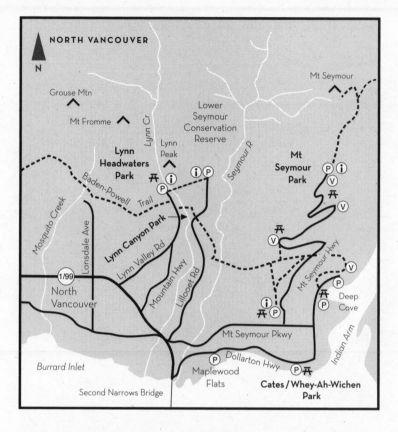

NORTH VANCOUVER

N

Grouse Mtn

Mt Fromme

Lynn Cr

Lynn Peak

Lynn Headwaters Park

Baden-Powell Trail

Lower Seymour Conservation Reserve

Seymour R

Mt Seymour

Mt Seymour Park

Mosquito Creek

Lonsdale Ave

Lynn Canyon Park

Lynn Valley Rd

Mountain Hwy

Lillooet Rd

1/99

North Vancouver

Mt Seymour Hwy

Deep Cove

Indian Arm

Mt Seymour Pkwy

Burrard Inlet

Dollarton Hwy

Maplewood Flats

Cates / Whey-Ah-Wichen Park

Second Narrows Bridge

Lower Mainlanders take their first snow-sport lessons here, and with good reason. The groomed trails are wide and gentle; those in search of more challenging terrain hike to a series of small peaks beyond the range of the chairlifts, particularly to First Pump and Second Pump. A friendly family feeling pervades Mount Seymour, which is why it retains a loyal following among even the most accomplished local snowboarders and "new school" skiers. Recently, snowshoeing the gentle trails that lead from the base of the Mystery Peak chairlift towards Dinkey Peak and Goldie, Flower and First lakes has begun to rival the popularity of hiking these same routes in summer. The tube and toboggan area is divided into both free and ticketed zones and is a magnet for families on winter weekends, particularly on sunny afternoons. *Note:* Dogs must be on leash at all times and are not permitted on backcountry trails.

Mount Seymour, North Vancouver

> **VIEWPOINTS**

Part of the pleasure of visiting Mount Seymour is the drive. Mount Seymour Road ascends 12 km (7.4 mi.) from sea level to a large parking lot beside the winter facilities at 1 034 m (3,392 ft.). Along the way are several picnic areas adjacent to spectacular viewpoints. It is difficult to overstate how sweeping the prospects are from the Vancouver Lookout at the second switchback and the Deep Cove Lookout at the fifth switchback.

If you enjoy hiking to viewpoints, Mount Seymour Park offers a wealth of moderate trails. Use extreme caution when exploring the park's open summits, especially in the region around Mount Bishop, at 1 508 m (4,947 ft.) the tallest peak in the park. Weather conditions change quickly during storm season, and the route between peaks quickly becomes obscured. Each year, this mountain confounds an unwary hiker or two.

In summer, once the snow has melted, short hiking trails lead from the parking lot at the top of Mount Seymour Road to Dinkey Peak and Goldie, Mystery and Flower lakes. Distances to these spots are short, the elevation gain is minimal, and hikers are rewarded with views of Greater Vancouver that are among the best in the Lower Mainland.

For a more extended hike, try the First Lake Trail to Dog Mountain from the parking lot at the top of Mount Seymour Road. Plan on taking 2 hours to complete the 5-km (3.1-mi.) round-trip journey. Wear waterproof boots, as this trail is often soggy. If you set your sights on reaching Mount Seymour's summit, try the moderately difficult 4-km (2.5-mi.) hike to Mount Seymour's First and Second Pump peaks. The trail traverses Brockton Point on its way to the peaks. Owing to the panoramic view from here, this is a very popular trail.

Other hiking routes on Mount Seymour include the 10-hour, 14-km (8.7-mi.) round-trip trek to Elsay Lake. Only experienced, well-equipped hikers should attempt this difficult route. The initial section of the trail covers the same route as that used to reach First Pump Peak. From there the trail to Elsay Lake passes Gopher Lake, then narrows as it crosses the most exposed section of the mountain. Trail markers are often difficult to locate in bad weather along this rugged portion of the trail, and hikers should not hesitate to turn back if the weather begins to deteriorate. An emergency shelter is located at Elsay Lake.

> ## BADEN-POWELL TRAIL

A 5-km (3.1-mi.) portion of the 48-km (29.8-mi.) Baden-Powell Trail that runs between Horseshoe Bay and Deep Cove passes through Mount Seymour Park. Although there are no major creeks or rivers to cross, plenty of small brooks and streams carry moisture down off the slopes of Mount Seymour. Many are bridged, but you can expect to do a little rock hopping across others.

Begin from the shaded parking area and picnic grounds at the Baden-Powell Trail's well-marked junction with Mount Seymour Road (see map page 57). From here, it's a 15-minute walk to the junction of the Baden-Powell and Mushroom trails. (A metal trail marker indicates that this is 42 km/26 mi. east of Horseshoe Bay.)

The historic Mushroom parking lot is marked by a sign that explains the important role once played by this site, where travellers to cabins on Mount Seymour left their vehicles before proceeding on foot. A short distance beyond are the Vancouver Lookout picnic grounds, a great place to take a break after making the effort to get this far.

To rejoin the Baden-Powell Trail, simply retrace your steps, or take the Buck Access Trail—a joy of a trail, overflowing with green essences—east from the Vancouver Lookout parking lot to where it joins Old Buck Trail, a 25-minute journey. Old Buck Trail is solidly built to accommodate both wheels and heels as it descends to meet Mount Seymour Road. Cross the road to rejoin Old Buck Trail. Although gated against vehicular traffic, this is part of the bicycle trail system in Mount Seymour Park, where many of the pathways are open for riding. Descend to the intersection with the Baden-Powell Trail, 15 minutes from the Buck Access Trail junction. Mount Seymour Road is 10 minutes east of here. If you want to connect with a bus, you can follow Old Buck Trail 2.2 km (1.4 mi.) downhill to the park headquarters. Buses stop on nearby Mount Seymour Parkway.

East of the parking lot on Mount Seymour Road, the Baden-Powell Trail enters a much rougher section than the smoother trail that leads west towards the Lower Seymour Conservation Reserve (see chapter 8). In the short distance between Mount Seymour and Indian River Road, there are boardwalks, bridges, stairs and a ladder to negotiate. Go left at Indian River Road for a short way to where the trail picks up again beneath the hydro lines. From here east is one of the prettiest sections as views of Indian Arm open up. There is one particularly rewarding location atop an open cliff, worth the scramble up beneath the hydro lines for its views of both Indian Arm and Burrard Inlet.

When you have gone as far east as possible, the Baden-Powell Trail cuts south towards Deep Cove. In an hour, you'll be out at its terminus on Panorama Drive, a short distance north of Gallant Avenue. This is as good a place as any to begin or end a visit to the trail, with a park, a pub and coffee shops nearby. At busy times, there's still ample parking in the lot just south of the beach.

> **CYCLE TRAILS**

In response to the growing number of cyclists who ride the lower slopes of Mount Seymour, BC Parks has reinforced several trails, such as the Old Buck Trail, to withstand the impact of mountain bike tires.

This not only assists riders but also provides a smooth surface for those pushing strollers. For a classic cross-country tour of the park, begin at the base of Mount Seymour just inside the provincial-park gates with an ascent of the Old Buck Trail. After a grunt up Old Buck, follow a route that touches on the BC Hydro power line service road, the Baden-Powell Trail, Dale's Trail, the Bridle Path and the notoriously steep Severed Dick Trail. Parts of this loop, particularly the technical drops where riders must call on all of their skills to pull off a clean run without having to dismount, are quite challenging. Allow 90 minutes to bike-and-hike the entire loop and keep your eyes on the trail markers. On more than one occasion, even experienced riders have lost their way.

For more information, including maps and trail information, visit www.env.gov.bc.ca/bcparks/explore/parkpgs/mt_seymour.

11

DEEP COVE &

. . . . .

- > DISTANCE: 10 km (6 mi.) northeast of the Ironworkers Memorial (Second Narrows) Crossing, in North Vancouver

- > ACTIVITIES: Boating, cycling, hiking, dog walking, paddling, picnicking, playground, swimming, viewpoints, walking

- > ACCESS: Take Exit 22 from the Upper Levels Highway (Highway 1/99) just north of the Ironworkers Memorial Crossing and follow Mount Seymour Parkway east to Deep Cove Road. Turn left and proceed north into the village. Alternately, take Exit 23 at the north end of the Ironworkers Memorial Crossing and follow Dollarton Highway east to Deep Cove Road. Bus service on Dollarton Highway (#212 Deep Cove) originates from the Phibbs Exchange at the north end of the Ironworkers Memorial Crossing. Call TransLink for schedule information, 604-953-3333, or visit translink.ca.

FOR ALL the change that's happened on the North Shore, Deep Cove has managed to retain an abiding serenity. The fact that the village lies at the end of the road helps. Surely this is what its counterpart, Horseshoe Bay, must have been like before BC Ferries hijacked that neighbourhood.

As well as being a jumping-off point for explorers heading up Indian Arm, it has a spruced-up main street and a kayak and canoe shop—handy if you're in need of advice or repairs.

> ## SAY NUTH KHAW YUM HERITAGE PARK/
INDIAN ARM PROVINCIAL PARK

At the height of paddling season, Deep Cove's harbour swarms with rowers, stand-up paddleboarders, canoeists and kayakers whose wind-milling paddle techniques project an appearance of an army of long-

Indian Arm

legged water striders. On Saturday mornings from late May to early October, the beach in front of the Deep Cove Canoe and Kayak Centre hums with activity. Every Girl Guide and Boy Scout in the Lower Mainland seems to converge on the strand, toting enough equipment to last a week, let alone an overnight camp out. Typically, they head to North Twin Island on the east side of Indian Arm—wherever they can squeeze in. This news undoubtedly comes as a relief for those paddlers headed farther north up the fiord. Campsites are not that plentiful along the shoreline of horseshoe-shaped Say Nuth Khaw Yum Heritage Park/Indian Arm Provincial Park, a swath of protected land set aside in 1997. The prospect of spending a night surrounded by youthful exuberance is almost as daunting as the 18-km (11-mi.) paddle to Indian Arm's northern end, where the two largest campsites at Berg's Landing and Granite Falls lie.

Upon consideration, that's more paddling than most adult arms can handle—let alone young teenage ones—which is what makes Deep Cove Canoe and Kayak Centre's 3-hour "Explorer" series of paddle outings increasingly popular.

Although paddling activity on the waters of Indian Arm has undergone a huge increase since the establishment of the provincial park, it's nothing compared with that of motorized boats. The recently built yacht club out-stations at the north end of the Arm are far more popular. On a good weekend, there are probably 50 to 100 boats now where there used to be only a few dozen. That's what happens when you give people a big dock, some outhouses and a green space. It can be just as busy there as here in Deep Cove.

That's really saying something, especially when one considers that the centre is maxed out on weekends for the capacity of the facility, the beach and the village. They can put 100 paddlers at any one time on the water. That's as much as Deep Cove can handle without affecting the surrounding residents. And if the ethnic mix of paddlers on Deep Cove's beach on weekends, particularly between April and October, is any indication, paddling is one sport that appeals to a broad cross-section of Metro Vancouver residents.

It's hard to express the profound interconnectedness of the people and the water. A Tsleil-Waututh legend tells of a two-headed serpent called Scnoki, whose arched body once spanned the entrance to Indian Arm, and of a young warrior who was shown in a dream how to put the creature to sleep so that it never again threatened paddlers. In the Coast Salish language, the park's name, *say nuth khaw yum*, translates as "serpent's land."

If you want to experience that transcendent bond for yourself, all it takes is a short paddle on Indian Arm to establish a link of your own. This applies to both sea kayaking and canoeing, though when the wind, the waves, the tidal currents and the sometimes formidable wakes of stinkpots commingle, those in canoes may find conditions far more challenging than they bargained on. As the Boy Scouts say, be prepared. From past experience, savvy leaders know the merits of getting an early start while the ocean is as flat as their well-ironed neckerchiefs.

One of the challenges facing paddlers on the journey up Indian Arm's west side is the relative scarcity of rest stops. At roughly the halfway point, several small landing sites occur at Brighton and Orlomah beaches. Depending on the height of the tide, more or less space will await you. Still, it's good to take a stretch. Paddlers are welcome to land on the beach at the south side of Camp Jubilee on Orlomah Beach but should avoid the camp's dock and campus. (Port Moody's Camp Jubilee Retreat and Conference Centre opened in 1936 at the base of Mount Seymour. For more information, visit campjubilee.ca). Another resting spot lies just north of Orlomah Beach at Thwaytes Landing on the west side of Indian Arm. This 48-ha (119-acre) Metro Vancouver Parks reserve site includes 1 100 m (3,610 ft.) of shoreline. It bears the name of Captain Tom Thwaytes, who in 1927 with his wife, Anya, a Russian princess, built the original heritage home still standing today. The rocky beach provides a welcome and scenic rest area to kayakers and canoeists. Landing on the shore is best at high tide.

As you progress further north, two of the arm's most striking natural features present themselves. You'll hear the roar of Silver Falls long before you see it. In fact, the surrounding forest conceals the cataract so completely that the only way to fully appreciate its turbulence is to paddle as close as possible to the shoreline. As you make your way from here towards Berg's Landing, sheer granite walls covered with a lurid green lichen called questionable rock-frog rise vertically from the ocean. Keep an eye out for seals here.

If you'd like to plan an overnight excursion, several choices exist on each side of the arm. For those heading up Indian Arm's western coast, Berg's Landing is the site of a former logging camp and offers a selection of grassy sites on the water and set back in an alder grove. Fresh water is available from Bishops Creek, which empties into Indian Arm at Berg's.

For information on Say Nuth Khaw Yum Heritage Park/Indian Arm Provincial Park, visit www.env.gov.bc.ca/bcparks/explore/park pgs/indian.html.

The Deep Cove Canoe and Kayak Centre (call 604-929-2268 or visit deepcovekayak.com) is located in Deep Cove Park off 4900 Gallant Avenue near the intersection of Branbury Road (Deep Cove's main street) and Rockcliff Road.

Takaya Tours offers 5-hour motorized eco-cultural explorations of Indian Arm, including stops to view pictographs. For details, contact the Tum-tumay-whueton Kayak Centre in Belcarra Regional Park (604-936-0236).

Millennia before the first Europeans to visit Indian Arm—Spanish naval captain Dionisio Alcalá-Galiano and his crew—arrived, the Tsleil-Waututh First Nation (pronounced *slay-wa-tooth*) had already established villages on both sides of Indian Arm: Whey-ah-wichen, or Facing the Wind, where Cates Park now sits just around the corner from Deep Cove, as well as Tum-tumay-whueton on the Port Moody side at the current site of Belcarra Regional Park (see chapter 14). Indian Arm's significance for the Tsleil-Waututh is the fiord's key geographical location in the heartland of their territory, a highway between communities both at the mouth of the inlet and at its top end where there are two small reserves at the mouth of the Indian River. This region was their breadbasket, both on the water and hunting in the hills. Tsleil-Waututh means "people of the inlet." That alone states how important this place is to their nation.

In June 2007, the Tsleil-Waututh finalized an agreement with the District of North Vancouver to establish a permanent base for Takaya Tours in Cates/Whey-ah-wichen Park located off the Dollarton Highway. For information on their cultural odysseys and canoe tours, phone 604-904-7410. For sea kayaking courses and equipment rentals, contact Cates Paddling Centre, 604-985-2925.

> PEOPLE OF THE INLET

TAKAYA TOURS sprang from a collective vision spearheaded by Leonard George whose father, the late Chief Dan George, founded the troupe Children of Takaya ("wolf") in the 1950s. Dan George's intent was to teach traditional songs and dances—and thus maintain Tsleil-Waututh culture—under the guise of entertainment. Today's tours, which include both land- and ocean-based cultural experiences, are an experiment in Aboriginal eco-tourism, an attempt to bridge the cultural gap between Vancouver's Native and non-Native communities by emphasizing the similarities and differences. This marks the first time that the cultural traditions of the local Tsleil-Waututh have been shared with outsiders. Takaya Tours celebrates all people sitting in the same canoe, paddling in the same tradition.

BURNABY

PORT MOODY

12

BURNABY MOUNTAIN CONSERVATION AREA AND DEER LAKE PARK &

. . . . .

> DISTANCE: 15 km (9.3 mi.) east of Boundary Road in Burnaby

> ACTIVITIES: Birding, cycling, dog walking, fishing, paddling, picnicking, viewpoints, walking

> ACCESS: The most convenient way to reach Burnaby Mountain from Vancouver is to take Hastings Street east to Burnaby Mountain Parkway, then turn north (left) on Centennial Way as the road begins to climb towards Simon Fraser University. The conservation area is at the end of Centennial Way and is well marked.

The main entrance to Deer Lake Park is located just south of the Trans-Canada Highway (Highway 1) in Burnaby. Take the Canada Way exit (#33). Turn left on Canada Way and immediately right on Sperling to Deer Lake Park. An alternative approach leads east from a parking area on Royal Oak Avenue between Kingsway and Canada Way. For bus information, phone TransLink at 604-953-3333 or visit translink.ca.

> ### BURNABY MOUNTAIN CONSERVATION AREA

Here's one of the most exotic parks in the Lower Mainland. Burnaby Mountain's proximity makes it perfect for a quick morning or afternoon getaway. No matter what your age, you'll feel as if you've entered another world. The location is stunning, with the city spread to the west below Mount Burnaby's long incline. Spacious fields offer plenty of romping room. Japanese ceremonial poles lend a truly fantastic appearance to the setting. The place where

Deer Lake

the poles are installed seems custom-made for works of such simple grandeur. A wide-open, grassy field descends the mountain's western slope in a series of gently rolling steps to meet the surrounding poplar forest. The poles were raised on the top third of the slope. Populating one of the steps is a group of perhaps 50 poles gathered as a community—some in pairs, some alone.

Although similar to the outdoor area beside the University of British Columbia's Museum of Anthropology, where several large ceremonial poles from a number of West Coast First Nations soar skyward, Burnaby Mountain's installation is different. The poles were carved by a Japanese artist, Nubuo Toko, and his son, who are among the Ainu people, Japan's first inhabitants, and were erected to commemorate the friendship between the sister cities of Kushiro and Burnaby.

The spectacular setting in the park inspired Toko to imagine it as Kamui Mintara, or Playground of the Gods. Set out in an orderly, eye-pleasing fashion, the poles represent the story of the gods who descended to earth to give birth to the Ainu. Familiar animal spirits such as the whale, bear and owl adorn the tops of the slender, bleached logs. Incised into the sides of some poles are suggestions of human forms, while other poles are simply ringed and notched like the pieces of an ultramodern chess set. Particularly pleasing are four poles set in a square and linked by diagonal cross-beams, with a killer whale riding atop. Nearby, the lone pole in the collection to be installed at right angles to the others supports a whale accompanied by the brooding figure of a raven gazing towards the west. All of the poles rise from gravelled pads, which gives the area a formal look. Harmony, balance and order reign here. Perhaps this is why a visit to Burnaby Mountain Conservation Area provides such a pleasant change for most people.

Not only is the vista to the west enchanting, but so, too, are the cliffside views down to Burrard Inlet, the sight of several bends in Indian Arm and the view north to the sprawling slopes and glacial expanses of Mamquam Mountain near Squamish. A fence keeps visitors back from the edge, providing a sense of security while still imparting a thrill.

The poles and views are not the sole attractions. Burnaby Mountain Conservation Area is ringed by a network of pathways that crisscross the perimeter of the SFU campus, including a 6.5-km (4-mi.) portion of the Trans Canada Trail. When spring temperatures heat the earth, the smell of the resin-rich buds of poplar trees fills the air, along with birdsongs. This is the ideal place to celebrate the annual seasonal renewal in the Playground of the Gods. Its formal rose garden is also a big draw for wedding parties who wish to be photographed among the blossoms. Horizons Restaurant is located next to the garden. Walking and cycling trails run through the forest uphill towards Simon Fraser University and in the woods below the ceremonial poles.

> DEER LAKE PARK

As quiet refuges go, Burnaby's Deer Lake Park defies the odds. Traffic on nearby thoroughfares conspires against tranquillity, or so one might think. Thankfully, a forested buffer zone mitigates all but the distant hum of rubber tires. For much of the year, bird calls—such as a varied thrush's single, sustained note—predominate. So, too, do sounds of human hilarity as novice paddlers struggle to synchronize their strokes to avoid colliding with other watercraft clustered offshore of the park's boat rental facility.

No kayak or canoe experience? No problem. Deer Lake is the ideal learning environment. If you come with a boat in tow, so much the better. The shallow beach beside the parking lot at the lake's eastern end is the perfect place to hand-launch one. With the exception of toy speedboats, only non-motorized craft are sanctioned. Just mind the gaggle of Canada geese, interspersed with colourfully coiffed red-breasted mergansers, that jostle for handouts. The diminutive lake spreads before you with little hidden from view. Modest sandbars extend from the open fields that rise above the western shore and beckon for closer inspection. If you set a good pace, you can circle the lake in little more than a half-hour. But what's the rush? Make like the anglers, who, having set their lines, sit back and quietly bide their time between nibbles and strikes. For details on boat rentals at Deer Lake, phone 604-839-3949 or visit deerlakeboatrentals.com.

As seen from the lake, North Shore peaks dominate the horizon line above the forested perimeter. Even finer gaga mountain views appear if you walk the pathway along the lake's southern bank. In fact, to fully enjoy this nature sanctuary, combine the two approaches. Once you've paddled the perimeter, come ashore and explore two of the attractive homes glimpsed from the water. Over the past half-century, as part of a long-term community vision to acquire all the private property around the lake, the park

> **THERE'S NO FIELD LIKE AN OLD FIELD**
. . . .

OPEN SLOPES preside over Deer Lake's western shoreline just east of Royal Oak Avenue. This meadow is of special importance to wildlife, particularly birds. It is classified as "old field," a former cow pasture that years ago was left to go wild; Burnaby Parks now manages the hillside as a nature reserve. In the late 1980s, Burnaby built a unique biofiltration pond here, complemented by a wildlife viewing platform. Aquatic vegetation planted in the pond, such as cattails, removes oily particles and other contaminants from storm sewers that drain the slope. This living filter prevents sedimentation and phosphates from entering Deer Lake farther downhill.

has expanded from 10 ha (24.7 acres) in the mid-1940s to over ten times that size now. In the process of transitioning Deer Lake into a public waterfront park, the city acquired the largest precinct of heritage properties of any urban centre in Canada and now owns 35 heritage sites around the lake, from small cottages to an Arthur Erickson–designed home, with only four or five private properties left in the acquisition plan. This all started as a dream in 1912 after the Oakalla Lands were turned into a prison. The idea really coalesced in the 1960s among citizens and the municipality. In future, this will be Burnaby's Stanley Park.

While you appraise Erickson's two-storey, post-and-beam Baldwin House, tucked into the woods beside Deer Lake, the Hermetic dictum, "As above, so below," likely takes on an entirely new interpretation. Completed in 1965, the pavilion-style home is a world removed from Erickson's concrete magnum opus atop Burnaby Mountain, Simon Fraser University, which opened that same year. In order to preserve the house, as well as the nearby Eagles Estate, Burnaby partnered with Victoria-based The Land Conservancy (TLC), which established its regional office at the Eagles Estate Heritage Garden.

After one look at Baldwin House, who wouldn't want to spend a few days relaxing there? As it turns out, doing so is entirely possible. The non-profit land trust had been looking for office space when approached by the City of Burnaby. In 2003, TLC staff moved into the 1930s-era home built for Violet and Blythe Eagles. In 2005, a similar arrangement to acquire the Baldwin House followed suit. Renting special properties like the Baldwin House is the way TLC connects people with the work they do. TLC currently owns five properties spread around the province, including one in Tofino. For details on The Land Conservancy, including rental rates on the Baldwin House, visit blog.conservancy.bc.ca or call 604-733-2313.

Whether you simply day trip or plan a weekend getaway to Deer Lake Park, make sure to stop by Eagles Estate. Interpretive tours are offered during weekday office hours. Savour the tranquillity that pervades the heritage garden, recently restored to its former glory. When TLC moved in, the yard was covered with ivy and blackberry bushes. With patient tending from local volunteers, the garden has reemerged from the overgrowth to once again display its original elegance. To fully appreciate the renaissance, simply sit beneath one of the blossoming trees where the hillside falls away to the lake below and revel in this peaceful legacy.

During annual spring and fall bird migrations, it pays to scan the horizon from the viewing platform at the lake's western end. You'll see not only raptors such as hawks, merlins and peregrine falcons making their way, but also turkey vultures winging between the Interior and their winter homes in the Fraser Delta. Silken-voiced meadowlarks and barn owls have begun to frequent the former pasture as well. Along the shore, Virginia rail and cinnamon teal share space in the shallows with the occasional angler. Each spring, the Freshwater Fisheries Society of B.C. (bcfamilyfishing.com) stocks Deer Lake with rainbow trout to encourage city dwellers to toss in a line. Just remember to have a freshwater fishing licence if you do.

For years, wildlife educator Al Grass (see chapter 9) has been keeping a detailed record of birds seen around Deer Lake for BC Wildlife Watch as part of an extensive wildlife inventory being carried out by the municipality. What makes this park so fascinating even for those who have difficulty pinning names on all but the most common birds is the sheer number of feathered creatures liable to be encountered. On a casual walk, visitors can easily spot upwards of 40 species. Creeks and gullies indent the hillside directly above the lake's south shore. Dense foliage here provides the perfect shelter for the diminutive western screech owls.

For a map and further information on both parks, call the Burnaby Parks and Recreation office, 604-294-7450, or visit www.city.burnaby.bc.ca/visitors/attractions/prkstr.html.

13

BURRARD INLET AND
PORT MOODY ARM PARKS &

. . . . .

> DISTANCE: As much as 15 km (9.3 mi.) east of Boundary Road

> ACTIVITIES: Birding, cycling, dog walking, in-line skating, kite-flying, paddling, picnicking, playgrounds, skateboarding, swimming, viewpoints

> ACCESS: New Brighton Park sits on the north side of McGill Street across from the PNE site in Vancouver. Turn north off McGill onto Commissioner Street and follow the signs.

To reach the Heights Trail, head to the north end of Gilmore Street in Burnaby or follow the Portside Trail east of Vancouver's New Brighton Park.

To reach Barnet Marine Park, drive east from Vancouver on Hastings Street into Burnaby. This route leads to the Barnet Highway (Highway 7A). In 2.5 km (1.6 mi.), you'll see the signed entrance to the park on your left.

Rocky Point Park is located in Port Moody, an easy 30-minute drive on weekends from downtown Vancouver via the Barnet Highway (see map page 82). Drive along St. Johns Street, Port Moody's main street. Watch for signs that point to Rocky Point Park. Turn north on Moody Street and follow it to an overpass above the railway tracks that leads to the park. For schedule information on the #160 bus to Port Moody from Vancouver, call TransLink, 604-953-3333 or visit translink.ca.

VANCOUVER'S INNER HARBOUR is a fascinating whirl of marine activity. Huge freighters come and go, slipping in and out of port with the help of tugboats, those little dynamos that ride herd on their foreign-flagged charges. Watching them in action, along with seals, gulls, herons and cormorants, is an engaging way to spend a few hours. On sunny weekends, the harbour fills with pleasure craft that range in size from slim racing canoes to fat cruise ships.

Some of the best vantage points for viewing the action are a series of waterfront parks located on the shores of Burrard Inlet. Getting to any of them involves a quick trip from Vancouver—New Brighton Park, for example, is inside the city limits near Burnaby.

> ### NEW BRIGHTON AND MONTROSE PARKS

Although you may often have driven down McGill Street past the Hastings racetrack on the way to the Ironworkers Memorial (Second Narrows) Crossing, you may not have stopped to explore New Brighton Park. After all, traffic moves through this area at a good speed, and making the turn into the park requires some foresight. Not that you'll find it difficult; you simply have to slow down to make the turnoff into the park. The entrance is well signed, but that doesn't make the park any easier to spot, hidden as it is by a railway overpass. In summer, there are plenty of other cars in the parking lot. New Brighton boasts a heated outdoor pool that attracts many families here on the east side of town.

In the off-season, the pool is fenced in and off-limits unless you fly in. On spring and fall days, ducks have it to themselves; floating on the calm waters of the pool, they look like ideal bathtub duckies. The nearby Cascadia grain elevators cast their reflection on the pool's surface. The rich smell of this year's grain crop being loaded onto a waiting freighter is so thick you'd think you could make bread from the air itself.

It's a short walk from the pool to the small pier for a look across Burrard Inlet at the Lions (Two Sisters), which are perfectly twinned when seen from here. This is one of the best vantage points in the city from which to view these iconic peaks. Perhaps this is why in 1863 the first buildings put up by Europeans in what is now Vancouver were situated here, at the Hastings townsite. A heritage plaque gives details of how the Douglas Road linked this spot with New Westminster and for years carried visitors to a resort that flourished in the days before the wheat pool arrived.

Judging from the currents that suck and eddy around the pier's pilings, ocean swimming never has been much of an option, but there are a couple of sheltered beaches on which to roam out of the cool breeze. The open playing fields around the shoreline lend themselves to tossing a Frisbee, flying a kite or romping with a dog.

If you're keen for an extended walk or pedal, head east from the park entrance along Portside Trail past the grain elevators to link up with the Heights Trail in Burnaby's Montrose Park.

Early spring is one of the best times to visit Montrose Park, when the first signs of green appear in the dense second-growth forest. Salmonberry bushes lead the pack as tightly curled leaves and delicate wine-coloured blossoms sprout from their skinny, shoulder-high branches. In April, it's still possible to look down through the forest to Burrard Inlet east of the Ironworkers Memorial (Second Narrows) Crossing and CNR bridges, and directly north up the Seymour River Valley that divides Lynn Peak and Mount Seymour. A palpable moodiness cloaks the scene as clouds scud across the North Shore, parting occasionally to reveal the glistening whiteness of fresh snow on the summits.

Strengthening rays of sunshine shaft down through bare branches as you follow east along first the 1.5-km (0.9-mi.) Heights Trail that links with the 2.2-km (1.4-mi.) Scenic Park Trail. A sign posted beside a pedestrian bridge spanning a train tunnel at the entrance to the CNR bridge marks the Burnaby–Vancouver border. Older than the Ironworkers Memorial bridge, which soars across Burrard Inlet, the level railway bridge sports two massive weights used to raise and lower its midspan, allowing ocean freighters to access Burrard Inlet's eastern arms.

Behind the wide trail, the hillside rises steeply towards the Burnaby Heights neighbourhood, unseen above. This route was once proposed as a scenic drive for motorists. In the 1970s, opposition to such a roadway prompted local officials to preserve it as a pedestrian greenway instead. Information markers installed by the Trails Society of British Columbia detail such Trans Canada Trail tidbits, including the history of Crabtown, a waterfront community that once thrived here.

When you want to get more of a feel for the inland reaches of the Pacific Ocean where it meets Vancouver's shores, head to Barnet Marine Park. As its name implies, this park provides visitors with access to the waters of Burrard Inlet's Port Moody Arm. You don't need a canoe or kayak to enjoy yourself here; there is much to experience on land. Preschoolers will find the spacious sandbox very entertaining, and larger expanses of sand form a wide beach that will appeal to kids of all ages. *Note*: Dogs are not allowed in the park.

Thick foliage hides any view of the park from the road, and railway tracks obscure the shoreline. From the parking lot, walk across the tracks to reach the green spaces. If you've got strollers and toddlers with you, you may wish to drop them off with an adult at the end of the road and then return uphill to park. Parking for people with physical disabilities is available closer to the water, near a viewing pier. True to the park's marine nature, there is a boat launch for canoes, kayaks or sailboats. Belcarra Regional Park (see next chapter) lies directly north across the narrow inlet. The waters close to shore are serene because no motorized boats can be launched from here.

Burnaby has improved the grounds of Barnet Marine Park tremendously over the past few years, and it now has one of the prettiest beaches in the entire Burrard Inlet area. A large boomed-off swimming section fronts the hard-packed sandy beach. Picnic tables with barbecue stands are shaded by tall poplars. Swings, slides and toy ponies are enclosed in a large sandbox beneath their boughs.

The park is located on the site of Barnet, a small town that flourished with the help of a lumber mill from 1889 until its demise in 1949. All that remains today are several large concrete towers and a squat scrap burner hunkered on the beach. In spring, piles of fresh sand awaiting spreading are mounded up beside a pier perched on tall pilings and provide a challenge for young hill-climbing explorers. The wide curves of Barnet's shoreline lead off to the west and east. Watch for the occasional pelagic cormorant, its long neck iridescent in the sun, as it paddles around, working the shoreline with its long thin bill. It's just one of many species of waterfowl you might see here. Other wildlife that inhabit the park include coyotes; signs warn visitors not to feed them.

A service road runs west through Barnet Park and a good distance beyond towards the Shellburn oil refinery. Follow it on foot or by bike for a look up Indian Arm, across to Deep Cove and Cates/ Whey-Ah Wichen Park, and at much maritime activity. Large freighters lie at anchor, with the green slopes of Mount Seymour rising behind. The setting is so sheltered that it is easy to imagine how welcoming Vancouver's inner harbour has always been to sailors. That same sense of peace extends to all those in need of a refreshing outdoor experience. The gracious lines of the Ironworkers Memorial Crossing stand half-revealed in the distance. In early mornings and late afternoons, watch for the distinctive blue cars of the West Coast Express commuter train. The engineer has a heavy hand on the whistle as the train passes beside Burrard Inlet. Seeing it roll by adds a special thrill to a visit here.

> ## ROCKY POINT PARK
Travellers have been coming to Port Moody for centuries. Native people had summer homes here long before Canadian Pacific's transcontinental rail line first reached the West Coast in November 1885. Port Moody was chosen as its terminus. Only in subsequent years did the line expand into the upstart town of Vancouver.

If you ever owned a toy train set, you may enjoy visiting the real thing. The Port Moody Museum is housed in a restored 1905 train station on Murray Street near the foot of Moody Street, next to the park. See the museum hours posted at vcn.bc.ca/pmmuseum, or call 604-939-1648. If you're just passing by, there's plenty to be seen

> ## BOLTING ON PAYDAY
· · · · · · · · · · · ·

IN THE 1920s, the McNair Mill introduced the first portable gasoline engine-powered saw in Canada. It was used for cutting large-diameter cedar logs into bolts a metre or more in length. The bolts were sent down the mountainside to the mill on a flume. On payday, some of the more adventurous loggers would ride a log down the flume rather than take the long way down.

Old Mill Park, Port Moody

just by looking in the windows. On a siding next to the museum is a 1920s CPR passenger car, "Venosta," named for one of the many stops along the vast cross-country rail line.

Rocky Point Park has a lengthy pier running out into the shallow waters of Port Moody Arm's eastern end. There's swimming here, both in the ocean and in a freshwater pool. The concentration of outdoor activity began to expand here in the 1990s with the creation of the Inlet Trail, a leisure pathway that runs east from Rocky Point Park past five pocket parks that ring the inlet's shoreline along the way to Old Orchard Park, about a 5-km (3.1-mi.) round trip around the elbow-shaped inlet. In fact, the trail consists of parallel tracks: a dirt route, augmented in places by a narrow boardwalk, appeals to walkers; its paved twin proves a boon to cyclists, in-line skaters, baby buggy–pushing parents and just about anyone and anything on wheels. *Note*: A fenced off-leash dog area with a separate small dog area is located in the park adjacent to Slaughterhouse Creek, which can be accessed from Murray Street.

In 2000, the PoMo Rotary Bike Trials Park opened. Sheltered by the Moody Street overpass, it was specifically built with trials bike riders in mind. The first urban trials park built in North America, it features logs, boulders and a wooden platform shaped like the prow of a boat for cyclists to hop around on.

That was followed two years later by the adjacent PoMo Rotary SK8 Park with ramps and rails, stairs and tabletops designed for skateboarders and BMX bike riders. About the same time, the Old Mill Boathouse was rebuilt for rowers and dragon boat, canoe and kayak paddlers. And in 2006, a new pavilion, water spray park, toddlers' wading pool and band shell were installed.

On foot, you can cover the Shoreline Trail one way in less than an hour, half that by bike. But you'll quickly discover that there's more to see and do along the way than meets the eye, so budget at least twice that much time for exploration. In fact, during spring and fall bird migration, you can spend quite a while hidden behind two blinds overlooking the inlet's mudflats where transient shorebirds and permanent residents, such as great blue herons, congregate. Hidden in the woods just off the trail is the Noons Creek Hatchery from which thousands of chum salmon fry are released each spring.

By far the most intriguing site lies at the trail's halfway point in Old Mill Park. This is the former location of the McNair Mill. Massive concrete footings, which once supported beehive burners where logging scraps were incinerated, rise like truncated step pyramids above the shallows. Tiny crabs skitter underfoot amid countless bricks strewn across the foreshore, many of which bear the imprint of the historic Clayburn kilns in Abbotsford.

Salmonberry bushes hem the trail. In wet seasons, the little streams and creeks that pass underneath gurgle like newborns. Here, at the very east end of the inlet, the wind often blows so strongly in your ears that you can't hear any sounds—industrial or wildlife—just the cleansing strains of nature calling.

14

BELCARRA AND
BUNTZEN LAKE &

. . . . .

> **DISTANCE:** 30 km (18.6 mi.) east of Boundary Road

> **ACTIVITIES:** Dog walking, fishing, hiking, mountain biking, paddling, picnicking, swimming, viewpoints, walking

> **ACCESS:** Belcarra Regional Park and Buntzen Lake Recreation Area lie on the north side of Port Moody Arm across from Burnaby. From Vancouver, head to Port Moody on Hastings Street and the Barnet Highway (Highway 7A). Turn east onto St. Johns Street and north six stoplights later onto well-marked Ioco Road. Ioco Road soon turns left at an intersection marked by a green Metro Vancouver Parks sign pointing the way to the park. (If you're headed to the village of Anmore and Buntzen Lake, continue straight ahead onto Heritage Mountain Boulevard.) Turn right at the Ioco School and follow First Avenue towards the village of Belcarra. (An alternative route to Anmore and Buntzen Lake via Sunnyside Road appears on the right just after you've passed through Ioco.) Just before Sasamat Lake, signs direct traffic left towards Belcarra Park. *Note:* There is no vehicle access to the park from the community of Belcarra, where parking is restricted to residents only.

For schedule information on the C24 Belcarra and Anmore route via the #160 bus to Port Moody from Vancouver, call TransLink, 604-953-3333, or visit translink.ca.

SINCE 1996, major changes have occurred in the parkland that surrounds the communities of Port Moody, Belcarra and Anmore. Three separate stakeholders—Metro Vancouver, BC Hydro and BC Parks—oversee recreational land here; the Metro

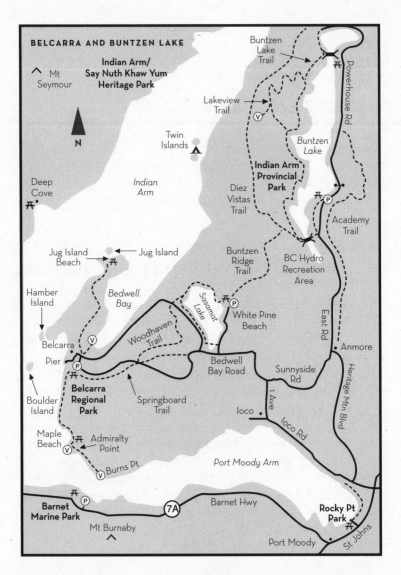

Indian Arm/
Say Nuth Khaw Yum
Heritage Park

∧ Mt
Seymour

N

Buntzen
Lake
Trail

Powerhouse Rd

Lakeview
Trail

Ⓥ

*Buntzen
Lake*

**Indian Arm
Provincial
Park**

Ⓟ

Academy
Trail

Deep
Cove

*Indian
Arm*

Twin
Islands

Diez
Vistas
Trail

Jug Island
Beach

← Jug Island

Buntzen
Ridge
Trail

BC Hydro
Recreation
Area

East Rd

• Anmore

Hamber
Island

*Bedwell
Bay*

*Sasamat
Lake*

Ⓟ

White Pine
Beach

Belcarra

Ⓥ

Woodhaven
Trail

Bedwell
Bay Road

Sunnyside
Rd

Heritage Mtn Blvd

Pier

Ⓟ

Boulder
Island

**Belcarra
Regional
Park**

Springboard
Trail

1 Ave

Ioco •

Ioco Rd

Maple
Beach

Ⓥ

← Admiralty
Point

Ⓥ Burns Pt

Port Moody Arm

Barnet
Marine Park

Ⓟ

⑦Ⓐ

Barnet Hwy

**Rocky Pt
Park**

Mt Burnaby
∧

Port Moody

St Johns

Vancouver's Belcarra Regional Park, BC Hydro's Buntzen Lake Recreation Area and Say Nuth Khaw Yum Heritage Park/Indian Arm Provincial Park border one another. Thanks to the efforts of a local citizens' group, the Buntzen Ridge Wilderness Recreation and Parks Association, trails connecting the three parks that once served only hikers and horseback riders have been upgraded to accommodate a mixed group of outdoor enthusiasts, including mountain bikers. Strategically placed "Shared Trail" interpretive signs have helped to minimize conflict between users.

This is one of the most varied destinations for day trippers in the Lower Mainland. There's far more ground to explore here than can be covered in a week, let alone a day. Walk oceanfront trails in Belcarra Park, hike lakeside trails on Buntzen Ridge, swim in freshwater Sasamat or Buntzen lakes, mountain bike through the forest of Indian Arm Park that surrounds Anmore and Belcarra, picnic on Buntzen's grassy lawns, launch a kayak into Indian Arm or paddle a canoe in Buntzen Lake. Decide how big a piece you want to bite off, pack a lunch and away you go.

> ### BELCARRA REGIONAL PARK

Belcarra welcomes about 850,000 visitors a year. Granted, the park bulges with swimmers, paddlers, picnickers and mountain bikers in summer months. In the off-season, though, it reverts to the quiet little hideaway it was when Metro Vancouver Parks first began acquiring land here in the early 1970s. *Note*: Dogs must be on leash at all times.

Belcarra is an Irish name meaning "fair land on which the sun shines." Approximately 4,000 years before the arrival of Judge William Norman Bole, the Irishman who christened this corner of Indian Arm and Burrard Inlet, ancestors of the local Tsleil-Waututh First Nation called it *Tum-tumay-whueton*, meaning "land" or "biggest place for people" or just plain "home." Since 1971, three significant archaeological sites have been unearthed in this area that highlight its importance over the millennia. One large midden, a mound of shells and shards, rises above the beach. From it you have an unobstructed view west across the waters of Indian Arm and Burrard Inlet, which sustained the Native population. Small wonder that First Nations peoples treasured this land as their winter home.

In 1923, the Harbour Navigation Company developed resort facilities here. Vancouverites rode the ferry to visit the dance pavilion, wharf and cabins. All but the cement stairway to the beach is now gone, but tour boats from Vancouver still come here in the summer with groups who picnic and play on the large open lawns. Anglers and crabbers use the dock. The Belcarra picnic area has reservable picnic shelters and even a reservable wharf. Call 604-432-6352 for more information. During summer months, kayak rentals are available Friday through Monday. For details, contact the Tum-tumay-whueton Kayak Centre: 604-936-0236.

As you near Belcarra Park, you will see several small parking lots beside the road. These are for the benefit of cyclists and hikers who wish to explore the forested 4-km (2.5-mi.) Springboard Trail without having to drive all the way to the main parking lot. The trail links Sasamat Lake with Belcarra's waterfront on Indian Arm beside the picnic area, concession stand and open park grounds.

At the picnic grounds, there is a choice of activities. Head for the beach, stroll out on the dock or stretch your legs along some of the scenic oceanfront trails.

> ### ADMIRALTY POINT TRAIL

One of Belcarra's most welcoming trails begins at the main parking lot and heads south through second-growth forest to several good viewpoints. Boardwalks assist footing on a steep-sided section that overlooks Burrard Inlet. A 30-minute walk will have you at Admiralty Point and the Maple Beach picnic area. It won't take long before your eyes begin to pick out things on the forest floor that rarely appear in Vancouver neighbourhoods. Chocolate-brown mushrooms the size of freshly baked muffins glisten at the foot of fire-charred snags covered by velvety, emerald-green moss. Sword ferns colonize the sides of soaring alders, giving the trunks a bristly outline. The graceful skirts of western red cedar branches shelter low-lying salal bushes that line the trail. At places like Cod Rock and Periwinkle Notch, paths lead out to panoramic viewpoints of Burrard Inlet. Kayakers and canoeists paddle by.

Hours of afternoon sunlight warm the shores of Belcarra on clear days. On cloudy days, an air of quiet reflection hangs over the trail. Besides Burrard Inlet and Mount Burnaby to the south, you can also see Deep Cove to the west and Mount Seymour rising above the entrance to Indian Arm, a fiord that stretches 18 km (11.2 mi.) north.

The most beautiful beach in Belcarra presents itself at Whiteshell

Bank, just minutes beyond Admiralty Point, as the trail bends south-east and leads beside Port Moody's outer harbour. The pathway to the beach was obviously fashioned long before this became a park. Indeed, in the early 1980s, squatters were finally ousted after having enjoyed this location since the 1950s. Thanks to their efforts over the years, rocks on a portion of the little beach were cleared away. Over time, pulverized shells streaked the sandy surface a powdery white. Drifts of delicate green periwinkle carpet the foreshore, suggesting human occupation. Confirmation of this is provided by a companion hydrangea bush whose greenish-blue blossoms add yet another splash of colour to the surroundings. Here is a quintessential West Coast setting: a quiet cove outlined in cedar where small streams splash out of the forest and down into the ocean. Gulls wheel above as a harbour seal bobs up to check you out.

Visitors in wheelchairs seeking a challenging workout will find the Springboard Trail's hardened surface to their liking. Take an able-bodied person to help on some steep, switchback sections west of Woodhaven Swamp.

> ## JUG ISLAND BEACH TRAIL

One of the lengthier walks in Belcarra leads to Jug Island Beach, which overlooks Jug Island. Depending on your pace, it will take between 30 and 45 minutes to reach it from the Belcarra picnic grounds. Jug Island Beach Trail begins in the woods beside the covered picnic shelter. Much of the route is either up- or downhill, with a series of wooden staircases for assistance in the steepest sections. Although there are few views along the way, one branch of the trail leads out to an opening beside Bedwell Bay. From here you look east to the slopes of Eagle Ridge and the broad flank of Coquitlam Mountain rising above unseen Buntzen Lake. Farther along, a new branch of the trail leads through a fragrant pine forest to another lookout on Bedwell Bay.

The beach trail leads through a forest of second-growth hemlock and alder as well as broadleaf maple. In summer, the dense leaf and needle canopy is an omnipresent green. Come autumn, the leaves

Buntzen Lake

turn shades of gold, and once they fall, their shades range from deep purple to rich terra cotta. So dense is the layer of leaves covering the trail that little, if any, of the bare earth can be seen.

Jug Island lies offshore at the north end of a narrow peninsula and can be viewed from a small beach at the end of the trail. The island has steep, rocky sides with no visible landing sites. Looking north from the little beach, you can make out the concrete walls of the hydro station whose turbines are driven by water from Buntzen Lake. Visible beyond Jug Island are Raccoon and Twin islands in Say Nuth Khaw Yum Heritage Park/Indian Arm Provincial Park (see chapter 11). A number of wilderness campsites on Twin Islands make them a desirable destination for paddlers who set off from Belcarra's shore. The broad, glaciated slopes of Mamquam Mountain dominate the skyline to the north. Mount Garibaldi's peak juts up to the left of Mamquam.

> ## SASAMAT LAKE

In the hills above Belcarra are two freshwater lakes, Sasamat and Buntzen. The sandy White Pine Beach on Sasamat Lake is among the most popular in the Lower Mainland, perhaps because the water here is so warm. As well, a pleasant walking trail circles the lake (about half as big as nearby Buntzen Lake) beneath the shelter of graceful western red cedars. A 200-m (656-ft.) floating bridge spans the south end of Sasamat Lake and provides welcome relief from the close quarters of the forested trail. *Note*: Dogs are not allowed on beaches in Belcarra Park.

One of the region's best-built hiking and cycling trails links Belcarra with Indian Arm Park. The Buntzen Ridge Trail begins from the south end of parking lot F above White Pine Beach at Sasamat Lake. It switchbacks 2 km (1.2 mi.) to link with the Saddle Ridge Trail (see next section) on Buntzen Ridge, to the west of Buntzen Lake.

> ## BUNTZEN LAKE RECREATION AREA

Buntzen Lake draws its water from a tunnel connected to the Coquitlam reservoir and is much chillier than Sasamat. A wealth of riding, hiking and cycling trails leads north from here beside the long lake and onto the ridges above. Those who enjoy exploring by water can rent a canoe year round at the nearby Anmore Grocery (604-469-9928). As Buntzen is closed to powerboats, you'll revel in the quiet as you paddle past loons and Canada geese. In 1970, BC Hydro, which draws water down from the lake to run two hydro generating plants on Indian Arm, developed Buntzen for recreation, pouring a wide, gently sloping sand beach. *Note*: Dogs are permitted in a fenced portion of the main beach area; there are picnic areas where dogs are allowed. Dogs must be on a leash except in the two designated off-leash areas or on the off-leash trail.

Buntzen Lake's South Beach picnic area is laid out in a tidy fashion. Large, well-spaced picnic tables sit under a forest of Douglas-fir, and broad lawns run down to the beach. You can drive to the dock to unload boats. It's possible to swim from the beach or docks—one of which is wheelchair accessible—to a small treed island just offshore with a rocky point for diving. Another such island lies a short boat ride north of the dock. The lake is stocked with kokanee, cutthroat trout and Dolly Varden char, among other species. It will take you half an hour to paddle the length of the lake, if you're in a hurry. Otherwise, Buntzen is the kind of place where, once you've arrived, there's no need to rush anything.

Avoid the park during peak weekend hours in July and August; it's just too busy. Otherwise, plan your trip for as early in the day as possible to avoid traffic and long walks from the overflow parking lots. Strategically placed information kiosks at South Beach give prospective boaters a detailed look at the shoreline and help determine where to head on this 6-km-long (3.7-mi.-long), narrow, steep-sided lake. Maps posted at the kiosks are also of great assistance to cyclists, walkers and hikers interested in circling the lake via a series of roads and trails. For much of the distance, these mostly level routes hug the lake. In addition, there is a network of more challenging trails that climb to viewpoints above the lake's east and west sides. Printed maps with detailed route descriptions are available at the aforementioned sign during summer months. Contact BC Hydro to obtain a copy, 604-469-9679, or visit www.bchydro.com/recreation.

Cyclists and those pushing strollers will particularly enjoy the well-maintained gravel road that runs for 3 km (1.9 mi.) along the lake's eastern shore from the South Beach parking lot to the powerhouse near North Beach. Those who'd prefer a lakeside walk should try the 8-km (5-mi.) Buntzen Lake Trail, which circles the lake. Allow 4 to 5 hours to walk the trail.

The well-marked Academy Trail provides a more challenging route. This pleasant 4-km (2.5-mi.) hard-packed pathway is a shared equestrian-hiker-cyclist trail. A good place to begin exploring Academy Trail on foot or by bike is from the first parking lot on the right as you enter the recreation area. Academy Trail links up with Powerhouse Road halfway to North Beach. Although views of the lake are scarce along this trail, views of Mount Seymour on the western horizon more than compensate.

Watch for the well-marked entrance to the Halvor Lunden Trail just north of South Beach on Powerhouse Road (see below). Named for a renowned local trail builder, the trail comprises three loop routes: the Lindsay Lake Loop (15 km/9.3 mi.), the Swan Falls Loop (20 km/12.4 mi.) and the Dilly Dally Loop (25 km/15.5 mi.). Only experienced and fit hikers and mountain bikers should attempt these longer trails. The loops traverse the steep hillside above Buntzen Lake's east side in Indian Arm Provincial Park. Viewpoints on Eagle Ridge and a nest of 10 lakes make the effort worthwhile. Depending on your route, allow between 6 and 12 hours to complete the individual loops.

As both Powerhouse Road and the Buntzen Lake Trail approach North Beach, they pass the tunnel for water entering Buntzen from Coquitlam Lake. You'll hear the sound of the water flowing from the tunnel beneath Eagle Ridge well before it comes into view near North Beach. You can walk down from the road to view the tunnel on a staircase that also leads to the North Beach picnic area. If you continue a short distance farther along the road as it descends downhill, you'll arrive at an entrance to North Beach. An interpretive map is located where the lake narrows, next to an open playing field. This is also a good destination should you be exploring by boat. A warning sign advises boaters to keep well away from the tunnel. Paddling north from South Beach will give your arms a good workout. Because of Buntzen's sheltered setting, its surface is most often calm, and you'll find that the water in the lake is extremely clear.

Look for Swan Falls cascading down the eastern slopes above the lake, just as the road descends towards the pumphouse. The road continues in hard-packed condition as it rounds the north end of the lake past the large intake pipe that feeds water to the generators. For many visitors, especially those with children, this will be as far as you wish to go before retracing your route. Don't pass up a chance to cross the suspension bridge over the lake's north end before you turn back.

If you're up for more adventuring, you can choose to return along the west side of the lake on the Buntzen Lake Trail, a round-trip distance of 8 km (5 mi.). Alternatively, the Lakeview Trail (6 km/ 3.7 mi.), which leads uphill from Buntzen, provides a much stiffer challenge to those on foot or bike. Novices should not attempt this route. It involves a long series of ups and downs along a series of bumpy switchbacks. In contrast, the Buntzen Lake Trail, which skirts the shoreline, is far easier to handle.

If you choose to explore Buntzen Lake in a clockwise direction from South Beach, cross to the lake's west side on the boardwalk that leads over the lake's south end. Pumphouse Road leads 1.5 km (0.9 mi.) along the lake's west side as far as the Burrard Pumphouse. A 4-km (2.5-mi.) portion of the Buntzen Lake Trail leads north from the pumphouse along the west side of the lake. Allow 2 to 3 hours to walk the trail one way to North Beach.

As you climb above the lake's western shoreline, you enter Indian Arm Provincial Park. Four multi-use trails originate here, including a series of steep loop trails called Bear Claw, Saddle Ridge and Horseshoe. Thigh- and quad-burning 7-km (4.3-mi.) Diez Vistas Trail is the longest and most demanding route. Ten viewpoints (hence *diez vistas*) are sprinkled along the trail, which overlooks Burrard Inlet, Indian Arm, Eagle Ridge and Buntzen Lake. Near the junction of Diez Vistas and Saddle Ridge trails is the 2-km (1.2-mi.) Buntzen Ridge Trail, which leads to Sasamat Lake in Belcarra Regional Park.

COQUITLAM

PORT COQUITLAM

PITT MEADOWS

MAPLE RIDGE

15

COLONY FARM
REGIONAL PARK

· · · · ·

> DISTANCE: 25 km (15.5 mi.) east of Vancouver

> ACTIVITIES: Birding, cycling, dog walking, nature observation, picnicking, viewpoints, walking

> ACCESS: From Highway 1, take Exit 44 and follow signs to Lougheed Highway (Highway 7) east. Continue travelling east on Lougheed Highway to the traffic light at Colony Farm Road. Turn right and continue 1 km (0.6 miles) to the main parking lot. From the east along Lougheed Highway (Highway 7), travel through Coquitlam past the lights at Pitt River Road and Riverview Hospital. Turn left at the traffic lights at Colony Farm Road. If you're travelling by public transit, take the SkyTrain to Braid Station, then hop on the #177 Coquitlam Station bus.

JEWEL-LIKE REGIONAL parks garland Metro Vancouver like an evergreen necklace. From Bowen Island's Crippen Park to Abbotsford's Matsqui Trail, you can't help but feel blessed, even overwhelmed, exploring one.

Not so at Colony Farm in Coquitlam, at least not on first sight. All that greets the eye is a wide swath of fallow farmland on the south side of Lougheed Highway, just east of the Port Mann Bridge. Classified as "old field," the former cow pasture and cropland were left to go wild when the provincially owned farm, once part of Riverview Hospital, closed in 1983. Although the property doesn't jump out at you, the land is of special importance to wildlife, particularly birds such as colourful lazuli buntings, Bullock's orioles and black-headed grosbeaks that nest here.

Community Garden, Colony Farm Regional Park

During a visit to Colony Farm, I always look forward to drinking in the views from the open fields of the dike trails, the river, the mountains, the wildlife—especially the birds. To those looking for a mellow outing, the level bike trails themselves are worth a million dollars. To help visitors, particularly those without their own two-wheeled chariots, experience this for themselves, the Kwikwetlem First Nation operates a bike tour and rental company at one of the band's two reserves that border the regional park. During the week, as many as 120 young students per day tour the park, not just from the local Coquitlam school district but also from schools in Richmond, Vancouver and three other municipalities. While half the kids head out on bikes for tours, the rest attend classroom workshops on First Nations history and wildlife. Then they trade off. Kwikwetlem elders consider themselves caretakers of the Coquitlam River. They've lived for these days. For details on Colony Farm Bike Tours and Rentals, call 604-520-0090 or visit www.colonyfarmbiketours.com.

Indeed, the intertidal Coquitlam flows through the park and adjoins part of the nearby 25-km (15.5-mi.) Traboulay PoCo Trail.

Dikes that hold the shallow waterway in check are topped with welcoming crushed-gravel trails, which make for smooth, almost effortless pedalling. Shade cast by a predominantly black cottonwood and western red cedar forest provides welcome relief from both the sun and the din of traffic. The dikes also protect an extensive community garden that thrives on almost 3 ha (7.4 acres) of verdant soil. Growers have been reaping the rewards of their 23-square-metre (248-square-foot) plots almost since the community garden—unique in the regional park system—opened in 1997. Flower gardens are magnets for hummingbirds and butterflies. With row-on-row of plots butted up against each other, many featuring protective coverings, the appearance is like an armada of houseboats moored together.

At the hottest times of the year, finding such an oasis is good fortune indeed, particularly at early morning and evening times when a cooling breeze wafts off the nearby Fraser River where the Coquitlam makes its confluence. Stillness envelops the hillsides and hazy peaks. Clusters of crimson berries hang heavy from the branches of red elderberry and black hawthorn bushes. Drifts of fireweed pattern the fields at the foot of Mary Hill. This is where you'll want to be. Enjoy a picnic supper beside the community garden gazebo. Then, best of all, stroll the lanes to admire the bounty erupting from the little jewel boxes.

For more information, visit metrovancouver.org/services/parks_lscr/regionalparks/Pages/ColonyFarm.aspx.

16

MINNEKHADA
REGIONAL PARK

. . . . .

> DISTANCE: 17 km (10.5 mi.) east of Vancouver, in Coquitlam

> ACTIVITIES: Birding, dog walking, hiking, nature observation, picnicking, in-line skating, viewpoints, walking

> ACCESS: From Vancouver, take either Highway 1 to Exit 44 (United Boulevard North/Mary Hill Bypass) or the Lougheed Highway (Highway 7) to Port Coquitlam–Coquitlam. As Highway 7 passes through Port Coquitlam's town centre, watch for the green Metro Vancouver Parks sign indicating the turnoff to Minnekhada at Coast Meridian Road. Turn north at the lights at this interchange. To reach the lodge entrance follow Coast Meridian for several blocks to Praire Road. Turn right on Prairie, then left on Cedar Drive to Oliver Road. From here, the park is an easy 10-minute drive. To reach the Quarry Road entrance, stay on Coast Meridian, then follow Victoria Drive.

A DREAM SHARED by many Canadians is owning a little cabin in the woods, a safe haven where we can retreat for a momentary respite from the sounds and sights of the city. In the 1930s, that yearning enticed B.C.'s Lieutenant Governor of the day, Eric Hamber, to construct a Scottish-style hunting lodge in a far corner of Coquitlam. Tucked up against the steep slopes of Burke Mountain overlooking the Pitt River, the two-storey lodge sits atop a ridge that backs on a marshy pond in what is now Minnekhada Regional Park.

You'll discover the same soothing remoteness to this forested location that once satisfied viceregal pastoral longings. In 1983, Metro Vancouver acquired the property and subsequently expanded it to 225 ha (556 acres), over half the size of Stanley Park.

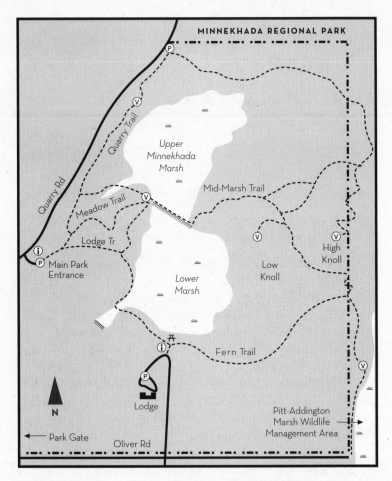

Upper
Minnekhada
Marsh

Quarry Trail

Quarry Rd

Mid-Marsh Trail

Meadow Trail

Lodge Tr

Main Park
Entrance

Lower
Marsh

Low
Knoll

High
Knoll

Fern Trail

N

Lodge

Pitt-Addington
Marsh Wildlife
Management Area

← Park Gate

Oliver Rd

Following the most recent ice age, knobby knolls unique in the region thrust up from the Fraser Valley in Minnekhada. From the tops of these modest but steep hills, visitors enjoy a panoramic look-out over a network of marshes ringed with leafy softwood trees.

Minnekhada is particularly attractive when the leaves start to change colour. A touch of frost at the higher elevations around the park brings out red and golden tones. Fog settles in the folds of the mountain but burns off with the warmth of the sun, revealing silver birches in changing hues. Spiral staircases of fungi cling to some of the older trunks. Walking is easy on the soft forest floor, cushioned by generations of fallen leaves.

Minnekhada's Marsh Trail

Two large ponds ringed by marshes sit squarely in the middle of the park. A figure-eight trail skirts the water's edge. When a winter cold spell hits and the ponds freeze over, this is a fine place to bring your blades. A light coating of snow serves only to heighten the vividness of the rich greens of the ferns and mosses on the forest floor and cliff faces of the rocky knolls that lend Minnekhada a lumpy demeanour.

The first of three entrances to the park leads along Oliver Road past Minnekhada Farm's heritage buildings to the lodge at the park's southern end. (A short distance farther east on Oliver Road is another approach to the park on the PoCo and Coquitlam Dike Trails beside the Pitt River. See next chapter for details.)

There is an information kiosk next to the lodge, as well as parking and several picnic tables beside one of the outbuildings. From Minnekhada Lodge, you can quickly walk to the Lower Marsh pond on Lodge Trail or follow Fern Trail east towards Minnekhada's boundary with the Pitt-Addington Marsh Wildlife Management Area. This rolling trail leads to a lookout over the marsh that requires only a moderate climb. Plan on taking 30 minutes to reach it.

The main entrance to the park is from the parking lot off Quarry Road. An information board at the trailhead often carries news of bird sightings. From here, you have a choice of approaches to the ponds and marsh area, as well as to the lodge. Soon after you enter the main trail, it divides. Lodge Trail leads off to the right. Meadow Trail to the left soon divides again. Quarry Trail meanders around some pretty areas where moss and forest intermingle. Bridges span the wetter parts, finally bringing visitors to the shores of the north or upper pond. Meadow Trail leads to a lookout over the ponds before descending to cross an earthen dam that divides the two ponds. Log Walk leads to the dam along more level ground. The banks of the ponds are thick with bulrushes, and there are several open spots where you can sit with binoculars and search for birdlife.

If you're feeling energetic, climb to the top of High Knoll to take in the view of Golden Ears to the east, the nearby Fraser and Pitt rivers, and the Cascade Mountains south across the Fraser Valley. The park's distinctive knolls are largely free of underbrush, and hiking is easy amid the groves. The steepness of the High Knoll does make climbing it a challenge. However, the trail is well constructed, and you can reach the top within an hour from the parking lot. If your time is limited or you're not inclined to climb, a shorter section of trail leads through a lovely stand of cedars and western hemlocks to the lookout at Low Knoll. From here, you can look back down on the ponds and west to Mount Burke.

After clambering around the narrow trail that leads around Low Knoll, head east to the Addington Lookout shelter. At magic hour, the reddish-gold sunlight accentuates a broad expanse of copper-coloured marsh grasses. Vivid green-feathered heads of male mallards provide further points of colour in the channels off the Pitt River. Orange-banded varied thrushes perch patiently in the hawthorn trees that line Quarry Road in front of Minnekhada Lodge. A field of knee-high blueberry bushes backlit by the last rays glows with a maroon hue.

Minnekhada Park is just one part of a large wilderness area on the west side of the Pitt River. As you become more familiar with the region, you can extend your visit to include the PoCo and Coquitlam Dike Trails and the Pitt-Addington Marsh Wildlife Management Area (see next two chapters).

17

POCO AND
COQUITLAM DIKE TRAILS

. . . . .

> DISTANCE: 25 km (15.5 mi.) east of Vancouver, in Port Coquitlam and Coquitlam

> ACTIVITIES: Birding, boating, cycling, dog walking, fishing, view-points, walking

> ACCESS: From Highway 1, take Exit 44 and follow signs to High-way 7B/United Boulevard North, which leads to Port Coquitlam–Coquitlam via the Mary Hill Bypass. As you near the Pitt River Bridge, stay in the right-hand lane, and take the Coquitlam exit on Highway 7 at its intersection with the Mary Hill Bypass. From High-way 7, turn north onto Coast Meridian Road and east on Dominion Avenue. Follow it to its terminus, next to the Pitt River dike, on top of which runs the PoCo trail. Alternatively, once you're on Coast Meridian, follow the green Metro Vancouver signs towards Min-nekhada Regional Park (see previous chapter).

THERE IS often such an enchanting stillness on a section of the PoCo (short for Port Coquitlam) and Coquitlam Dike Trails that it feels as if you're sealed inside a capsule and set apart from the nearby world. So calm is the surface of the Pitt River that it exactly mirrors the surrounding mountains in all their glory. On a clear day, your vision, under a pale-blue sky, is of a world so impeccable that it will erase all of the smudges and fingerprints left on your mind by the cares and concerns of everyday life.

There is a trend in many local municipalities to create or expand urban greenways and make them more wheelchair accessible.

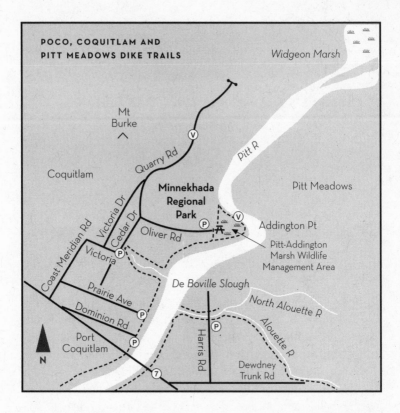

Widgeon Marsh

Mt
Burke

Quarry Rd

Coquitlam

Pitt R

Pitt Meadows

**Minnekhada
Regional
Park**

Victoria Dr

Cedar Dr

Oliver Rd

P

V

Addington Pt

Pitt-Addington
Marsh Wildlife
Management Area

Coast Meridian Rd

Victoria

P

Prairie Ave

De Boville Slough

North Alouette R

Dominion Rd

P

P

Port
Coquitlam

P

Harris Rd

Alouette R

N

7

Dewdney
Trunk Rd

Coquitlam and Port Coquitlam have done this. Part of their circuit winds along the banks of the Pitt River, one of the more active rivers to flow into the Fraser. The Pitt's motion is affected by the tidal action on the Fraser, and, depending on the time of day, its waters can be moving either north or south. The banks of the Pitt have been built up to prevent flooding on the adjacent lowlands.

Families with carloads of bikes and the occasional stroller make these dike trails their year-round destination when a quick outing is called for. It gets everyone out of the house; the kids can ride on ahead at their own rate while those on foot fan out at a more sedate pace. The trail leads north beside the river for more than 10 km (6.2 mi.), far enough to let cyclists really know they've spent some time in the saddle when they dismount, particularly after a round trip.

PoCo Dike Trail

> ### DOMINION AVENUE ENTRANCE

When you leave your vehicle behind and climb up onto the dike, your eyes must adjust to the wide views east across the river to Pitt Meadows' open prairie. Log booms march north towards Pitt Lake along both banks, and there is plenty of open water in the river's channel to accommodate flocks of waterfowl. You may have to duck as squadron upon squadron of geese rise honking from the river, cresting the dike at low altitude before making their descent to feed in the open green fields to the west. Lunchtime! The birds have been resident on the Pitt for such a long time that they even have a section of marshland—Goose Bar—named for them.

Although during warmer months, this region is a swath of mixed greens, by late fall and early winter, this exposed piece of wetland looks washed of colour. Flaxen hues predominate along the dike and on the slopes of Mount Burke to the northwest. This makes the thick evergreen forest covering much of Minnekhada's High Knoll at the far northern end of the dike trail stand out in exaggerated relief.

> ## DE BOVILLE SLOUGH

No matter from which direction you explore the dike, you'll have to spend some time away from the river where the PoCo Dike Trail cuts inland to circumvent De Boville Slough, whose snaking course provides shelter for ducks and spawning salmon. All the land north of the slough, including Mount Burke and the dike trail to Minnekhada, lies within Coquitlam.

Stay with the Coquitlam Dike Trail that hugs De Boville Slough's north side. It will bring you back out to the banks of the Pitt River in a matter of 5 minutes. Blackberries grow along this section of the trail in great numbers; despite the best efforts of the well-organized pickers with their gloves, hooking poles and loppers, there will still be lots left if you visit here in September.

> ## ADDINGTON POINT

Back beside the river, the country alongside the trail becomes even more rural, with tilled fields running right up to Mount Burke's steep sides. In another 10 minutes, you'll reach the caretaker's heritage home beside Addington Marsh. Visible on the slope of the

> ## PADDLIN' THE PITT

IF YOU are planning to adventure by canoe, kayak or small hand-carried boat, there is a launch at the Pitt River Boat Club (3765 Lincoln Ave.; 604-942-7371; www.pittriverboatclub.com). To find it, go north on Coast Meridian, turn right on Prairie Avenue, left on Devon Road and right on Lincoln Avenue. The boat club is at the end of Lincoln.

knoll ahead is a sheltered lookout over the marsh, a good place to stop and picnic, for this is where the dike trail ends.

Just north of the caretaker's house, another long trail curves out over the marsh, with two-storey observation towers poised above the wetland in several places, hardly visible from here. You can add another half-hour of cycling to your journey if you roll out here. Or, if you're hankering for a little vertical relief after all the level riding or walking you've just experienced, consider climbing the trail behind the shelter to the top of Minnekhada's High Knoll.

Metro Vancouver Parks maintains a trail that runs north of the lookout shelter to several additional viewpoints overlooking the marsh. This trail leads out onto the marsh, linking with the trail you passed earlier on your way past the caretaker's home. The lodge at Minnekhada is only minutes away. You can see it in the distance, nestled in the forest, as you approach Addington Point. A narrow paved road leads off to it from the left side of the dike as you near the shelter. (For more information on the lodge, see previous chapter.)

Fields of bright foliage colour the eastern shore in an area called Pitt Polder (see next chapter). Mount Burke with its dark forest closes in on the west side of the trail beside the Pitt-Addington Marsh. You've come a long way to reach this point. Catch your breath before turning back, and remind yourself that the view on the return journey will be refreshingly different from what it was on the way here.

> # 18

PITT MEADOWS:
RIVERS AND POLDER &

. . . . .

> DISTANCE: 50 km (31 mi.) east of Vancouver, in Pitt Meadows

> ACTIVITIES: Birding, boating, camping, cycling, dog walking, fishing, hiking, nature observation, paddling, picnicking, viewpoints, walking

> ACCESS: To reach Pitt River Greenway, follow Highway 1 east to Exit 44 in Coquitlam. Take the United Boulevard off-ramp, which connects with the Mary Hill Bypass (Highway 7B) and leads across the Pitt River Bridge via the Lougheed Highway. (You can also take the Lougheed Highway east through Port Coquitlam–Coquitlam as an alternate route.) Cross the bridge and turn right at the Harris Road intersection. Drive south along Pitt Meadows' main street to Harris Landing beside the Fraser River.

To reach the Pitt Meadows dike system and Grant Narrows Regional Park, drive east of the Pitt River Bridge or west of the Golden Ears Bridge on the Lougheed Highway (Highway 7). Turn north on Harris Road at the traffic lights where a large sign points to Pitt Lake. You begin to drive through agricultural land at this point, past prosperous-looking dairy farms and nurseries. A bridge leads across the Alouette River. Turn right on McNeil Road, then left on 132nd Avenue and left again at Neaves Road, following it north past the Swaneset Bay golf course. Neaves crosses both the south and north arms of the Alouette River. Beyond the narrow bridge that spans the North Alouette, the road becomes rougher as its name changes from Neaves to Rannie. Grant Narrows Regional Park lies 10 km (6.2 mi.) north of here.

The opening of the Pitt River Greenway in 2008, combined with the completion of the new Pitt River Bridge in 2010, makes it much easier now to explore the forested trails at the confluence of the Fraser and Pitt rivers. Pedestrians and cyclists can adventure north along the Pitt River and inland along parts of the Alouette River dike system to Sturgeon Slough. The final phase from there to Grant Narrows Regional Park (see below) will take decades to complete pending the decommissioning of a gravel quarry.

Fortunately, there are plenty of alternative trails at hand, including a 26-km (15.6-mi.) stretch that links Pitt Meadows and Maple Ridge with Coquitlam and Fort Langley via the Golden Ears Bridge. To get to know the greenway better as it comes into its own, explore the dike network in Pitt Meadows, parts of which are designated as the Trans Canada Trail. The low-lying fields of the largely rural community are ringed with dikes to hold back the waters of not only the Fraser but also the Pitt and Alouette rivers. To those who explore on foot or by wheel, these wide, raised berms offer great views of the surrounding countryside, including a fortress of peaks in Golden Ears Park. Since the dikes are already in place, the cost of establishing a greenway along, and in places beside, them was relatively modest. The Pitt Meadows and Maple Ridge recreation departments installed washrooms and parking, as well as built a 2-km (1.2-mi.) interpretive loop trail at Hastings Landing, the Pitt River Greenway's main trailhead.

One of the best places to enjoy a walk beside the Fraser on the greenway is in the riparian zone between the dikes and the riverbank beneath the rough-barked black cottonwood trees. That's just what you'll find at Harris Landing, the eastern terminus of the Pitt River Greenway, which, when completed, will stretch for 31 km (19.2 mi.) and connect with Grant Narrows Regional Park at the south end of Pitt Lake. At the moment, the Pitt River Greenway leads 20 km (12-mi.) west and north to Ferry Slip Road beside the Pitt River Bridge and beyond to Sturgeon Slough and lets you tie in a cycle on the dike with a road ride through Pitt Meadows' charming historic town centre on Harris Road.

> ## PITT MEADOWS DIKE TRAIL

As they flow down off the ridge below Alouette Mountain, the two arms of the Alouette River curl back and forth through Pitt Meadows. As the twin tributaries of the Pitt River move west, they become increasing more influenced by the currents in the Pitt whose motion in turn is driven by the nearby Fraser River. Water levels rise and fall according to the intertidal rhythms at play. The arms merge east of Harris Road.

To the indigenous Katzie people, this place was known as sa'nesa?t, "the place where people go to fish," not to mention cultivate wapato—a tuberous potato-like root— and native cranberries.

People walk, jog, cycle and ride horseback along 26 km (16 mi.) of dike trails that link Pitt Meadows and Maple Ridge with Coquitlam and Fort Langley. That's far more than most visitors attempt at one go, but it's motivating to know that you can if you like. Dream big as you make your way along this well-marked section of the Trans Canada Trail. For added inspiration, superb views span the horizon as Mount Burke and Mount Baker bookend the spires of Golden Ears Park. The quiet out here is one of the biggest surprises, just minutes from one of the Lower Mainland's busiest thoroughfares. Ride up on the Pitt River Bridge to experience the contrast.

The best place to begin exploring is the parking lot on the south side of the bridge over the Alouette on Harris Road. You can launch a hand-carried boat here as well. Portions of both the north and south sides of the dike trail are designated as the 11-km (6.8-mi.) Osprey Route that leads west to the Pitt River Bridge and the 19-km (11.8-mi.) Blue Heron Route that leads east and follows both sides of each arm. Information and detailed route maps are available from the Tourism Maple Ridge and Pitt Meadows Visitor Info Centre (12492 Harris Road; 604-460-8300; www.mapleridge-pittmeadows.com), and from the visitor kiosk at the Maple Ridge Public Library (130–22470 Dewdney Trunk Road).

> ## PITT POLDER

After the settled character of Pitt Meadows' cultivated farmland, there is a sudden shift to one of remoteness as you head beyond the

Alouette River Dike Trail

bridge over the North Alouette River into a region called Pitt Polder. Polders are low-lying sections of land near rivers and oceans, dried out using a technique perfected in the Netherlands, a country famous for its ability to pry land from the sea. It takes a polder—the word is Dutch in origin—about 20 years to become productive agricultural land. The northern half of Pitt Polder is part of the 2 882-ha (7,122-acre) Pitt-Addington Marsh Wildlife Management Area. A colony of endangered greater sandhill cranes nests in a part of the polder that is closed to visitors from April 1 to June 30 to ensure the nesting birds are not disturbed.

> ### GRANT NARROWS REGIONAL PARK
Looking for a place to head on a moment's notice that will give you a sampling of our local wilderness: mountains, trees, water, wildlife—

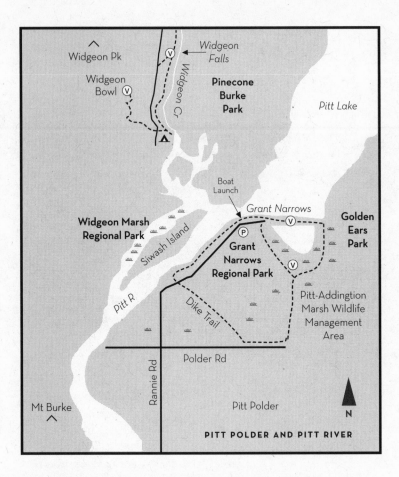

Widgeon Pk

Widgeon Bowl ⓥ

Widgeon Cr

Widgeon Falls ⓥ

Pinecone Burke Park

Pitt Lake

⚑

Boat Launch

Grant Narrows ⓥ

Widgeon Marsh Regional Park

Siwash Island

ⓟ

Grant Narrows Regional Park

ⓥ

Golden Ears Park

Pitt R

Dike Trail

Pitt-Addingtion Marsh Wildlife Management Area

Rannie Rd

Polder Rd

Mt Burke

Pitt Polder

N ⬆

PITT POLDER AND PITT RIVER

the works? One of the best and most accessible such spots is Grant Narrows Regional Park, where Widgeon Creek and the Pitt River meet. And with the trails through Pitt-Addington Marsh Wildlife Management Area leading right up beside it at the foot of thickly forested Alouette Mountain (site of the UBC Malcolm Knapp Research Forest), this part of Pitt Meadows offers a complete outdoor experience.

Grant Narrows Regional Park serves as a gateway for several different user groups headed in a variety of directions. By land, visitors can begin walking or cycling around the Pitt-Addington Marsh wildlife area, with its extensive series of dike trails and imposing observation towers. Boaters can venture onto the waterways of Pitt River and Pitt Lake or paddle southwestern B.C.'s largest freshwater marsh on nearby Widgeon Creek.

In the mid-1990s, Metro Vancouver took control of a large area of Widgeon Marsh, now a regional park in its own right, at the mouth of the creek where it flows into the Pitt River. Together with the public lands at Grant Narrows and Pitt-Addington, this constitutes a sizable package of protected habitat. For information on Grant Narrows Park, visit www.metrovancouver.org/services/parks_lscr/regionalparks/Pages/GrantNarrows.aspx.

> ## PITT-ADDINGTON MARSH WILDLIFE MANAGEMENT AREA

Exploration of this fascinating wetland can be undertaken by either a perimeter route that loops around the marsh or the rougher, rolling Nature Dyke Trail that leads through the heart of the marsh. Both originate from Grant Narrows within steps of each other.

The perimeter dike trail forms a long arch along the south end of Pitt Lake to the slopes of Alouette Mountain. Climbing an observation tower provides relief from the flatness of the dike. Out here, the broad, level surface of Pitt Lake—the second-largest freshwater tidal lake in the world—stretches out in front of you.

The dike roadway is wide and smooth until it reaches the mountain slopes. It narrows south of here, with the UBC Malcolm Knapp Research Forest on one side and the marsh on the other. An observation tower rises above the dike's intersection with the Nature Dyke Trail. If you prefer to take the long way back to Grant Narrows, continue south. It eventually meets a side road on your right that will take you back out to Rannie Road. Plan on taking 2 to 3 hours to complete this circle route.

Depending on the season, the Nature Dyke Trail can be muddy and strewn with trees brought down by beavers. Some of the larger trees still standing are netted with wire in an attempt to protect them from the castor's chisel-like chompers. It's not unusual to see bear scat. The eerie noise emitted by a snipe's tail is one of the few sounds. There's a palpable tranquillity here, particularly when a mist cloaks the polder and clouds snag the knolls across the way in Minnekhada Park. Nary a power line or telephone pole intrude on the landscape reflected on the surface of the glassy wetland where swallows swoop and dive above the marsh channels.

> PITT RIVER AND WIDGEON CREEK

One of the pleasant aspects of visiting Grant Narrows is that you don't need to own a boat or canoe to explore the waterways here. Daily canoe rentals are available on site from March through October. The current rate is $52 for the day for two adults. At present this service is provided by Ayla Canoe Rentals (604-941-2822; www. aylacanoes.com).

The advantages of exploration by canoe or kayak are numerous: fewer people (though on a busy day Ayla may rent as many as 100 canoes—be there by 11 A.M. if you want one), more scenic vistas and the chance to approach wildlife in a quiet, less-threatening manner. The current allows boaters to drift beside creek and riverbanks in silence, sometimes viewing birds and other animals at a much closer range than on foot. *Note*: The weather in this area can turn quite windy with little warning. As a result, canoeists should not venture out onto Pitt Lake. Be content to explore Pitt River's shoreline or the quieter backwaters in the marsh or Widgeon Creek.

On the Pitt River itself, large log booms are tethered to mooring posts at regular intervals, especially along the eastern shore. These booms help cut the wake of passing motorboats. Once you've left the boat launch, paddle south between the shoreline and the booms. In these quiet waters, you'll have the best chance of observing ospreys nesting on the tops of the mooring posts.

Paddle downstream to where cottages appear on the opposite shore and cross over to explore the backwaters along the river's western side. From the east, large Siwash Island conceals the river's bank at the foot of Mount Burke. The channel between the bank and the island is shallow, with marsh marigolds blooming in summer. A very wild scent fills the air. This is Metro Vancouver's Widgeon Marsh Regional Park, a wildlife sanctuary with numerous signs prohibiting hunting—especially of widgeons!

Crossing Pitt River from Grant Narrows Park to reach Widgeon

Creek takes only 10 minutes. However, as mentioned, this is the most exposed section of the journey, where canoeists are liable to encounter winds blowing south off Pitt Lake late in the day. If paddling a canoe is a relatively new experience for you, or if there is a novice in your party, take a few minutes to practise in the area around the dock before setting out across the river. Canoeing definitely requires well-coordinated teamwork. Be sure to check the detailed map posted on the park's information kiosk before launching to familiarize yourself with the geography of the marsh. *Note*: Basic canoe instruction for novice paddlers is included in the rental price from Ayla Canoe Rentals.

Once you're in Widgeon Creek's main channel, a sense of tranquillity prevails. You're bound to find at least one great blue heron stalking along Siwash Island's marshy shore on your left as you head upstream. The creek soon divides into two long arms. The branch to the left leads upstream to hiking trails in Pinecone Burke Provincial Park and to Widgeon Falls; the right arm ambles into a series of secluded backwaters perfectly suited for wildlife observation and fishing.

By late in the summer, water levels are at their low point for the year in Widgeon Creek. Chances are that if there are more than two of you in the canoe, you'll have to hop out to float it across a sandbar or two. These are only momentary hindrances, and there are far worse trials in life than dipping your feet into the fresh waters of Widgeon Creek. But do keep these occasional wades in mind when choosing footwear. A pair of river shoes that you can slip in and out of easily will come in handy.

A provincial campground is located on the banks of Widgeon Creek an hour's paddle northwest of Grant Narrows. Along the way to the campground are fine sandy areas well suited for sunning and picnicking. Tall cottonwood and hemlock trees line the shore in many places. Sitka spruce stand apart from the rest, easily identified by their solitary splendour. The creek lazily winds its way into the folds of the nearby mountains, whose slopes rise sharply towards unseen peaks. Silence envelops the valley. Rocky knolls, characteristic geologic formations in the Pitt River flood plain, thrust up in advance of the mountains.

Widgeon Falls

The sight of other canoes pulled up on a broad bank of the creek will alert you to the fact that you've arrived at the campground in Pinecone Burke Park. Above the pullout is a broad grassy field from which a road lined with poplars and maples leads gently uphill and will bring you close to Widgeon Falls within 40 minutes. *Note*: Because of poor maintenance, BC Parks does not advise using the Widgeon Falls Trail.

Widgeon Falls drops through a series of smooth granite boulders. Much of the year, the force of the water rushing through here will keep visitors at their distance. During hotter, drier times of the year when water levels drop, it's possible to walk out on the rock shelf beside the creek for a better look. On a sunny day, the water in the creek is a beautiful blend of green shades. At any time of year, the sound of water dropping over the falls dominates all else, enclosing visitors in a capsule of white noise.

For information on Pinecone Burke Provincial Park, visit www.env.gov.bc.ca/bcparks/explore/parkpgs/pinecone.html.

GOLDEN EARS
PROVINCIAL PARK &

. . . . .

- > DISTANCE: 11 km (6.8 mi.) north of Highway 7 in Maple Ridge, about 50 km (31 mi.) east of Vancouver

- > ACTIVITIES: Boating, camping, climbing, cycling, dog walking, hiking, paddling, picnicking, swimming, viewpoints, walking, windsurfing

- > ACCESS: Take either the Lougheed Highway (Highway 7) or Highway 1 from Vancouver. (Travelling east on Highway 1, take Exit 44, just west of the Port Mann Bridge. Follow signs to Highway 7B/ United Boulevard North, which leads to Maple Ridge via the Mary Hill Bypass.) As Highway 7 enters Maple Ridge from the west, it intersects with Dewdney Trunk Road. Turn left at the lights here and follow Dewdney east to 232nd Street, where you make another left turn. Provincial-park signs direct you to Golden Ears. (There are also signed approaches on Highway 7 in downtown Maple Ridge.) Follow 232nd as it crosses the Alouette River, then turn right on Fern Crescent as it passes through the municipal Maple Ridge Park. (This park is an excellent destination for groups looking for camping facilities, a treed setting and a playing field. Call the Municipality of Maple Ridge, 604-463-5221, for information.)

WITHIN THE boundaries of 62 540-ha (154,540-acre) Golden Ears Park, it is possible to swim, boat and camp at Alouette and Pitt lakes; to walk or mountain bike along trails to the two waterfalls pouring off Gold Creek into Alouette Lake; or to hike to the Golden Ears themselves or several other peaks that rise high above the lake. The park is large enough to accommodate all these activities within its borders and still have plenty of wilderness left over into which few visitors venture.

As you enter the provincial park, you will be met by a strikingly large carving of a white mountain goat, symbolic of the fascinating wildlife found at higher points in the Coast Mountains around Golden Ears. Close at hand, horse trails forming a network parallel the road and lead off into the surrounding forest. There are conflicting opinions as to the origin of the name Golden Ears. Veteran members of the Alpine Club of Canada and long-time residents of the Fraser Valley recall that the mountain was previously known as the Golden Eyries, nesting place of eagles.

Note: Dogs must be on a leash, no longer than 2 m (6 ft.) long, including in campgrounds and on trails within 1 km (0.6 mi.) of the Parkway Road. Trails beyond 1 km (0.6 mi.) of the Parkway Road are considered backcountry, and dogs may be off leash but must be under control at all times.

> ### ALOUETTE LAKE

Beyond the park gates, you have a leisurely drive for 7 km (4.3 mi.) until the first of several parking lots appears. Along the way is an information kiosk, where maps of the park are on display. Farther along is the road leading off to park headquarters and diminutive Mike Lake, and shortly thereafter is the turnoff to the Alouette Lake day-use area at the lake's south end. As this road nears the day-use area, parking for the Spirea Universal Access Interpretive Trail appears on the right.

> ## SPIREA UNIVERSAL ACCESS INTERPRETIVE TRAIL

THIS TRAIL, the first of its kind in a B.C. park, affords those with disabilities a natural-history experience. Unique interpretive signs in a variety of languages appear along the trail, much of which is covered by boardwalk. These signs also feature solar-powered audio systems for hearing-impaired trail users and brass re-creations of some of the park's natural features for the visually impaired.

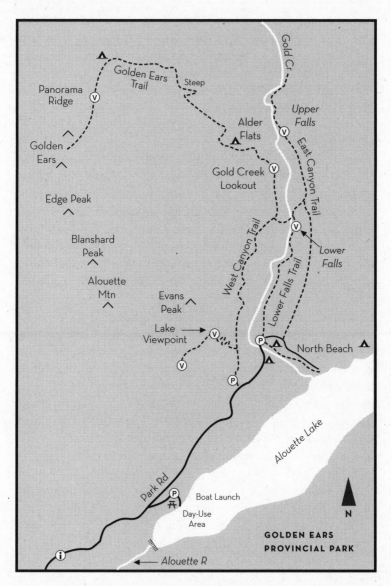

Dogs are permitted off leash in only two swimming areas: at the North Beach day-use area near the outflow area of Gold Creek into Alouette Lake and at the Alouette day-use area between the boat launch and the canoe rental shop. Dogs are strictly prohibited at the south Beach Parking Lot #2 and Campers Beach.

A beautiful wide beach lies at the south end of Alouette Lake, next to an unobtrusive BC Hydro dam. There are a large boat launch and a dock at the north end of the beach, and during the summer months you can rent canoes and kayaks. Rentals are on a first-come, first-served basis. If you arrive before noon, there is usually a good chance of getting one.

> ## NORTH BEACH

Near the end of the 12-km (7.5-mi.) road that runs through Golden Ears is the entrance to the Gold Creek and Alouette campgrounds, with an astounding 343 campsites between them. (For reservations, call 604-689-9025 or visit discovercamping.ca.) For many, camping here is their first introduction to overnighting in the outdoors. Long weekends in May and October are particularly popular with school, Girl Guide and Boy Scout groups. Adjacent to the Gold Creek campground is a parking lot for the West Canyon Trail, which leads to the Golden Ears themselves (see below).

Beyond the West Canyon Trail parking lot the road crosses a one-lane bridge over Gold Creek. The North Beach campground at the north end of the road has an additional 55 campsites. If you're just here for the day, leave your vehicle in the day-use-only Gold Creek parking lot. A gentle walking trail leads from this parking lot along the north bank of the creek to a broad, sandy gravel bar where the creek meets the lake at North Beach. The short (2-km/1.2-mi.) walk is one of my favourites. Decades of duff deposited on the forest floor give the trail a welcoming sponginess that will put a spring in your step. The clear blue-green water in boulder-filled Gold Creek delights the eye. Mostly level, the trail climbs slightly as it nears the lake. At this point, the creek widens and deepens, and you get some of the prettiest views of its colour. Out on the gravel bar at North Beach, look west to Evans Peak, which dominates the horizon.

If you explore the lake by boat, numerous submerged snags soon make you aware that this was once a forested valley. The east side of the lake is particularly heavy with snags, and the shoreline there drops straight down to the water with few landing sites. The northwest side of the lake features both wilderness camping and makeshift picnic sites, accessible only by water. Many visitors paddle to these sites from the south end of Alouette Lake. It's an hour or more's steady paddling from there to North Beach, and the shoreline between the two is not particularly inviting. Better to launch from the parking lot beside the outdoor learning centre at North Beach. Its post-and-beam construction is typical of the local Katzie First Nation bighouse tradition. Situated on a promontory above North Beach, the centre has a commanding view of the lake.

Within an hour of leaving the dock at North Beach, you can land at a variety of small beaches. There's plenty of driftwood on which to spread out a towel or tablecloth. The hills behind are thick with evergreens, but exploration is remarkably easy as there is only light undergrowth. Alouette Lake warms up in summer to provide some of the best freshwater swimming in the Lower Mainland. You can also explore Moyer Creek, whose boulder-filled course leads back into the hillside. There is a good view of the Golden Ears from this northern section of the lake.

Alouette Lake is long enough that it presents an opportunity to do some serious paddling. Beware the winds that rise around noon and blow from the south throughout the afternoon; don't expect to make very good time heading back towards the boat launch during this period. The best times to be out on the water are in the morning and in the late afternoon, when the lake is still.

> ## GOLD CREEK TRAILS

In addition to the short trail to lakeside described above, Lower Falls Trail runs beside Gold Creek as it flows downstream from the upper and lower falls. The falls on Gold Creek descend through a canyon, twisting over a set of rock staircases. The best viewpoints are at the top and bottom of the falls. There are two approaches to these spots. You will find both trails outlined on the large map located near the entrance to the Gold Creek parking lot.

Gold Creek originates far to the north in Golden Ears Park. For most of its course, it is wide and fairly straightforward. As it nears the lake, it's suddenly confined by an imposing rock face, part of which has fallen away. At the upper falls, you can observe the most dramatic descent of the creek—and at as close a range as your nerve will allow. The rock shelf through which the creek falls is flat enough in

Alouette Lake

places to permit a daring observer to venture out for a close inspection of the volume of water tumbling by. The waterfall reflects the hues of the sky and the green of the trees, but the most entrancing colours come from the golden boulders and bluish stones in the creekbed.

Lower Falls Trail heads upstream at a gentle grade. At first you pass through a stand of second-growth western hemlock and vine maple. Just past the "1 km" marker the forest suddenly gives way to alder and cottonwood trees. Views of the mountains open up to the west. Alouette Mountain stands tall above Evans Peak, which is closer in the foreground. On high, those small patches of white may be snow or mountain goats; it's hard to tell at this distance, even with the help of binoculars. The closer you get to the falls, the more other peaks across the valley reveal themselves. The Blanshard Needle, Edge Peak and the twin Golden Ears stand grouped in profile. Even if this is your first visit to the park, you'll find the mountains look familiar because of their visibility on the horizon east of Vancouver.

This is a pleasant area and quite popular on weekends. The 3-km (1.9-mi.) Lower Falls Trail is a wide bed of cedar bark and makes for easy walking. Along the way, there are several good picnic spots, quite accessible to the creek for swimming in the fresh soft water. There are campsites at places on the other side of the creek, reached via the West Canyon Trail. Walking time to the falls is an easy hour or less one way.

Short of an arduous climb to their peaks, one of the best views of the Golden Ears appears as you walk along the East Canyon Trail. This trail runs along the canyon above the creek and goes directly to the upper falls and beyond for a short distance. It begins uphill towards the North Beach campground from the Gold Creek parking lot. Longer than the Lower Falls Trail by approximately 1 km (0.6 mi.), this route takes twice as much time to complete because of its rolling course. Small orange distance markers show up with regularity along the way. This is a good workout for those on mountain bikes.

The trail climbs gradually uphill as the voice of Gold Creek rises through the forest from below. At the "2.5 km" sign lies the wreckage of an old log bridge that has been swept aside. An old metal gate stands partially covered by rocks. From here, the trail climbs somewhat more steeply. After another 0.5 km (0.3 mi.), watch for the turnoff to the upper falls. A rough trail, part of which is a broad, dry creekbed, leads downhill a short distance to a good viewpoint. The sound of Gold Creek as it plunges over the falls is relentless, overwhelming and hypnotic. Approach with extreme care.

> ## WEST CANYON TRAIL

The several routes to the falls on Gold Creek are part of a dozen hiking, cycling, walking and riding trails within the park. Golden Ears Park is 55 km (34 mi.) long from its southern border to its northern boundary, where it connects with Garibaldi Park, of which it was once part. The Coast Mountains within which the park lies form a rugged and often impenetrable barrier of peaks and valleys. Weather conditions can change quickly in this region. Be prepared for any eventuality. *Note*: Biting insects can be a nuisance in this area in warmer months, so come prepared with repellent.

West Canyon Trail is one approach to the lower falls. At first the West Canyon Trail leads above and away from Gold Creek. There is evidence of the old logging railway that once ran through the canyon along the way to Alder Flats. After 5 km (3.1 mi.), you'll reach a sign pointing down a branch trail to the lower falls. At low-water seasons it's possible to ford the creek below the falls, provided you're prepared to roll your pant legs way up.

Note: Beyond the West Canyon Trail, BC. Parks no longer maintains the Golden Ears Trail. Access to Panorama Ridge and the Golden Ears is recommended only to those experienced in backcountry travel and mountaineering.

> ## 20

KANAKA CREEK
REGIONAL PARK &

. . . . .

> **DISTANCE:** About 30 km (18.6 mi.) east of Vancouver, in Maple Ridge

> **ACTIVITIES:** Birding, boating, dog walking, fishing, hiking, nature observation, picnicking, swimming, viewpoints, walking

> **ACCESS:** Kanaka Creek Regional Park, located on the eastern outskirts of Maple Ridge, has three principal approaches, each offering different points of interest. To get to the launch site and creekside trails at the Fraser Riverfront section of Kanaka Park, take the Haney Bypass east from Highway 7 in downtown Maple Ridge and watch for green Metro Vancouver Parks signs to the park as well as the creek itself, which passes under the road. There is a small CPR railway bridge here and a parking lot next to it on a service road. The two other entrances are off Highway 7 on the Dewdney Trunk Road at 252nd and 256th streets. Both are well marked and lie 11 km (6.8 mi.) upstream from the Fraser.

IN THE building of the West, the Chinese were not the only labourers attracted from across the Pacific. Hawaiians also came to this region, where they established several small communities, intermarried with Natives on the North Shore and left their name, the Polynesian word for "man," to grace one of our regional district parks, Kanaka Creek. In the 1830s, preceding the arrival of the Hawaiians, Kwantlen Natives established a camp here under the guns of nearby Fort Langley, seeking protection from their marauding northern Native neighbours.

Although the entire area is a warren of well-used trails and riverfront dikes, you'll seldom meet many people in this park, which

121

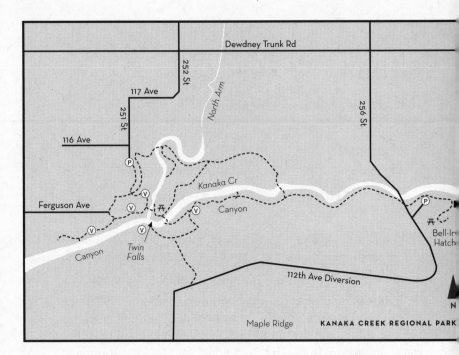

Within the map:

Dewdney Trunk Rd

252 St

117 Ave

North Arm

251 St

256 St

116 Ave

P

Kanaka Cr

Canyon

Ferguson Ave

V

V

V

V

P

Bell-In Hatch

Twin Falls

Canyon

112th Ave Diversion

N

Maple Ridge

KANAKA CREEK REGIONAL PARK

---

comprises about 405 ha (1,000 acres) and runs along both sides of
the creek. Golden Ears Park is the major draw in this area, and it
siphons off most of the visitors.

> **FRASER RIVERFRONT**

Kanaka Creek flows into the Fraser River's north side, across the
river and just east of Derby Reach and Barnston Island. You can
explore the marshlands at this junction with a light boat, launching from any of the Fraser Riverfront access points. The gently flowing creek makes a series of lazy backwater S-turns both above and
below the Highway 7 bridge before reaching the faster-moving Fraser. Among the streams flowing into the lower Fraser, it is one of the
few still in its natural state.

The banks of the creek are composed of slippery clay, so be careful when launching; rubber boots are recommended. The creek
meanders through tall stands of bulrushes and past open fields bordered with graceful poplars as it approaches the Fraser. It's wide

Rainbow Bridge, Kanaka Creek

enough for two boats, though it's unlikely that you'll encounter many.

These last bends in Kanaka Creek before it joins the Fraser are home to birds and fish, coyotes and rabbits, living undisturbed in their wildlife sanctuary except for the rumble of an occasional train passing nearby. Blue herons often stalk fish from the riverbanks; they fly over from their colony in the woods of Derby Reach. If you're not in a boat, a three-storey observation tower above Kanaka Creek's sweeping oxbow lets you spy on them while they work.

A short walk or bike ride on the creekside trail past the tower brings you to the Fraser, where you can head up- or downstream. A small staircase descends to the river, an observation post gives broad views of the river, and a gracefully arched bridge spans the mouth of the creek. West to the heritage pier at old Port Haney, little about the Fraser has changed much in decades. There's always commercial and recreational boat traffic on the river.

> ## TRANS CANADA TRAIL

Just east of Fraser Riverfront off Kanaka Way lies a short but pleasant section of the Trans Canada Trail that crosses Kanaka Creek on the Rainbow Bridge. The span overlooks the creek as tall black cottonwoods tower above. Thickly matted penstemon, a perennial flowering herb, overhangs the riverbank like a bouffant hairdo.

> ## CLIFF FALLS

The entrance off 252nd takes you a short distance down the road to a parking lot beside a municipal playing field. From here, a short, steep trail leads down to one of two bridges that span twin waterfalls created by the confluence of separate arms of Kanaka Creek. The north arm originates a short distance from the falls; the east arm begins farther back in the Blue Mountain Forest near Alouette Lake.

Fossils in the stones by the sandstone canyon walls and a slippery grey clay along the banks are distinctive features of this area.

There are several picnic tables and a fire pit in a cleared area just above the falls, surrounded by signs emphasizing the danger of the cliffs. Numerous trails wind down to the creeks, and walking the streambed in either direction is not difficult once spring water levels have dropped and water temperatures have risen. Swimming is easy, and you have your pick of a number of small pools, from ankle- to neck-deep.

The well-worn trails alongside the eastern arm of the creek make you realize how popular this area was with earlier inhabitants. Old wooden staircases, bridges and small dams lead through the forest, which rises and falls on each side of the creek in dramatic fashion. Salmonberry bushes are everywhere.

> BELL-IRVING HATCHERY

Use the 256th Street entrance to reach the Bell-Irving salmon hatchery, where you will also find a great deal of information on the park. Since the hatchery opened in 1983, millions of salmon fry—most of them chum, with some coho—have been released. You may wish to witness the event, a spring ritual for local schoolchildren. Contact the hatchery at 604-462-8643 for information.

If you leave your car here, it is a half-hour hike downstream to the falls. Follow the trail along the south side of Kanaka Creek that begins directly across 256th Street from the hatchery. Along the way, you'll discover many inviting approaches to the creek where you'll want to spend some quiet time. The trail follows the south side of the creek and involves some climbing through the sheltering forest. Despite extensive logging in earlier years, there are still some impressive-sized trees here.

For more information on Kanaka Creek Regional Park, call Metro Vancouver Parks' East Area Office at 604-530-4983 or visit www.metrovancouver.org/services/parks_lscr/regionalparks/Pages/KanakaCreek.aspx.

FRASER VALLEY NORTH

21

ROLLEY LAKE
PROVINCIAL PARK &

. . . . .

> **DISTANCE:** 70 km (43.5 mi.) east of Vancouver, in the district of Mission

> **ACTIVITIES:** Birding, camping, dog walking, fishing, nature observation, paddling, picnicking, playground, swimming, walking

> **ACCESS:** Via the Lougheed Highway (Highway 7) or the Trans-Canada Highway (Highway 1). Traffic on the Lougheed can be stop-and-go until it reaches the Pitt River; you can avoid this by using the Trans-Canada (Highway 1) to link up with the Lougheed at the Pitt River Bridge. Travelling east of Vancouver on the Trans-Canada, take Exit 44 just before the highway crosses the Port Mann Bridge, then head east on the Mary Hill Bypass towards Maple Ridge and Mission.

Once on Highway 7, you can save yourself a few more minutes by taking the Haney Bypass through Maple Ridge. Watch for the large overhead sign indicating a right turn off Highway 7 towards Mission. The bypass rejoins Highway 7 east of Maple Ridge, and you are well on your way to Rolley Lake and the Stave Lake region. The highway follows the curves of the Fraser River. East of Maple Ridge, the countryside becomes more rural. The turnoff to Rolley Lake is at the mill town of Ruskin; the park lies 10 km (6 mi.) north of Highway 7. Turn north off Highway 7 onto 287th Street and drive uphill past the Ruskin Dam to an intersection with the Dewdney Trunk Road. At the sign here, turn right and drive east to Bell Road, where a sign reads "Rolley Lake 2 km." Turn left here.

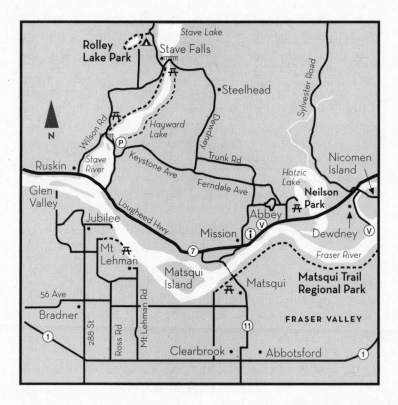

ROLLEY LAKE PARK, which has been a provincial park since 1961, itself is tucked away in the wooded hills of the Mission district east of Maple Ridge. Rolley Lake is a small lake with nothing hidden around its circumference except the 64 campsites (six of which are double-occupancy) in the nearby woods, several minutes' walk from the shoreline. Benefiting from a gentle drop-off, a sandy beach on the lake's open south side is a kid magnet. *Note*: Dogs are not allowed on the beach and must be on leash at all times in the park.

An ancient corduroy road, along which logs were hauled to old Port Haney, is in remarkably good condition considering the passage of time. You can see signs of the road when you walk the trail that begins west of the day-use parking lot and leads past the outhouses set back in the woods behind the beach. This trail soon turns into the old corduroy road. Remains of rotting cedar shakes let you know you're in the right place.

In the 70 years since the loggers left, the forest around Rolley Lake has regrown amid what's left of the old growth. Fallen nurse logs, each supporting three or four offspring, are slowly repopulating the forest floor. A boardwalk trail leads across a wet zone at the southwestern end of the lake, away from a modest-sized beach and picnic area. Here, in the stillness, a practised eye can identify dozens of species of birds during the 90-minute walk around the lake. Pileated woodpeckers with their distinctive red heads (*pileated* is derived from the Latin *pileus*, meaning "felt cap") are among the winged residents often spotted.

A steep slope climbs above Rolley Lake's shady north side. Several small streams flow down off the hillside at wet times of the year. The water in the streams is a deeper red than a woodpecker's cap as it becomes tinted by the cedar mulch through which it runs. At intervals along this side of the lake, small wooden docks float under a canopy of long hemlock boughs, making ideal places to fish for rainbow and cutthroat trout or to use those binoculars to search out the profiles of herons standing sentinel in the marsh at the lake's northeastern corner. The catch allowance (for humans) is two per day; there is no limit on the amount of fun that young and old alike can share while tossing in a line. You can park yourself on one of the docks to enjoy the stillness, with no fear of being interrupted by the sounds of outboards—no motorized boats are allowed

> ## THEM'S THE SHAKES

SETTLERS SUCH AS James and Fanny Rolley began arriving in the Mission district in the 1880s. The couple to whom the lake owes its name homesteaded here for a decade before moving to nearby Whonnock. Remains of the logging camps that took over and cleared off most of the cedar are still evident around the lake's western perimeter. The Japanese crew that worked much of the forest pulled out in the 1930s when the last of the red cedars and Douglas-firs were gone.

Rolley Creek waterfall

on the lake. For the best results, plan to fish here as early in the spring as possible while the lake is still well stocked with cutthroat and rainbow trout. Anglers 16 years of age and older must have a freshwater fishing licence.

The campsites at Rolley Lake seem exceptionally spacious compared with those at many other parks in B.C. Much of the surrounding forest is a mix of western hemlock and mature vine maple. The forest floor is open and soft underfoot from centuries of cedar mulch. Children will find plenty of material to construct small forts and lean-tos in the underbrush. The vine maples naturally bend to form shelters that look surprisingly similar to the framework of Native sweat lodges. Note that the use of sticks and underbrush from campground and park areas for fires and tent structures is not permitted.

The camping season at Rolley Lake begins in early April and lasts through mid-fall; a campsite costs $28 per day. You can reserve a campsite here by calling 604-689-9025 or visiting discovercamping.ca. This is an extremely popular park, and space is at a premium in July and August. But you will have the place practically to yourself at most other times, such as those special days in May and September before school ends or after it has reconvened. Each site comes furnished with a bright-yellow cedar picnic table and fire pit with cooking grill. The campsites are clean, and there is plenty of water (though it smells slightly sulphurous) and firewood, with indoor toilets and tiled showers next to a children's adventure playground.

As you sit quietly, listen for the soft peeping of the bushtits, flocks of which come by to feed on insects. You'll hear them before you spot their dark shapes high in the boughs of the hemlocks. They drop from branch to branch, hanging upside down as easily as right side up, moving from bush to tree in straggling flocks. Another visitor, one of the early risers, is the Douglas squirrel, as black as the back of the Steller's jay, who'll be by later in the day to clean any leftover crumbs from your table.

In the mountains north of Rolley Lake are far larger species of wildlife, such as black bears, so be careful to pack all food away at night. On a large-scale map of the province you can see that a wilderness corridor, in which large and small animals have dominion, stretches from here north past Harrison Lake and all the way to Lillooet. When the end of summer signals the return of campers to the city, the woods and lakes here welcome the reappearance of wildlife that has spent the past few months in northern seclusion. Large birds such as eagles and Pacific loons are back with youngsters grown almost as big as their parents.

Follow the small stream that drains from the lake's northeastern end down into nearby Stave Lake. A waterfall drops away through the forest in several stages. The best view of it is from a wooden bridge on the hillside below the campground. To find it from the day-use area, take the path from the lake to the camping area. The walk to the falls begins to the right of a pit toilet near campsite 27 and takes an easy 10 minutes. Although the trail continues beyond this point to a road beside Stave Lake, there is little to recommend this steep, narrow route unless you crave a stair climb–like workout. Allow 10 minutes one way.

For more information, visit the BC Parks Web site at www.env. gov.bc.ca/bcparks/explore/parkpg/rolley_lk.

22

RUSKIN AND ENVIRONS &

. . . . .

> DISTANCE: About 60 km (37.3 mi.) east of Vancouver

> ACTIVITIES: Boating, cycling, dog walking, fishing, nature obser-
vation, paddling, picnicking, swimming, walking

> ACCESS: Signs indicate the turnoff north to Hayward Lake from
the Lougheed Highway (Highway 7) in Ruskin. A parking lot is
located at the south end of the Railway Trail beside the Ruskin
Dam, about 4 km (2.5 mi.) from Highway 7 on Wilson Road. The
south end of the Reservoir Trail and the Ruskin Recreation Area
are located on the east side of Ruskin Dam. A single-lane road leads
across the dam to them. (See Fraser Valley map, page 129.)

FOR A little backwoods town in the north Fraser Valley, Ruskin
has a lot going for it. In the course of a day trip here, visitors
can walk or bike the 6-km (3.7-mi.) Railway Trail along the
west side of Hayward Lake, hike sections of the 10-km (6.2-mi.)
Reservoir Trail, picnic at the Ruskin Recreation Site while observing the annual salmon run in the nearby Stave River and, for the
price of a saltwater fishing licence, head home with a guaranteed
catch. All in all, not too shabby a selection when you're in the
mood for a simple outing.

In the late 1800s, Ruskin was one of several riverfront towns—
Whonnock and Albion are two others along this stretch of the Fraser
west of Mission—settled in what is traditional Kwantlen First Nation
territory. By the light of kerosene lanterns, newcomers looked to
electricity as leading-edge technology. To meet this need, a dam
and hydro generating plant were constructed at Stave Falls, 10 km
(6.2 mi.) upstream from the Fraser along the Stave River. In the

early 1900s, the shortest incorporated railway in Canadian history ran from Ruskin to Stave Falls, carrying supplies for the dam and returning loaded with cedar logs, shakes and shingles. Cedar logging ended here long ago. Today, most of the mills that line the Fraser River are quiet. In their place are new, value-added endeavours such as the log-hewn Shingle and Shake Pub on Wilson Road and a network of recreation trails around nearby Hayward Lake, built by a trail crew of ex-loggers with funding from BC Hydro and Forest Renewal BC.

> ### RAILWAY AND RESERVOIR TRAILS

Since BC Hydro opened the Railway Trail to the public for recreation in the 1980s, the former railbed has been widened in places and made smoother. The trail runs 6 km (3.7 mi.) between the Ruskin Dam and a large picnic ground at North Beach beside the Stave Falls Dam. By bike, allow 2 hours for the round trip, including breaks, and as much as twice that on foot.

For the most part, this is a gentle grade with a few steep sections that will get your heart rate up, especially if you're bike hiking. Along the way, it skirts the remains of seven partially submerged trestle bridges. Each trestle is a well-worn design piece—an arrangement of thick posts and cross-beams that serves to remind that architecture is a blend of both construction and art.

Overhung in places by a sheltering forest canopy, much of the Railway Trail is ideal for an outing in cloudy weather. Stately stands of second-growth Douglas-fir rear skyward like sentinels. Several loop trails veer off from the Railway Trail and climb the steep hillside above Hayward Lake, in actuality a reservoir formed between the Ruskin and Stave Falls dams. Benches are placed at each switchback so that visitors can catch their breath while enjoying a view deep into the nearby glens. In fall and winter months, ivy and fern glisten like malachite. Small streams lace the hillside and trill a soothing background accompaniment. A stretch of boardwalk winds across Bob Brook, where it empties into a bay where paddlers often pause for a picnic.

The Reservoir Trail links with the Railway Trail to provide a continuous 16-km (10-mi.) loop around the lake. Highlights along the

Stave River, Ruskin

Reservoir Trail include a 150-m (490-ft.) floating bridge near the Ruskin Dam and a viewpoint of Steelhead Falls near the Stave Falls Dam. All of the wood on both the Railway and Reservoir trails was milled from recycled hydro poles and log booms.

> ### RUSKIN RECREATION AREA
Although there is a picnic ground at the north end of Hayward Lake, in fall the best place to picnic either before or after a workout on the trails is at the Ruskin Recreation Area, just below the Ruskin Dam. A short walk from the parking lot leads to a series of spawning channels on the Stave River. From October to December the river and channels are choked with hefty chum salmon, followed by a run of smaller coho salmon. The Stave is full of energy as thrashing salmon launch themselves into the air in the midstream current. Close to shore, schools of battered but still breathing chum, coloured like

speckled marble, silently scull past the decomposing bodies of those who've finished their epic journey. An ecstatic chorus from circling flocks of gulls sings them homeward. Equally thrilled are the families who have come to snag a few fish for themselves.

Although wide spawning channels have been dug on each side of the river, the best viewing is from the Ruskin Recreation Area. To reach it, take single-lane Ruskin Road across the top of the dam from Wilson Road and descend the east side to the nearby site gates. A boat launch (also gated) is on your left as you enter. Several picnic tables are located on a benchland above the Stave River. A short trail descends to the river, with a bridge crossing the spawning channel and leading out onto the banks of the river itself. Downstream from the recreation site, you can see Ruskin and the wide expanse of the Fraser River.

> ### STAVE LAKE AND NORTH BEACH

Two more recreation sites are located at the north end of Hayward Lake, reached by driving up Wilson Road to the Dewdney Trunk Road and proceeding east to the small settlement of Stave Falls (a community of a hundred homes at the time of the dams' construction). One is a boat launch on Stave Lake; the other is the wheelchair-accessible recreation area at North Beach on Hayward Lake. The two lakes are separated by the Stave Falls Dam. North Beach is dotted with picnic tables and is a busy place in good weather. At other times, it can be so deserted that it's almost spooky. Only hand-powered boats or boats with electric motors are permitted on Hayward Lake. Larger, more powerful boats must launch on Stave Lake at a site 1 km (0.6 mi.) north of the North Beach turnoff.

As you enter the North Beach recreation area, you will see the beach and picnic area just beyond the parking lot. The boat launch for Hayward Lake is just beside the parking lot. A charming gazebo graces the grass lawns surrounding the beach. The history of the Stave Falls Dam project is depicted in archival photographs at an interpretive display nearby. If you're in the mood for a short walk or ride, take Harry's Trail to a bluff overlooking the reservoir.

For further information, visit www.bchydro.com/recreation.

23

MISSION AND
ENVIRONS &

. . . . .

> **DISTANCE:** 80 km (50 mi.) east of Vancouver

> **ACTIVITIES:** Boating, cycling, fishing, dog walking, historic sites, nature observation, paddling, picnicking, swimming, viewpoints, walking

> **ACCESS:** Take the Lougheed Highway (Highway 7) east to Mission. Watch for the Travel Info Centre, located on the north side of the highway just past Mary Street, where you can obtain a Mission Visitors' Guide with detailed street maps of the area. (See Fraser Valley map, page 129)

To find Fraser River Heritage Park, turn north off Highway 7 on Third Avenue at its convergence with Mary Street. The park entrance is at Mary and Fifth.

To get to Westminster Abbey from Highway 7, take Stave Lake Road to the Dewdney Trunk Road. Turn right and go east along Dewdney. Watch for the abbey on your right just past the intersection of Dewdney and Goundrey Street.

To find Ferncliff Gardens, turn north off Highway 7 onto the Dewdney Trunk Road, drive three blocks, then turn right on Henry Street. Continue down Henry to its end, where it turns into McTaggart Street (which becomes a dirt lane), then turn right at the Ferncliff Gardens sign. A lovely Tudor-style farmhouse sits sheltered behind a cedar hedge; the main barn and garden office lie just beyond at road's end.

To reach Neilson Park, drive north from Ferncliff Gardens on McTaggart, turn left on McEwen, then turn immediately right on Edwards Street and follow the signs to the park from here.

IMAGINE BEING lucky enough to live on a ridge on the north side of the mighty Fraser River, overlooking the Matsqui Prairie, with towering Mount Baker as the centrepiece of your view. Residents of Mission enjoy this natural spectacle every day, weather permitting. You can, too, when you visit Westminster Abbey, any of several well-kept parks or, from August through early October, hidden Ferncliff Gardens. There's also much to choose from in the vicinity of Mission, including a drive to Cascade Falls Regional Park—built with access for the disabled in mind—or a cycle tour of Nicomen Island.

> FRASER RIVER HERITAGE PARK

Located at an important geographical point where the Fraser River makes an elbow turn on its way to the Pacific, Mission is tied historically to the Cariboo gold rush of the 1850s but with a slightly different twist. With the influx of tens of thousands of miners pursuing gold came grief for the First Nations people through whose lands the prospectors travelled. In 1860, Father Fouquet, a French priest with the Oblates of Mary Immaculate, founded St. Mary's Mission to provide shelter, counselling and schooling for Native people. It was the first and largest residential school of its kind in the Pacific Northwest. In 1959, the federal government rebuilt the school 3 km (1.9 mi.) east of the old site. Each year in July, the Mission Powwow draws participants and spectators to a three-day festival of Native singing, drumming and dancing held on the grounds of the new school, off the Lougheed Highway just east of the Travel Info Centre.

The remains of the old mission were cleared in 1965, and in its place is the expansive Fraser River Heritage Park. You can still see footprints of the old buildings near the bandshell. On the east side of the park is a small cemetery surrounded by a grove of tall, sturdy hemlocks. Father Fouquet is buried here in a section set aside for Oblate priests.

A log chalet, the Norma Kenney House, is located at the park entrance. It serves as a reception centre and is home to the Blackberry Kitchen, a good place to pause for refreshment in summer, and the Valley Treasures gift shop, which features work by local craftspeople. Fraser River Heritage Park is also the site of the annual Mission Folk Festival.

Westminster Abbey from Ferncliff Gardens

> **WESTMINSTER ABBEY**

Westminster Abbey, home to a Benedictine monastery and Mission's most imposing landmark, was completed in 1982. The abbey stands atop a ridge overlooking the Fraser River valley. Treat yourself to a visit for the view—even better than at Fraser River Heritage Park—and a choral vespers service in the abbey. The simplicity of the unaccompanied chanting stands in remarkable contrast to the imposing character of the abbey itself, designed by Vancouver architect Asbjorn Gathe. In late afternoon, when the slanting rays of the sun shine through the modern stained-glass windows, the abbey's interior is bathed in shades of burnt orange and cool blues, highlighting a series of 21 bas-reliefs mounted on the walls. Visiting hours at the monastery, where the ancient Benedictine credo has always been to show hospitality to guests of all faiths, are weekday afternoons from 1:30 P.M. to 4:30 P.M., and 2 P.M. to 4 P.M. on Sundays. The 30-minute vespers service begins at 5:30 P.M. on weekdays and 4:30 P.M. on Sundays.

If you are here just to visit the grounds, formerly a family farm and still operated by the self-sufficient monks, make your way along the path that leads south from the abbey's parking lot. It gently winds up to one of the most commanding viewpoints found anywhere in the Fraser Valley, a must-see for visitors. Large knolls thrust up from the valley floor to the east; across the wide Fraser from the agricultural lands of Hatzic and Nicomen Island, the well-ordered Matsqui Prairie lies before you to the south, surmounted by Sumas Mountain and Mount Baker.

> **FERNCLIFF GARDENS**

At certain times of the year, from the abbey viewpoint, you can see a small but intense patch of colour on the eastern slopes below: Ferncliff Gardens. After the tulips and daffodils have finished blooming in the nearby Bradner region (see chapter 31), nature goes into a bit of a lull. But not for long. Across the river, Ferncliff Gardens provides one of the most beautiful floral displays in the valley, especially from May to October. Not only is the variety of blooms awesome to see, but the setting is second to none.

Ferncliff Gardens was started in 1920 in Hatzic, 3 km (1.9 mi.) east of downtown Mission. Once a thriving commercial berry-growing centre, Hatzic today more closely resembles a bedroom community. Signs of redevelopment are already everywhere around Ferncliff, and as the years go by it will become even more of an oasis.

Specializing in irises, peonies, day lilies and dahlias, the gardens feature hundreds of varieties, which bathe the landscape with a spectrum of brilliant hues from May to October. From August to mid-October when dahlias flower, visitors are welcome to Ferncliff to make their selections or simply admire owner David Jack's personal garden. When blossoming finishes, the bulbs, tubers and rhizomes are harvested and shipped out to buyers. The challenge faced by anyone who visits here is to come away without dreaming—in high definition, of course—of creating his or her own backyard Ferncliff. For more information on viewing dates and times at Ferncliff Gardens, call 604-826-2447 or visit ferncliffgardens.com.

> HATZIC AND NEILSON PARKS

Photographers will enjoy the views of Ferncliff Gardens from the open slopes of nearby Hatzic Park (its entrance is off Draper Street). This is also a good place to picnic after a visit to the gardens. Better suited to this same purpose is nearby Neilson Regional Park, located on the west side of Hatzic Lake and an easy 5-minute drive from Ferncliff. Open fields slope down to the shore of Hatzic Lake from the parking lot. There are numerous picnic tables, a swimming beach and a salmon spawning channel on Draper Creek that teems with activity come November. (*Note:* No pets are allowed in Neilson Park.) You can launch a hand-carried boat here and spend some leisure time exploring Hatzic Lake. From out on the water, Westminster Abbey's bell tower appears on the skyline.

> NICOMEN ISLAND

A good venue for road cycling lies east of Mission on level-surfaced Nicomen Island. Entirely rural, this countryside is as sleepy as it gets out here in the Fraser Valley. After the Lougheed Highway passes Hatzic Lake, it runs through the small town of Dewdney, then

> HATZIC ROCK

STÓ:LŌ FIRST NATIONS have lived beside the Fraser for millennia. A visit to the X̱á:ytem Longhouse Interpretive Centre on the Lougheed Highway in Hatzic helps explain traditional Aboriginal fishing technology as well as the significance of an enormous rock, renowned as one of the Fraser Valley's "stone people." Profiles of three chiefs can be discerned on the rockface that is X̱á:ytem's (pronounced *hay-toom*) centrepiece. Older than Stonehenge and the pyramids of Giza, the recently excavated site produced artifacts that have been carbon dated to about 9,000 years ago. Two cozy pithouses capture a sense of the ambience of those long-ago times. The centre's cedar longhouse also features a fascinating collection of traditional baskets as well as displays of weaving and carving. For information, call 604-820-9725 or visit xaytem.ca.

crosses a bridge onto Nicomen Island. (Just before the bridge, River Road leads off to the right and follows the shoreline of Nicomen Slough past a pub and a number of wharves to Dewdney Nature Park, where there's a boat launch for exploring the Fraser River and Nicomen Slough.) You may wish to leave your vehicle beside the bridge at Dewdney and use your bicycle to explore the dike trails around the perimeter of Nicomen Island as far east as the rustic town of Deroche, located where Highway 7 crosses from Nicomen back onto the mainland.

If you're inclined to sample some of the local cuisine, one of the most entertaining spots is the Mission Springs Brewing Company with its eclectic blend of classic automotive and logging memorabilia for decor, including a 1949 GMC pickup truck suspended from the ceiling. Children will particularly enjoy pulling the chain that triggers a steam whistle (not nearly as annoying a sound as one might imagine) while those with a mind to play a little pick-up volleyball will head for the sandy outdoor courts positioned beside the brewery on a promontory that overlooks the Fraser. The Mission Springs Brewing Company is located west of Wren Street off the Lougheed Highway in Mission. For more information call 604-820-1009 or visit missionspringsbrewingcompany.com for information.

24

HARRISON HOT SPRINGS
AND **ENVIRONS** &

. . . . .

> **DISTANCE:** 130 km (81 mi.) east of Vancouver in the North Fraser
Valley

> **ACTIVITIES:** Boating, camping, cycling, dog walking, fishing,
paddling, picnicking, playgrounds, swimming, walking

> **ACCESS:** Harrison Hot Springs can be reached by a variety of
routes. The quickest approach is via Highway 1 east of Chilliwack.
Take Exit 135 and follow north on well-marked Highway 9 as it
crosses the Fraser River, then twists and turns through Agassiz and
on to Harrison Hot Springs. A slightly longer approach is via Highway 7, east of Mission, which passes through Harrison Mills near
its intersection with Highway 9.

Kilby Provincial Park is located at Harrison Mills, 15 km (9.3 mi.)
west of Agassiz on Highway 7. To reach Sasquatch Provincial Park,
travel 6 km (3.7 mi.) north of central Harrison Hot Springs along
the eastern shore of Harrison Lake.

TUCKED IN the folds of the Coast Mountains, Harrison Hot
Springs boasts a beach that would be the pride of any seaside
town, let alone a lakefront one. Add to that both public and
private hot spring pools, and you have the makings of an exquisite
aquatic experience year round.

If you're curious about the source of the hot springs, from which
scalding water is piped into a public swimming pool as well as the
pool of the town's anchor tenant, the Harrison Hot Springs Hotel,
head west of the hotel along a well-maintained pathway suitable

for those in wheelchairs. Within minutes, you'll arrive at what first appears to be a curved roof mausoleum built of cinder blocks.

Closer inspection reveals that this is indeed the source of the hot springs, which percolate from a rocky outcropping at a sizzling 62°C (144°F). A cement foundation isolates the springs from the lake water from where it is then pumped through a pipeline into town. By the time you get to soak in either the hotel or town pool, the temperature has been moderated to a more welcoming 40°C (104°F). Although the main source of the springs is off-limits, a companion seep flows from a pipe into a pond immediately beside the brick building. This one is even hotter: 68°C (154°F). Try keeping your hand in it for longer than a second—if you can.

Watch for a rougher trail that leads west from the source. Although it climbs steeply for a short distance through the cool interior of a dense forest, this route leads to a smaller expanse of beach at Sandy Cove. The crescent-shaped stand slopes out into the lake in a much shallower approach than the town's main beach. As a result, water here is warmer for swimming than elsewhere on the glacier-fed fiord. Pick up the trail again at the west end of the beach as it loops around Whippoorwill Point for views south along the Harrison River.

All of 15 km (9.3 mi.) long, the Harrison River is one of the shortest in the province as it empties from the 68-km-long (42.2-mi.-long) lake bearing the same name to the Fraser River. And it's one of the easiest to explore, beginning from the town's beach. Floating along is guaranteed to provide you with a view to the south of Cheam Peak and the surrounding ridge, which looks all the world as if this setting were in the Alps. I recommend the town's Visitor Info Centre, housed in a small roadside home three blocks from the lake, as an ideal source for local information (499 Hot Springs Road; 604-796-5581; www.tourismharrison.com).

> SASQUATCH PROVINCIAL PARK
Three provincial campgrounds nestle beside two of the four lakes within Sasquatch Provincial Park. There's ample room for overnighters at the 177 campsites (currently $21 per night), and there's enough recreational diversity spread over its rolling 1 220 ha (3,015 acres) to satisfy the choosiest of day trippers.

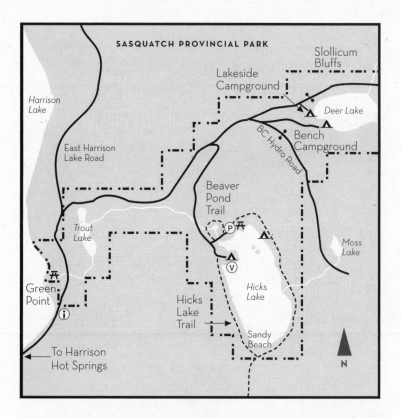

Slollicum
Bluffs

Lakeside
Campground

Harrison
Lake

Deer Lake

East Harrison
Lake Road

BC Hydro Road

Bench
Campground

Beaver
Pond
Trail

Trout
Lake

Moss
Lake

Green
Point

Hicks
Lake

Hicks
Lake
Trail →

Sandy
Beach

To Harrison
Hot Springs

N

At the entrance to the park is the grassy Green Point picnic area, beside the shores of Harrison Lake, which features dozens of wooden tables, many with barbecues; an open play area; and a beach with great exposure to the afternoon sun. This is important, as the waters of Harrison Lake, a deep fiord, are cold year round. *Note*: Wheelchair access at Sasquatch is limited to the Green Point picnic area.

East of Green Point, the road turns from pavement to gravel as it passes beside small Trout Lake, entirely surrounded by thick green growth. About 3 km (1.9 mi.) farther east, the park road divides, with one branch leading 2 km (1.2 mi.) south to Hicks Lake, the other same distance east to Deer Lake. Gates restrict motorized vehicles to the main road, but several old logging roads leading off through the park are perfectly suited for exploration by bicycle. The road to the lakes climbs through a saddle in the slope of the modest-sized

Sandy Cove, Harrison Lake

mountains surrounding Harrison Lake. Sasquatch Park was logged
many years ago. Today, the sheltering forest is more deciduous than
evergreen. Broadleaf maple, white birch and poplar present an allur-
ing sight in autumn when the leaves change colour. From spring
through early fall, birdsongs fill the air and mingle with a chorus of
frogs until late evening.

Deer Lake is a rather simple body of water that reveals itself from a vantage point on the beach at its western end. There's a children's play area just uphill from lakeside with slides and a jungle-gym setup. Only quiet electric motors are allowed on boats that put in here, whereas on nearby Hicks Lake gas-driven motors up to 10 horsepower can be used. Other than in July and August, visitors with small boats will usually have the lakes to themselves. Simply launch from the beach or drive down to a small dock tethered at the south end of the beach.

The circumference of Deer Lake can be easily paddled in an hour without rushing. From the beach, you can also walk a lakeside trail out to a sandy point where fishing or swimming may suit your mood. Or you can cycle the fire and service roads that run well back into the surrounding mountains. For those who wish to get away from the beaches beside the campgrounds, there are more isolated sandy stretches at the far end of either lake that can be reached by boat. Watch for mountain goats in the early-morning light on the slopes of Slollicum Bluffs, which rise above the lake's north side.

Hicks Lake is twice as large and not as open as Deer Lake. Several points of land jut out into the lake from which to fish or catch a view of the mountains rising on the southern horizon. As you approach Hicks, you'll see signs pointing in several different directions. Decide whether you want to head over to the day-use parking

> ## AGASSIZ CIRCLE FARM TOUR

ONE OF the most rewarding aspects of trekking to Harrison Hot Springs is the numerous farms and craft cottages along the way, including the artisan cow and goat cheeses made at The Farm House Natural Cheeses and the drive-through Sparkes Corn Barn, both in Agassiz. You're guaranteed to go home with a heavier load than when you arrived, even if you are slightly lighter in the pocket. The annual Agassiz Fall Fair and Corn Festival takes place mid-September. For information, check out agassizfallfair.ca. For information on Fraser Valley Circle Farm Tours, visit circlefarmtour.ca.

Harrison River, Harrison Mills

lot next to a boat launch and picnic area or proceed to the campground, where there is also a beach and picnic area. Trails link all
the areas together, and it's only a few minutes' walk between the
day-use area and the campground. For the best views, check out
the beach beside the campground amphitheatre: the peaks of the
Skagit Range near Chilliwack Lake stand out on the southern horizon. There are also some good fishing spots here on a point of land
in front of campsites 2 to 17 (some of the most desirable locations,
along with sites 36 to 41).

Put your boat in at the Hicks Lake launch site or walk or cycle
the trail ringing the lake to Sandy Beach at the south end, perhaps
targeting it as your picnic destination if you're travelling light. You'll
reach the beach in 1 hour after a stroll in the shade along an old logging road. Partway around is the group campsite, in front of which is
a good beach. An easy swim offshore are two small forested islands,
perfectly sized for adventure exploration with children and a good
place to cast in a fishing line. Rainbow trout thrive in these waters,
as the sight of ospreys attests.

Campsites at Sasquatch may be reserved in advance by calling 604-689-9025 or by visiting discovercamping.ca. For more information, visit the BC Parks Web site at www.env.gov.bc.ca/bcparks/explore/parkpgs/sasquatch.

> **KILBY HISTORIC SITE**

In rhythm with the vernal and autumnal seasons, the gates at the Kilby Historic Site on the banks of the Harrison River swing open in April and close in November, offering a window to both the valley's past and a future as lively as a newborn lamb. As it has for the past three decades since being acquired by the province from the Kilby family, who set up shop in Harrison Mills in 1904, the historic site hums with life thanks in large part to the commitment of local volunteers from the Fraser Heritage Society. For fruit pie lovers, chef Vera Point of the local Chehalis First Nation helms her kitchen in the Orientation Barn, where the smell of fresh baked goods wafts out the windows of the former stable into the grassy compound that surrounds the imposing heritage store and former hotel complex. Of particular significance is a Gravenstein apple tree planted in 1926, the oldest of its kind in the region, which stands propped up in all its gnarled glory beside the equally venerable Kilby General Store.

Long before the construction of a dike system sturdy enough to hold back the waters of Fraser River, whose confluence with the Harrison lies a short distance downstream, the newly arrived Kilby family wisely mounted their fledgling two-storey store and hotel on pilings high above the flood plain. Nothing else akin to its quaint grandeur remains from the glory days when, in the wake of the Cariboo gold rush and the advent of the transcontinental railway, sawmills sprang up at riverfronts like Harrison Mills and spurred settlement in the valley. For over 70 years, goods from the Kilby General Store's well-stocked shelves filled shopping baskets while its upstairs rooms in the Manchester House Hotel housed workers.

These days, day trippers journey to Harrison Mills and the nearby farming centre of Agassiz for recreation at Kilby Provincial Park, for the annual Fraser Valley Bald Eagle Festival in November, and for a self-guided circle farm tour of the region in search of locally created crafts and artisan produce, much of which is on sale at the Harrison River Restaurant and orientation centre housed in a reconstructed wood-planked barn originally raised in 1917 alongside the Kilby General Store. Kilby represents values and traditions of a day gone by that people feel good about and like to be reminded of—a slower lifestyle.

A recent arrival at Kilby is a crossbred Dorper–St. Croix sheep named Benji, a red ribbon winner at the Agassiz Fall Fair. Her owner donated her to the Kilby Historic Site's Waterloo Farm, which includes potbellied pigs, Shetland ewes, a billy goat and a cocky rooster. The long-term goal is to open an animal education centre for kids at Kilby that will eventually be enlarged to include ponies.

Pack a picnic and head out to the North Fraser Valley. If you've got a canoe or kayak, bring it along as well. And don't forget the binoculars. Not only does the Kilby Historic Site offer an attractive place to enjoy a fresh-air outing, but the nearby provincial park on the shore of Harrison Bay does as well. A sandy beach beckons wind surfers, while a boat launch offers the opportunity to paddle while bald eagles and the occasional breaching white sturgeon soar above the surface.

Details of the historic site as well as current information on special events are posted at www.kilby.ca. For information on Kilby Provincial Park, visit www.env.gov.bc.ca/bcparks/explore/parkpgs/Kilby. For information on the Fraser Valley Bald Eagle Festival, visit www.fraservalleybaldeaglefestival.ca

FRASER VALLEY SOUTH

> ## 25

HOPE AND ENVIRONS &

. . . . .

> **DISTANCE:** 165 km (103 mi.) east of Vancouver

> **ACTIVITIES:** Cycling, dog walking, historic sites, nature observation, picnicking, swimming, walking

> **ACCESS:** Drive 138 km (85.7 mi.) east to Hope via the Trans-Canada Highway (Highway 1). Follow signs to the Coquihalla Highway (Highway 5). About 15 km (9.3 mi.) east of Hope on Highway 5, take Exit 183. Drive west across the highway overpass to the Coquihalla Canyon Provincial Park and nearby Kawkawa Lake Park. (See map on page 157.) Alternatively, from Hope follow Kawkawa Lake Road, then Othello Road, a distance of 7 km (4.3 mi.). Kawkawa Lake is 2.4 km (1.5 mi.) north of Hope. The Othello-Quintette Tunnels are 4.4 km (2.7 mi.) farther north.

> **HOPE**

Hope's origins are in the fur trade. Fort Hope was one of the Hudson's Bay Company trading posts, built on the trail linking Fort Kamloops and Fort Langley. The British hoped for an overland route that would let them cross the mountains without having to tack south into American territory, and their hopes were realized when the trail opened in 1849.

Make a point of stopping in this pretty little river town. A Travel Info Centre kiosk and the Hope Museum are located at the south end of Hope's main street, which fronts on the Fraser River. Look for the waterwheel, part of the restored Home Gold Mine, mounted next to the kiosk. The Hope Visitor Info Centre (919 Water Avenue, 1-866-467-3842, hopebc.ca) publishes a visitor guide, *Daytrippers Paradise,* which comes complete with detailed maps of trails, including the Dewdney Mule and Kettle Valley Railway trails.

Othello-Quintette Tunnels near Hope

If you're looking for some baked goodies for your picnic, find your way to the bakery nearby. As you make your way around town, you'll notice large wooden carvings of animals mounted everywhere. A particularly colourful time to see Hope is the second full weekend in September, when the town hosts Brigade Days, a celebration of its pioneer past.

Long before Bard on the Beach, there was a Bard on the River with an all-star cast: Romeo and Juliet, Lear and Portia, Iago and Othello. Perhaps echoing the Xe:xá:ls, a mythical quartet that transformed people and objects into the present Stó:lō territory, Andrew McCulloch, general superintendent and chief engineer with the Kettle Valley Railway, brought the line's Coquihalla subdivision near Hope to life with whistle stops named after some of William Shakespeare's best-known characters.

That act was little more than window dressing compared with McCulloch's major opus: the Quintette Tunnels at Othello. The trail that leads through the four tunnels that once supported the track cost $300,000 to lay in 1914. Almost all of the work was done by hand—hence the enormous expense. This is still considered the costliest mile of railway track in the world. After the trains stopped running in 1965, Hope residents removed the wooden ties and smoothed out the rail bed into a broad recreation trail, now part of the Trans Canada Trail system that opened in 2000. To mark the opening of the Coquihalla Highway in 1986, the provincial government protected Coquihalla Canyon as parkland.

If you'd care to add your footprints to the paths of history in the Coquihalla Canyon, it's no more strenuous than strolling the Stanley Park sea wall. Should you tack on a stint of hiking on the Dewdney Mule Trail, you'll get the added bonus of climbing through a

> DEWDNEY MULE TRAIL

. . . .

DECADES BEFORE the railway blasted through the Coquihalla Canyon, a more discreet trail was cut on the slopes above the emerald-hued river by surveyor Edgar Dewdney. Beginning in 1860, he and a group of Royal Engineers started clearing a route that eventually led from Hope to Fort Steele, near the present site of Cranbrook in the East Kootenays. The Dewdney Mule Trail intersects with the Kettle Valley Railway on both sides of the Othello Tunnel complex and makes for a fascinating loop hike.

shady, old-growth forest with viewpoints above the canyon that stretch out towards imposing Mount Hope in the distance.

Along the Kettle Valley Railway route, you'll develop a new appreciation for the term *tunnel vision*, particularly in the middle of the longest of the four passageways, where light barely seeps in through each end. And as you step from the heat of the day into the coolness of the shafts, currents of soothing air waft over you, propelled along by the rushing motion of the nearby river. Short spans of bridges link one tunnel to the next, allowing tantalizing glimpses of the Coquihalla Canyon below, the river muscling its way through granite walls with all the emotional rage of Othello himself. The Bard would surely have approved. (*Note:* The park is officially closed November to March.)

> ### KAWKAWA LAKE PARK

The word *kawkawa* is a poetic term in the Halkomelem language that means "much calling of loons." Kawkawa Lake Park is a quiet, roadside municipal park with grassy picnic grounds fronted by a beach and boat launch. In summer, you'll appreciate the lake's warm water. Forest shades the background and shelters the road between here and Coquihalla Canyon Provincial Park.

If you are in the area during salmon spawning season, follow Kawkawa Lake Road east of Hope as it passes over the Coquihalla River. A municipal park is situated on the west bank of the river. On the other side, Union Bar Road leads off to the left past Kawkawa Creek, which flows into the Coquihalla at this point. A fish ladder for returning salmon has been constructed here, and you may be fortunate enough to see the spawning run in September. A boardwalk has been installed beside the creek to give a close-up view of the action.

> ## 26

SKAGIT VALLEY

. . . . .

> **DISTANCE:** 210 km (130 mi.) east and south of Vancouver

> **ACTIVITIES:** Birding, boating, camping, cycling, dog walking, fishing, hiking, picnicking, playground, nature observation, swimming, walking, windsurfing

> **ACCESS:** The road into the Skagit Valley begins off Highway 19 (Exit 168) on the western outskirts of Hope, about 150 km (93 mi.) east of Vancouver. Leave the Trans-Canada via the Hope Business Road exit (also signed as the beginning of the historic Gold Rush Trail route). Drive a short distance through the settlement of Floods—home to the Hope airport, with its field of light planes and gliders—to the well-marked Silver/Skagit Road turnoff in the settlement of Silver Creek. A sign at the start of the road, posted for the benefit of American visitors headed for an outpost of their country at the road's southern end, announces "Hozomeen 38 miles" (or 61 km). (Hozomeen is home to a small U.S. ranger station where recreational visits to Ross Lake are monitored.) There are no services along this wide and well-maintained road, so make sure to fill your tank at one of the local service stations in or near Hope.

COME SIT beside the crystal-clear waters of the Skagit River, deep within a long valley that stretches 70 km (43.5 mi.) south from the eastern Fraser Valley town of Hope to the Canada–U.S. border. Here's a place where you can follow the changing seasons: smell the rich humus as the earth begins to warm in spring, or listen to the wind in the dry leaves of the trembling aspen trees above, whispering that nature has entered the transition zone between summer and autumn. Walk or cycle the network of roads and trails, or paddle a boat to a wilderness site on Ross Lake for a

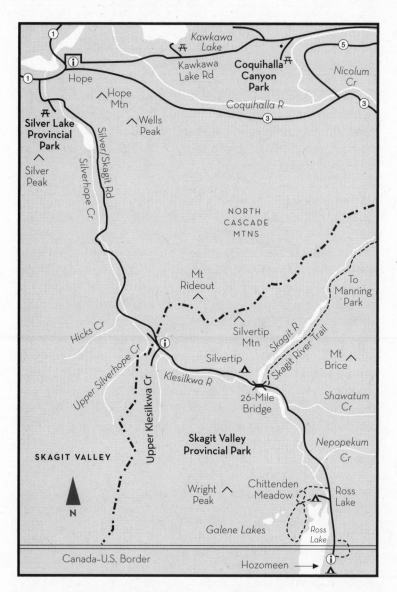

picnic. Fishing for rainbow trout in the Skagit's waters is still one of the biggest drawing cards here. Come the end of the day, there are plenty of camping spots from which to choose, should you be fortunate enough to have time to spend a night or two. On clear evenings, the Milky Way pours out across the open sky above you. By comparison, what we see in the city starscape are, indeed, *skim* pickings.

In spring and fall, this important migration corridor fills with dozens of species of birds and mammals on the move. Year round, its vastness is inhabited by hundreds of species of birds, reptiles, amphibians and most of the common B.C. mammals. Elk and mountain goats frequent the higher mountains. Several ecological reserves in the valley feature virgin stands of Douglas-fir, western red cedar and ponderosa pine.

> ### SILVER LAKE PROVINCIAL PARK

Silver/Skagit Road is paved for a short distance, then becomes well-graded gravel as it follows Silverhope Creek. Silver Lake Park lies 6 km (3.7 mi.) south. Drive 1 km (0.6 mi.) in from the main road to reach this small lake whose 25 campsites ($16 per night) are popular with locals; space is at a premium in warm-weather months.

Families come here to fish together, sometimes from old logs jutting out from the shoreline. The bottom drops off rapidly at the lake's north end, and the best swimming is at the south end of the park road. The road running along the west side of the lake leads down a narrow, treed lane to a sandy section on the bank of Silverhope Creek near where it enters the lake. This is a good picnic area, especially if you aren't planning to drive much farther south into the Skagit. Regular flooding has carved deep potholes in the

> ## TOPS FOR TROUT

AS SILVER/SKAGIT ROAD heads south of Silver Lake, it parallels one of North America's finest river systems for fishing. Along the way, first at Silverhope Creek, then at the Klesilkwa River and finally at the Skagit River, fly-fishers pull off at designated parking spots to try for rainbow trout. Open season is summer and fall, when there are several strong runs. Watch for postings along the way. The area around the Silvertip campground, where the Klesilkwa flows into the Skagit, is especially popular. Fishing is strictly catch-and-release here on the Skagit, with only barbless hooks permitted.

fast-flowing creek. Diving into them from the thick tree trunks on the riverbank is a chilly challenge.

Windsurfers on Silver Lake enjoy the breeze that frequently gusts through the valley and that gives the Hope region such a favourable reputation for gliding. Rugged cliffs rise above the east side of the lake, with Hope Mountain and Wells Peak's jagged teeth pre-eminent on the skyline. The high walls catch sunlight at the beginning or end of day in a way that emphasizes the subtle colours in them, shades of iron red above the evergreens. The trees at lakeside are aspen, water birch and cottonwood, all silver-green in summer, golden in autumn.

> ### SKAGIT VALLEY PROVINCIAL PARK

Nearly 40 km (25 mi.) south of Silver Lake along the winding gravel road a large wooden information kiosk marks the western boundary of 32 570-ha (80,484-acre) Skagit Valley Park. It's worth a stop to read about the natural history of the valley, which is the transition zone between the Interior and the Coast, a medley of coastal forest, open meadows populated with prairie species, subalpine and alpine areas, and marshes, all of which create a special biological mosaic.

Just south of the kiosk is the Silvertip provincial campground, one of the best-organized sites in the Skagit. From April to October there is a nightly charge of about $16 per site. Silvertip has 43 well-spaced campsites, seven of which sit on the north bank of the Skagit River.

The forest at this site is much more typical of the region than that at Silver Lake. Douglas-fir and red cedar blend with western hemlock and lodgepole pine. Ponderosa pines climb the slopes of Silvertip Mountain and Mount Rideout to the north. Cool breezes come down off the slopes of Mount Rideout (2 447 m/8,028 ft.). It has a twin, Mount Redoubt (2 730 m/8,956 ft.), due south across the border, the tallest peak of six that are grouped between Chilliwack and Ross lakes, including Nodoubt Peak.

At Silvertip, the Skagit River makes its grand entrance into the valley at 26 Mile Bridge, flowing in from its headwaters to the north in Manning Park. From here it heads to its eventual union with the Pacific near the town of Mount Vernon in Washington State's

Skagit County. There's a small day-use area on the north side of the bridge with four picnic tables and plenty of parking. An information marker posted beside the river recounts the history of the Whatcom Trail, a section of which lies on the opposite bank. The 1850s Cariboo gold rush tempted Americans to build a 430-km (267-mi.) supply trail from the town of Whatcom (now Bellingham) to the Thompson River. In this way, they hoped to circumvent customs and excise tax collectors stationed at the mouth of the Fraser River. The trail opened on August 17, 1858, but was abruptly abandoned two months later. Maintenance proved difficult, and the route itself was just too long.

> ### SKAGIT RIVER TRAIL

To get a walking workout, try a section of the popular 15-km (9.3-mi.) Skagit River Trail (the old Whatcom Trail) that runs northeast from 26 Mile Bridge to Sumallo Grove in Manning Park. The first 3 km (1.9 mi.) make for an easy bicycle ride before the trail begins a short, steep climb along the edge of an extensive ancient scree slope. (If you wish to explore farther, leave your bike here.) One note of caution: in late summer, be on the lookout for bears foraging for berries along this initial part of the trail.

Red trail markers affixed to trees count down the kilometres, beginning at 14 near the bridge and decreasing as you head towards Manning Park. Treats along the way include views of nearby Silvertip Mountain and its retreating glacier, a copse of rare wild rhododendrons that bloom red in June, sandbars exposed on the Skagit and a provincial ecological reserve at km 9 protecting the stand of tall cedar and fir here. Just before the trail reaches the reserve, it crosses 28 Mile Creek. At times of high water, crossing here is tricky. Tread cautiously.

> ### CHITTENDEN MEADOW TRAIL

The Skagit is a special valley because of its U-shaped profile, a rare configuration in southwestern B.C., where most valleys are steep-sided Vs dominated by high mountains. The trails through Chittenden Meadow, 16 km (10 mi.) south of the Silvertip campground, show off the valley's grandeur as the valley bottom spreads out

Skagit River anglers

before you. It's easy to see what attracted Washington politicians in the 1950s and '60s, who wanted to clear trees from the American side of the valley to create the Ross Lake Reservoir. The trees were cut, and, backed up behind the Ross and Diablo dams, the waters of the Skagit River are drawn down through hydroelectric turbines to provide power for the Seattle area.

From here on the Canadian side, it's equally evident why conservationists such as Wilfred (Curley) Chittenden, after whom the meadow is named, worked so hard to protect the valley from further flooding in the 1970s, when the governments of Washington and British Columbia seemed poised to expand the perimeter of the Ross Lake Reservoir north beyond the border.

Curley Chittenden was a legendary figure who died in 1995. Born in Bradner in the Fraser Valley in the early part of this century, the son of one of B.C.'s early explorers, he worked as a logger for most of his life. In 1953, he was contracted to clearcut 200 ha (500 acres) of the Skagit Valley floor, now the Canadian end of Ross Lake. Later, when the government asked him to log even more, including the stately ponderosa pines (unique in this region because they are so far west of their usual habitat), he categorically refused and instead began lobbying for the meadowland's preservation. Thanks to his vision, the pines and surrounding meadow were saved as part of the 32 508 ha (80,331 acres) set aside by the provincial government in late 1973.

A gentle trail meanders through Chittenden Meadow, leading past a series of interpretive markers. To reach the meadow, park beside the Skagit River and cross the suspension bridge. Trail maps may be available from the BC Parks kiosk located at the beginning of the meadow trail on the west side of the suspension bridge. The level, hard-packed Chittenden Meadow Trail branches off in several directions and leads towards Ross Lake. (A trail leads north from the west side of the bridge to several good fishing spots. Depending on your technique, you can either cast from the riverbank or don waterproof gear and wade in. You'll find a cozy campsite here beneath the sheltering limbs of five magnificent red cedars, from which there is a view of Silvertip and Shawatum mountains to the north and east.)

One of the best ways to tour the meadow is with bicycles along the old logging roads that double as pathways through the meadow. For example, from marker "4," follow a faint trail west that soon becomes much more distinct as it leads to a sign that points towards International Creek. Follow this trail as it leads through the overhanging forest, eventually emerging at the northwest corner of the lake. From here, ride through the field of stumps and tall grass back towards the meadow. A branch of the trail leads to the nearby Ross Lake campground. Allow an hour to do the trail by bike.

Cycling the trails imparts an enhanced sense for the flatness of the valley bottom that you won't otherwise experience as you pass beneath stands of tall cottonwoods. Come fall, their leaves turn a vivid gold. At that time of year there's such a stillness in the air that the leaves make a racket as they tumble down.

> ### ROSS LAKE PROVINCIAL CAMPGROUND
Ross Lake spreads across the international border at the south end of the Skagit Valley, 65 km (40.4 mi.) from Hope. A campground and day-use area here overlook the lake. Some of the 88 campsites are more exposed to the elements than at Silvertip, but most are sheltered in a forested area. Parents will find the nearby children's play area handy to the beach and boat launch, with a panoramic view south over the lake as well. From April to October, there is a charge of $16 per night for the use of a campsite. The park is set back a short distance from the main road. Chittenden Meadow is just 1 km (0.6 mi.) north of here.

Note: Depending on rainfall, the time of the year and the demand for power at the Diablo generating station, Ross Lake may be full to the brim ("full pool," as it's officially designated), or there may be stumps showing above the surface. In summer, the water in the big lake is much warmer than the cold river, making this an ideal place to swim. Call BC Parks at 604-869-7080 for current water levels.

> ### HOZOMEEN
Just south of the Ross Lake campground lies the international border. There are no lengthy line-ups for customs inspections at the Hozomeen crossing. As the connecting road only leads several kilometres south of Skagit Valley Park into the Ross Lake National Recreation Area (itself a portion of the much larger North Cascades National Park), there's no border patrol stationed here, only a team of U.S. park rangers who greet visitors with a friendly wave. There's no need for heightened security—the rugged backcountry

and flooded valley floor provide a natural barrier. In a heartening display of bipartisanship, a well-stocked rack of trail maps and visitor information for both Skagit Valley and Ross Lake parks fronts the A-frame ranger station. Stop here for information on wilderness campsites on 37-km-long (23-mi.-long) Ross Lake.

Just past the ranger station is a boat launch, a beach and a cleared area dubbed Winnebago Flats, with a dozen campsites beside the lake. All the amenities provided at the two provincial campgrounds north of here are also present at Hozomeen. A trail runs south along the beach to a distant headland, an enjoyable stretch for your legs. Although there is plenty of driftwood for campfires strewn on the beach, signs politely suggest you try camping without one. Loons, Canada geese and dabbling and diving ducks populate the shoreline along with hundreds of tiny frogs. Aside from their various calls, cries and croaks, this is a very quiet environment most of the time. It does get busy on the major American holidays in summer, when water levels are kept high.

On the benchland above the beach are dozens of additional campsites, although with diminished views of the lake. Drinking-water pumps, picnic tables and toilets are also located here. Unlike on the Canadian side, camping in Ross Lake National Recreation Area's Hozomeen campground is free.

As a warm-up to some of the longer hikes in the region, stretch your legs on the 1.3-km (0.8-mi.) Trail of the Obelisk that leads a short distance uphill east from the ranger station onto a ridge above the lake. Your destination is a metre-tall aluminum obelisk on the international boundary; similar markers are placed along the Canada–U.S. border from Tsawwassen/Point Roberts (see chapter 44) to Manitoba. Looking west across the valley, you can make out a thin clearing running straight up the mountain that marks the 49th parallel.

Hozomeen Mountain's distinctive peak is prominent on the southern horizon. The hike up its slope to Hozomeen Ridge is not particularly difficult and can be accomplished in 2 or 3 hours. Your reward will be a commanding view of Ross Lake, the Skagit Valley with the river's course clearly outlined and an eyeful of other North Cascade peaks.

CHILLIWACK LAKE

. . . . .

> DISTANCE: 141 km (87.6 mi.) southeast of Vancouver

> ACTIVITIES: Boating, camping, dog walking, fishing, hiking, nature observation, picnicking, swimming, viewpoints, walking, windsurfing

> ACCESS: Travel 85 km (52.8 mi.) east along the Trans-Canada Highway (Highway 1) to the Chilliwack Lake exit (#104), then east on No. 3 Road. You'll pass through the rural community of Yarrow. Continue east along Vedder Mountain Road. Just over the Vedder Bridge, turn south (right) onto Chilliwack Lake Road at a well-marked intersection. Drive another 42 km (26 mi.) to the lake, an easy 2-hour drive from Vancouver.

ALL IT takes is one trip to an exotic locale like the Stein Valley on the eastern perimeter of the Lower Mainland near Lytton to make you fall in love with the sight of very large trees. There are other locations closer to Vancouver where small groups of these gnarly giants still flourish—for example, Lighthouse Park (see chapter 2) in West Vancouver. Once you've caught the bug, you'll be driven to find whole hillsides and valley bottoms full of these huggable hulks. Perhaps it's their serene nature: all that bio-mass in motion without so much as a gurgle to be heard, just a sighing from high above.

If you've got the itch, head for Chilliwack Lake, where you can enjoy the company of some big trees with much, little or no effort—take your pick. Walk the provincial-park trail up Post Creek to Greendrop and Lindeman lakes near the north end of Chilliwack

Lake, or ramble through the ecological reserve of old-growth cedars beside the upper Chilliwack River at the lake's south end.

> CHILLIWACK LAKE PROVINCIAL PARK

In 1997, the borders of Chilliwack Lake Park expanded dramatically. BC Parks' original 162-ha (400-acre) toehold at the north end of the lake mushroomed when the provincial government added a further 8 960 ha (22,140 acres). Today, most of the Chilliwack River drainage north of the Canada–U.S. border is protected, as are the Post Creek and Radium Creek drainages. This is exciting news for Lower Mainland day trippers who have explored this area's trails and waters for decades. It's also beneficial to wildlife populations of grizzly bear, spotted owl and amphibians such as the Pacific giant salamander.

> The Pacific giant salamander is no Komodo dragon, but at 30 cm (12 in.), two-thirds of which is tail, the province's largest salamander is as startling to encounter as a large mammal.

If you decide to camp at Chilliwack Lake Park, you may be lucky enough to find room beneath some large ponderosa pines at lakeside. This is the western edge of the ponderosa pine's range. Any closer to the coast is just not dry enough for their liking. There are 146 campsites in all. The best ones are situated on a bluff overlooking the lake, with a wide sandy beach below. A fee of $16 is charged when the campground is open from April to October. There's also a boat launch here suited to large watercraft. Windsurfers love the winds that are almost guaranteed to blow across the lake daily. The lake is often whipped up by winds funnelling out to the coast, so be cautious when out in a small boat.

> LINDEMAN–GREENDROP LAKE TRAIL

There's no better time to visit the south Fraser Valley than in late summer. Prized picnicking and angling sites are sprinkled along the Chilliwack River Valley, and shaded trails thread through the slopes above the river's headwaters in Chilliwack Lake Provincial Park. Although river access comes easily at numerous roadside pullouts, you'll need to expend more energy to reap the benefits offered by

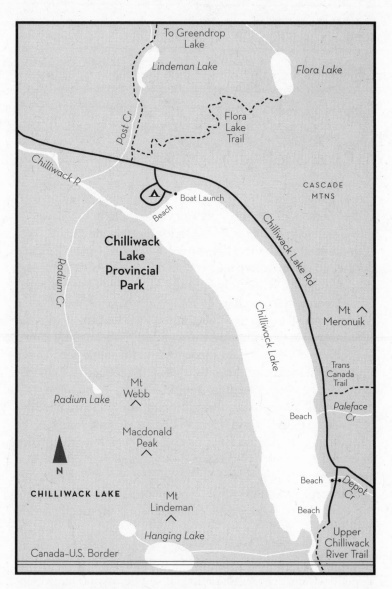

To Greendrop Lake

Lindeman Lake

Flora Lake

Post Cr

Flora Lake Trail

Chilliwack R.

Boat Launch

CASCADE MTNS

Beach

Chilliwack Lake Provincial Park

Chilliwack Lake Rd

Radium Cr

Mt Meronuik

Chilliwack Lake

Trans Canada Trail

Mt Webb

Radium Lake

Beach

Paleface Cr

Macdonald Peak

N

CHILLIWACK LAKE

Mt Lindeman

Beach

Depot Cr

Beach

Hanging Lake

Canada-U.S. Border

Upper Chilliwack River Trail

hiking routes such as the popular Lindeman–Greendrop Lake Trail. One of the rewards will be the entrancing sight of sunlight sparkling on the surface of the two lakes enfolded by craggy North Cascade Mountain peaks. Lindeman Lake is 3.4 km (2 mi.) return; Greendrop Lake is 10.4 km (6.2 mi.) return.

Chilliwack Lake shoreline by Depot Creek

Beside the trail's outset, lively Post Creek froths its way down the mountainside from high above, carrying a gentle breeze that helps keep biting insects at bay. Columns of old-growth Douglas-firs line the way. In less than an hour, you'll find yourself beside Lindeman, possibly the most beautiful subalpine lake in the Lower Mainland. Clear green at the shoreline, its chilly waters progressively deepen in hues from blue to indigo when viewed from the trail. If you plan to journey on to Greendrop, save a swim here for the return journey.

Picking your way around Lindeman's north side requires some tricky boulder hopping. Shoes with good ankle support will not only spare you the misfortune of twisting or wedging a foot in the scree, but they will also help improve balancing skills. Thankfully, staircases and boardwalks assist hikers around the steepest section of the lake. From there, the well-marked trail to Greendrop passes knee-high wild gooseberry bushes and delicate mountain orchids as it wends through a narrow, forested valley interspersed with open sections of scree. With the exception of the occasional whirring hummingbird, the air is thick with a rich stillness rarely experienced in daily life.

As you near Greendrop Lake, a sign posted at a fork in the trail offers two approaches, either across a wooden bridge or beside a small stream that occasionally fans out across the forest floor. Regardless of which route you choose, orange metal markers affixed to tree trunks helpfully guide the way. Whereas Lindeman Lake has a lock on looks, Greendrop's special feature is the spectacular size of the western red cedar grove on its waterfront. Although a trail marker beside Greendrop's wilderness campsite indicates that the Centennial Trail leads east from there into the Skagit Valley, attempts to find the faded route will prove futile to all but the hardiest of bushwhackers.

Portions of the Trans Canada Trail lead through the Chilliwack River Valley, particularly from several kilometres before the Thurston Meadows campsite to Chilliwack Lake. The 3-km (1.8 mi.) Tolmie Trail between Little Tamahi and Tamahi is another stand-out. It's a good hike, but sadly ATVs have ruined it for cyclists. For information on the Trans Canada Trail, visit www.trailsbc.ca.

> ## CHILLIWACK LAKE

The peaks of the Cascade Mountains' Skagit Range surround the shores of Chilliwack Lake. It's 14 km (8.7 mi.) from the north end of Chilliwack Lake to its south end. For much of the way, the rough road is level and runs alongside or just above the lake, crosses a bridge over Paleface Creek and becomes gated south of Depot Creek. There are wide, sandy beaches at the mouths of both Paleface and Depot creeks that require a scramble to reach.

> ## UPPER CHILLIWACK RIVER TRAIL

A well-worn track leads behind the beach at the lake's south end to where the upper Chilliwack River, which originates on the American side of the border, flows into the lake. Enormous old-growth cedars surround you almost as soon as you begin walking the pathway. Groves of these giants, some of them 3 to 4 m (10 to 13 ft.) in diameter, feed on the steady supply of water from the nearby river. The upper Chilliwack River usually crests in late June, then drops during the summer. Wide sandbars lie exposed in many places until autumn rains bring water levels up once more. The river gurgles along past the ecological reserve, where most of the riparian forest is preserved in a 3-km (1.9-mi.) stretch that leads to the Canada–U.S. border.

Press on along the main trail until you find another spot close to the international border. Fortunately, the clearing that marks the 49th parallel doesn't extend right down to the river, so the forest next to the river remains undisturbed.

> ## 28

CULTUS LAKE &

. . . . .

> DISTANCE: 100 km (60 mi.) southeast of Vancouver

> ACTIVITIES: Boating, camping, cycling, dog walking, hiking, pad-
dling, picnicking, playground, swimming, trail rides, viewpoints,
walking

> ACCESS: Follow the Trans-Canada Highway (Highway 1) for
90 km (56 mi.) almost to Chilliwack. Watch for signs indicating Exit
104 to Yarrow and the provincial parks at Cultus and Chilliwack
lakes. Once you've left the highway, you are on No. 3 Road. East of
Yarrow, Vedder Mountain Road skirts the base of Vedder Mountain.
Just before the bridge over the Chilliwack/Vedder River, turn uphill
(south), following the provincial-park signs. Cultus Lake is 4 km
(2.5 mi.) from this point.

MENTION CULTUS LAKE to many people and what immediately come to mind are images of speedboats, summer parties, water slides and, above all, crowds of campers. While
these impressions are certainly accurate during the hottest days of
summer, there is a quieter side to the lake and its environs in most
other seasons.

Cultus Lake has limited drainage aside from the Sweltzer River,
which flows out the north end. A small creek enters at the south end,
but otherwise, there is no source of fresh cold water to feed the lake
once the snowpack has melted from the surrounding slopes. In comparison to the frigid waters of nearby Chilliwack and Harrison lakes,
Cultus is a bathtub, which surely accounts for its popularity among
visitors for almost a century. Because of the warm water, too, fishing
in the park is good, with rainbow and cutthroat trout and Dolly Varden char to be hooked.

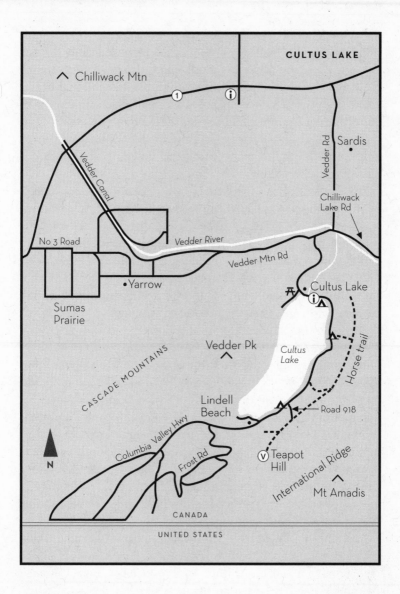

CULTUS LAKE

Chilliwack Mtn

Sardis

Vedder Rd

Chilliwack Lake Rd

Vedder Canal

No 3 Road

Vedder River

Vedder Mtn Rd

Yarrow

Cultus Lake

Sumas Prairie

CASCADE MOUNTAINS

Vedder Pk

Cultus Lake

Horse trail

Lindell Beach

Road 918

Columbia Valley Hwy

Frost Rd

N

Teapot Hill

International Ridge

Mt Amadis

CANADA

UNITED STATES

Cultus Lake was originally settled at its north end. There is still a small community of year-round residents here and another at Lindell Beach at the lake's south end, though most cottages are used only on a seasonal basis. Row upon row of small, well-kept cabins, built close together, ring the shores at both ends of the lake.

> CULTUS MUNICIPAL BEACH

Although much of the summer activity has expanded along the east side of the lake, it is at Cultus's north end that you will find some of the best swimming, especially if you have smaller children in tow. There is a playground, complete with a small slide, and a maze of docks on which to sun while keeping an eye on young bathers. On the nearby lawns of the municipal park, you'll find plenty of room to hold barbecues, with a picnic gazebo, tennis courts and washroom facilities close at hand.

To reach the municipal beach, turn right at the large wooden public-parking sign as you enter the town of Cultus Lake and drive the short distance to lakeside. Even if your destination is the nearby provincial park, this is an interesting location through which to stroll and admire the cottages. Some sport quaint names—Bide-a-wee, Laffalot, Dunroamin—and mounted atop one beachfront cabin are several pairs of ancient homemade water skis equipped with cut-off rubber boots, signs of earlier, more ingenious times.

> CULTUS LAKE PROVINCIAL PARK

Once past the mall, the go-kart track, the commercial water slides and the stable where trail rides may be arranged, Columbia Valley Highway, the main road around the lake, heads south for 4 km (2.5 mi.) towards the provincial park. Just past privately operated Sunnyside Campground is the park headquarters where well-informed staff can answer questions on recreational options in the surrounding district. You can reserve a site here by calling 604-689-9025 or visiting discovercamping.bc.

There are four campgrounds within the park, as well as three large picnic grounds. During summer months, the gatehouse at the entrance to the park is open 24 hours a day. If you are seeking camping space, this is the place to register. An overnight camping fee (about $30) is charged from April to October. Both Entrance Bay and Maple Bay have a boat launch, beach and picnic day-use area. For details, visit www.env.gov.bc.ca/bcparks/explore/parkpg/cultus_lk. *Note:* Dogs must be on a leash at all times and are not allowed in park buildings or beach areas except for areas set aside for pets at the Shale Beach area between the Jade Bay boat launch and the Entrance Bay day-use area and also between the Maple Bay boat launch and the Maple Bay day-use area.

The boundaries of the park encompass both sides of Cultus Lake, but only the southeast side is developed for recreation. To the northwest is open countryside where second-growth forest is beginning to establish itself. Much of the northwest side of the lake is made inaccessible by cliffs that plummet to the water's edge.

International Ridge rises steeply above the campsites and day-use areas on the southeast side of the lake. Several trails traverse the ridge. One particularly popular trail leads to a viewpoint on Teapot Hill, named by two surveyors in the early 1950s. While laying out boundaries for the 658-ha (1,626-acre) park, they found an abandoned teapot on the open face of the knoll that rises 750 m (2,460 ft.) above the lake, affording good views to the south, west and north.

Of the several approaches to Teapot Hill, the easiest begins on the east side of the road between Delta Grove and Honeymoon Bay. The entrance is marked by a gate and signposts. One sign reads "Road 918"; its companion points the way uphill to Teapot Hill. There is limited parking next to the trailhead. Interpretive signs are situated at various places along wide, well-worn Road 918. Near the top the road forks right while the well-marked trail to Teapot Hill leads uphill to the left.

The forest through which the road and trail run is made up largely of second-growth western hemlock and tall broadleaf maple. In autumn, as the maple leaves turn golden with the change in seasons, the forest around Cultus Lake is bright and colourful. The air is rich with the smell of humus, and the dry leaves crunch underfoot as you walk along. Total walking time one way from the road to the top of Teapot Hill is less than 1 hour.

From the top, the most interesting views are of Lindell Beach and south to the Columbia Valley, which opens and then narrows on its way into the United States, with several peaks of the Cascade Mountains rising in the distance.

A horse trail runs much of the way along International Ridge. It joins Road 918 near Honeymoon Bay. Feeder trails lead from both the Entrance Bay and Clear Creek campgrounds to the horse

Summer at Cultus Lake

trail, providing a pleasant alternative to the more straightforward approach to Teapot Hill via Road 918 mentioned above. The walk one way from Entrance Bay to Teapot Hill is less than 2 hours: from Clear Creek it's 90 minutes one way. The horse trail offers more variety than Road 918, as it rises and falls along the hillside.

> **COLUMBIA VALLEY**

The Columbia Valley Highway leads south from the park onto the benchland above the town of Lindell Beach. Lindell Beach is similar in flavour to the community at the north end of Cultus Lake. From here you may choose to drive through the Columbia Valley, an enjoyable 1-hour jaunt, or to explore the area by bicycle. In contrast to the narrow shoulders and highway traffic running the length of Cultus Lake, the roads south of Lindell Beach are far less busy, making them ideal for cycling.

Columbia Valley Highway divides just south of the Cultus Golf Park. It really doesn't matter which of the two forks, Frost Road or Columbia Valley, you choose to follow, as one feeds into the other near the U.S. border, creating a loop through the valley. Both major roads level out soon after cresting on the benchland above Lindell Beach and run 12 km (7.4 mi.) to the American border.

LANGLEY

SURREY

ALDERGROVE LAKE
REGIONAL PARK &

. . . . .

> DISTANCE: 70 km (43.5 miles) southeast of Vancouver

> ACTIVITIES: Birding, cross-country skiing, cycling, dog walking, group functions, in-line skating, paddling, picnicking, stargazing, swimming, viewpoints, walking

> ACCESS: Take the Trans-Canada Highway (Highway 1) east to the 264th Street exit (#73). Head south to 8th Avenue (Huntington Road), then turn east to reach the main park entrance at the intersection of 8th Avenue and 272nd Street. (There are equestrian and pedestrian entrances on the west and east sides of the park, 272nd Street and Lefeuvre Road, respectively.)

F OR ONE SEASON of the year—summer—Aldergrove Lake is a magnet for overheated kids on vacation. The rest of the time, it's a quiet corner tucked away on the border between Langley and Abbotsford in the southern Fraser Valley. Two main trails loop and interconnect as they thread through a tall, dense forest, eventually leading out into the brightness of an open meadow surrounding Aldergrove Bowl, a former gravel quarry that has now been successfully restored to green space. You can walk or cycle these inviting trails over the course of several hours or even cross-country ski them when conditions are right.

The rolling countryside around Aldergrove Lake is largely under cultivation, taken up by berry and dairy farms and plant nurseries. Little creeks crisscross the fields, culverted under roadways and bridged where they really display their girth. Salmon spawn in some,

Rock 'n' Horse Trail, Aldergrove Lake

especially when the creeks are running high after a fall rainstorm. Endangered species, such as the Salish Sucker and the Nooksack Dace, return in smaller streams, such as Pepin Brook, which flows through the park on its way to join the Nooksack River in nearby Washington State.

If you pull in here with high hopes that water levels in Aldergrove Lake have benefited from rainstorms too, think again. Imagine an enormous bathtub with the plug pulled: this is Aldergrove Lake in the off-season, from Labour Day to Victoria Day. Entirely artificial, shaped like a sandy racing oval with a concrete pad on its bottom, the lake can be bone dry. That doesn't deter kids from building sandcastles on the shoreline year round. The size of the parking lot confirms that the lake is very popular in summer, but most times the lot is as empty as the basin. (*Note:* Dogs are not allowed on the beach.)

A stone's throw from the lake on the north side of Pepin Brook is a large playing field and the Blacktail group picnic area with a covered barbecue shelter. (You can reserve the latter by calling the Metro Vancouver Parks' East Area Office at 604-530-4983.) Fringed with young maple trees, come October this is a colourful locale.

There's much more to Aldergrove Lake Park than first meets the eye. Set out along the pedestrian-only 4-km (2.5-mi.) Pepin Brook Trail, which mostly follows a ridge along the park's northern perimeter. The surface of this quiet woodland trail has a pleasant spring underfoot. On summer nights in August, stargazers gather in an open field beside the trail for astronomy programs provided by the park in cooperation with the Royal Astronomical Society and the Pacific Space Centre.

Walk or cycle the 7-km (4.3-mile) Rock 'n' Horse Trail, which intertwines with Pepin Brook Trail in places. You can usually expect to encounter horseback riders on this aptly named route. A Trail Users Courtesy Code posted at intervals reminds everyone of the procedures to avoid conflict: cyclists yield to pedestrians and equestrians, while pedestrians yield to equestrians. Take care not to spook any horses you may meet; slow down when approaching them and stand aside on the down side of the trail while they pass.

You won't need any prompting to mount a bicycle saddle and pedal off through the sheltering forest along this easygoing trail, suited to beginner- and intermediate-level cyclists who like to enjoy

> **TRANSFORMATIONS**

A MASSIVE ERRATIC BOULDER, a leftover from glacial times, is nestled in the woods near Lefeuvre Road. The Transformer, a supernatural character from Native mythology who went about changing animate beings into inanimate objects, might just have had a hand in this one. Transformations of other kinds have influenced the park since it was created in 1970. The recycled timbers used to build Hunt Bridge, located close to the pedestrian entrance on 272nd Street, came from Vancouver's old Cambie Street Bridge in 1985.

a view and a challenge at the same time. The farther you cycle, the better the trail gets. Just when it looks as if you'll spend your visit marvelling at tall broadleaf maple and cedar trees, suddenly the forest opens up and you're riding over hills beside farmland where berry bushes colour the horizon. Continue up and down, back and forth along the trail, enjoying views of Mount Baker's snow cone (cloud cover permitting). At sunset you can watch it turn shades of pink and red.

A gravel mine near the southeast corner of the park has been greened up and restored as a small lake and marsh/pond. Unlike those in Aldergrove Lake, water levels in the Aldergrove Bowl are stable year round—good news for canoeists and kayakers. For information on activities, plus updates on Aldergrove Lake Park's development, call 604-530-4983 or visit www.metrovancouver.org/services/parks_lscr/regionalparks/Pages/AldergroveLake.aspx.

Should your park outing leave you wanting more, paved shoulders on the Langley back roads around the park provide ideal routes for extended cycling and in-line skating excursions. They are wide and smooth, and best of all there is only a hint of traffic along most of the routes. Enjoy rural scenes as you ride or skate along. Mount Baker seems astonishingly close at hand. For quick access to the back roads, park at the entrance to Aldergrove Lake Park at 8th Avenue and 272nd Street and begin from here. The paved shoulders nearby on 272nd Street were developed for cyclists and in-line skaters. Signs posted by the Township of Langley point out the route to follow. A note of caution: Although you can in-line skate on the roadway that leads into Aldergrove Lake Park, a steep hill that drops down to the main parking areas and the lake will probably prove too challenging for novice skaters. Always wear a helmet and protective padding just in case.

Explore the region at your leisure as you make your way to and from the park by following the back roads south of Highway 1. The drive along the country roads of Surrey and Langley is a reward in itself. In autumn, front porches and roadside stands brim with colourful squashes and mound upon mound of pumpkins, the harvest from nearby fields.

> # 30
CAMPBELL VALLEY &

. . . . .

> DISTANCE: 55 km (34 mi.) east of Vancouver, in Langley

> ACTIVITIES: Cycling, dog walking, historic site, horseback riding, nature observation, picnicking, walking

> ACCESS: Follow Highway 1 southeast to the 200th Street exit and drive 14.5 km (9 mi.) south to either the park's 16th or 8th Avenue entrance. Or from Highway 99 South, take the 8th Avenue East exit and travel 7.5 km (4.7 mi.) to the South Valley entrance on 200th Street.

> ## CAMPBELL VALLEY REGIONAL PARK

In 1898, when Alexander Annand left Port Moody to take up farming in southwestern Langley Township, he had no greater intention than to homestead. Much of the better land from here north to Fort Langley on the Fraser River had already been claimed. But he must have been happy to have had water in the small wetland valley above, which he cleared forest for pasture. Home, barn and sheds went up, an orchard grew, time went by.

Annand eventually passed the farm into other hands, but his imprint is still visible in the hand-hewn lumber of the farmhouse and on the smooth surface of the surrounding fields. Below, where Little Campbell River seeps in, a trail leads to several level meadows from which wagons once hauled out hay to feed the livestock. Half forest and half marsh, the valley is a quiet haven for birds and is rich with berries.

This gently rolling region just north of the Canada–U.S. border lends itself to exploration on foot or horseback in the park, and by bike around the park's perimeter (see below). Over the years, Langley riders have kept open the trails that run east to Aldergrove. Since

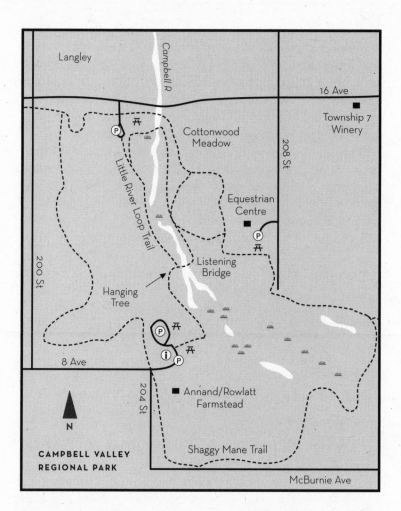

Langley

Campbell R.

16 Ave

Township 7
Winery

Cottonwood
Meadow

Little River Loop Trail

Equestrian
Centre

Listening
Bridge

208 St

Hanging
Tree

200 St

8 Ave

204 St

Annand/Rowlatt
Farmstead

Shaggy Mane Trail

McBurnie Ave

N

CAMPBELL VALLEY
REGIONAL PARK

September 1979, when Metro Vancouver Parks took control of more than 535 ha (1,322 acres) of the Campbell Valley, including the Annand farm, these trails have come into greater public use.

Campbell Valley Regional Park attracts more than 200,000 visitors annually, and although not all of them are on horseback, the flavour of the area is contagious enough to make anyone want to mount up. The Shaggy Mane Trail, which rings the park, runs 11 km (6.8 mi.), quite a distance on foot but an easy 2-hour ride. While the Shaggy Mane Trail runs around the perimeter, the valley itself is interlaced with trails of varying length, including several stretches of boardwalk over marshy sections. The trails are mostly level and scenic, especially the 2.3-km (1.4-mi.) Little River Loop Trail, which is also suitable for wheelchairs. Many features in this park, including specially adapted picnic tables, have been designed for people with disabilities. The park's groomed trails also provide a great advantage for parents with young children in strollers.

This is picnic country in summer. The perfume of wild roses and fireweed, blackberries and salal, distilled over the course of a hot day, carries down off the hillside between the Annand/Rowlatt Farmstead and the marsh. Most of the historic farm buildings have been restored, including two barns that date from 1903 and 1937. Visitors are welcome to explore them, although care must be taken not to disturb the privacy of the caretaker's family who live in the 1898 farmhouse.

In the 1970s, Campbell Valley and Belcarra were the first in what has since grown to be a 23-park regional network that stretches from Bowen Island to Abbotsford.

Adjacent to the farmstead is the Lochiel Schoolhouse, built in 1924 and relocated to the park in 1988. Peer in the windows for a nostalgic glimpse of desks arranged in neat rows with a map of the Dominion of Canada prominently displayed on one wall. The brightly lit school has a remarkable number of windowpanes.

Near the farm are a dozen tables, each with its own hibachi, arranged around the visitors' centre and garden at the 8th Avenue entrance. Directly below, but hidden by dense growth in summer, are the boardwalk and trails that run north to another picnic area at the 16th Avenue entrance. A Demonstration Wildlife Garden is planted beside the visitors' centre. The garden is ingeniously planted with trees, shrubs and small plants that attract wildlife such as butterflies. Ponds and hedgerows provide refuge for larger animals. Hands-on educational displays in the centre assist visitors to discover the park's rich natural and cultural heritage.

If you'd prefer to take a picnic basket on your walk into the park, head towards the Listening Bridge on the Little River Loop Trail.

Campbell Valley Regional Park

The bridge is easily located to the east of a clearing dominated by a large maple known ominously as the Hanging Tree. (There is no evidence that it was ever used to dispense vigilante justice.) Although there are several open areas along the western side of this valley trail, there are none on the east side, much of which is covered with boardwalk. The hillside is steepest on the east side beyond the bridge, where at one point a wide pathway leads off to the Cottonwood Meadow and the equestrian centre. Watch for comfortable benches on the boardwalk from which you can look back down the valley through tall stands of bulrushes. Don't let the number of visitors to Campbell Valley Park dissuade you from coming. Thick growth provides a sense of privacy with every bend in the trail.

The Little Campbell River watershed stretches for almost 30 km (18.6 mi.) from its headwaters in nearby Langley Natural Park to Semiahmoo Park in White Rock where it joins the Pacific. The river has an almost imperceptible gradient, which accounts for the mellow pace at which it flows through Campbell Valley. From the boardwalk, it's almost impossible to gauge where the river's main channel lies as it spreads out between benchlands to the east and west.

Little River Loop Trail

Several times each year special events are held at the park. The themes vary; one of the most popular is the annual Country Celebration, held on the third weekend in September. For further information, call the park at 604-530-4983, or visit www.metrovancouver.org/services/parks_lscr/regionalparks/Pages/CampbellValley.aspx.

> **CAMPBELL VALLEY WINERIES**

In the countryside around Vancouver, autumn is all about rich smells: fallen leaves and freshly sprung mushrooms give off earthy aromas, beds of late-blooming marigolds cloud the air with perfume, and trellises of ripe grapes emit telltale sweet notes as clusters cry out to be crushed for jelly or wine.

If you care to experience this chord of delight for yourself, leave your vehicle at Campbell Valley Regional Park and head out for an hour or three's bike ride *around* the park. As you explore these laneways, you'll find three wineries that dot the route. September through November is an ideal time to drop in for a taste of both new and old vintages, either from the bottle or straight off the vine, though the earlier in fall you go, the better your chances of sampling fresh grapes. Park your bike in front of Township 7 Vineyards' tasting room, as plenty of cyclists do on sunny weekends, and taste the plump, purple table grapes on the trellises originally planted 60 years ago by the former farm owners. Buy a glass of wine, sit out at one of the picnic tables spread among the rows of chardonnay and pinot noir varietals, and toast your good fortune at finding your way here.

Until recently, locals scoffed at the idea of cultivating grapes for anything grander than jelly. Claude and Inge Violet, whose French winemaking pedigree stretches back to the 17th century, challenged that perception when they founded the Fraser Valley's first winery in the 1980s. By the time they retired, Domaine de Chaberton had become one of the largest estate wineries in B.C., with an annual production of over 40,000 cases. Inge Violet still supplies some of the winery's trademark white wine varietal—Bacchus—from her nearby property.

Here's a suggestion: save any wine tasting for the tail-end of your ramble. Hop aboard your bike and start circling the park in a clockwise direction to make the most efficient use energy as you pedal the contoured hillside. The landscape rolls gently along with little loss or gain in elevation. The one exception is a steep notch where North Bluff Road, also called 16th Avenue, plummets into the narrow Campbell Valley. Be prepared for a short section of pumping no matter which approach you take. As a reward, one of the best views of this circumnavigation appears from the bridge that spans Campbell River. At this brief opening, the spires in Golden Ears Provincial Park (see chapter 19) dominate the northern skyline. This is one of South Langley's most picturesquely forested microclimates—it receives more sun and less rain than anywhere else in the Fraser Valley. Imagine you're biking in Europe, particularly beneath a stand of towering Lombardi poplars adjacent Township 7 Vineyards. Add vino to heighten the sensation and cap your tour. Voilà!

Domaine de Chaberton Estate Winery is located at 1064–216th Street. For information, call 604-530-1736 or visit www.domainedechaberton.com. Township 7 Vineyards and Winery is located 1 km (0.6 mi.) west of Domain de Chaberton at 21152–16th Avenue, a short distance from Campbell Valley Park's north entrance. For information, call 604-532-1766 or visit www.township7.com.

> ## 31

BRADNER, AND MATSQUI
TRAIL REGIONAL PARK

· · · · ·

> DISTANCE: 75 km (46.6 mi.) east of Vancouver

> ACTIVITIES: Camping, cycling, dog walking, fishing, nature
observation, picnicking, walking

> ACCESS: To get to Bradner, take the Trans-Canada Highway
(Highway 1) east to the 264th Street North exit (#73). Turn east on
56th Avenue (Interprovincial Way) to Bradner Road, then south
(right) on Bradner Road (288th Street) to enter Bradner.

To reach Matsqui Trail Regional Park, take Highway 1 to Abbotsford, then head north on Highway 11 towards Mission. Watch for the
green Metro Vancouver signs that point the way to the park near the
south end of the Mission Bridge. (See Fraser Valley map, page 129.)

IN THE gently rolling hills east of Vancouver, spring signals the start
of a festive season. Everyone keeps one eye out for the first robin,
the other for the first daffodil. Both are harbingers of winter's true
end. Whether you're wanting to celebrate spring, looking to shake off
cabin fever after a winter indoors or just seeking an opportunity to
dig your bicycle out of the garage, the Bradner region has a welcome
ready for you. Even if the spring breeze still has a chill edge to it, pack
a lunch, as there are sheltered spots beside the nearby Fraser River for
picnicking. If you time your arrival close to the Easter weekend, plan
to attend the Bradner Flower and Garden Show, held here annually
since 1928. Visit www.bradnerflowershow.com for details.

The festival, complete with its legendary bake sale and Easter
bonnet competition, is held in the Bradner Community Hall. A

small park with a gazebo across the road from the Bradner General Store is one potential picnic location.

In 1906, an English gardener, recently arrived in Vancouver, spotted a stump full of blooming daffodils. Fenwick Fatkin instantly knew that he'd found his calling in the New World. He bought property in Bradner, a small farming town in the Fraser Valley, and set about cultivating several varieties of this popular member of the amaryllis family. In 1928, Fatkin held a "parlour show" in his home, featuring 14 varieties of daffs.

These days, more than 400 varieties of daffodils bloom in the area's fields. In spring, the sight of daffodils and narcissi poking their yellow or white heads above the ditches is your first clue that you're close to Bradner. You'll soon start to come across roadside stands with bunches of daffodils for sale; some stands operate on the honour system: just choose your blooms and leave your money.

A network of back roads crisscross this plateau atop the Pemberton Hills bordering the Fraser River. No matter what your vantage point, you'll find yourself lifting your eyes north to one of the best full-face views of the Golden Ears and south to broad, glaciated Mount Baker. As you drive east or west of Bradner, you drop down into prairie land, with Fort Langley to the west and Matsqui to the east. The area around Bradner is perfect for either a leisurely inspection by car or an energetic bicycle ride. Many of the roads on the plateau are flat, and traffic is generally light. One caution: the shoulders of most roads are narrow.

If you drive out with bikes on board and are wondering where to leave your car, try the large parking area beside the Bradner schoolhouse or a second one at the north end of Bradner Road beside Jubilee Hall, several miles north of town. Just beyond the hall the pavement narrows, then becomes gravel for an exciting descent on the Langley side into the valley below. Around Bradner are a dozen roads to choose from, most of which feed into each other at one point or another. An occasional heritage marker will help direct you to some interesting vistas, but otherwise finding your way around this small region can be rather haphazard without a street map.

Have you ever stopped and shivered just because you were looking at a river? The Fraser makes that kind of impression on people. The thought of being caught in the grasp of a river as mighty as the Fraser is enough to make anyone's adrenal glands flutter. Conversely, walking, wheeling or horseback riding beside the river is enough to arouse shivers of delight in the dourest of souls, especially where the Fraser Valley begins to widen and flatten around Abbotsford. In spring, breezes bear a decidedly floral fragrance as they waft down into Matsqui Trail Regional Park from the daffodil fields surrounding nearby Bradner, a welcome counterpoint to the odours from local farmyards.

European settlers on both sides of the Fraser trembled when the river began to rise. High-water markers at the Dyke Crest Gauge mounted beside Matsqui's main trailhead illustrate the heights that flood waters reached over the past two centuries, including the record 8-m (26-ft.) mark in 1894, as well as lesser inundations in 1948 and 1972, and, most recently, in 1999, all of which prompted refortification of the dike system. As you explore the main trail, look down to see evidence of more modest, earlier levee-building endeavours that predate the existing barricade.

Thanks to a land purchase in 2009, Metro Vancouver Parks acquired more access to the Fraser and added an extension to the riverside trail below the dike, a 1-km-long (0.6-mi.-long) trail that links with the main route to form a loop. In particular, parents of young children will appreciate the improved path, as it provides easy access to sandy stretches of the river on which kids can toddle or practise their casting. Cyclists will also welcome the new riverside stretch, especially on breezy days when the dike trail acts as a wind break.

At first glance, Matsqui Trail appears short, but there's more here than meets the eye. Decide at the outset how much of its 14-km (8.4-mi.) length you're game to tackle. The park's main jumping-off point beside the Mission Bridge lies midway between the Fraser Valley Regional District's Sumas Mountain Park to the east and the City of Abbotsford's Douglas Taylor Park on the western perimeter. There are advantages to exploring in either direction. A favourite

Daffodil fields in bloom

portion is a 4.5-km (2.7-mi.) wilderness corridor that leads from rolling farmland through a Matsqui Indian Band reserve into a forested setting above the river before dropping down into a marshy area bisected by a small creek. This is a spectacular transition with a little bit of everything, created during an expansion done in 2000. Do this section on one visit; next time head east to Page Road at the foot of Sumas Mountain. As a benefit to runners, kilometre markers are posted along the way. Along the way, watch for sturgeon, which can breach as much as 1 m above water offshore of the trail's eastern extremity, where the Fraser bends around Strawberry Island. A sense of wild natural rhythms governs the landscape there. Depending on the time of year, there are snow geese in the fields and eagles in the cottonwoods. There are lots of First Nations connections along this stretch for traditional fishing rights as well.

A plaque affixed to Matsqui Trail's info board acknowledges the influence of the Fraser Basin Council on shaping the park's current identity. In 2000, the Vancouver-based council published a special report that detailed how park planners, Matsqui First Nation members, and a myriad of local citizens groups could begin the process of creating a greenway beside the Fraser from Sumas Mountain to Fort Langley. Valley bottoms are where 85 per cent of species live, and linking green fragments together will be key to environmental resiliency. According to the council's report, when the effects of climate change hit, these corridors will be critical for survival.

If you long to be awoken by a dawn chorus of songbirds returning to the Fraser Valley, consider camping at one of Matsqui Trail's three modest riverside sites, which are open from March to October. Except on hot summer weekends, there are usually vacancies. Many people who camp here are cycling the Trans Canada Trail, of which Matsqui Trail is a well-forged, spirit-shivering link indeed. Sites are available on a first-come, first-served basis. Call Metro Vancouver Regional Park's East Area Office at 604-530-4983 to determine if space is available, or just show up.

For more information on Matsqui Trail Park, visit www.metro vancouver.org/services/parks_lscr/regionalparks/Pages/MatsquiTrail. aspx.

> ## 32

FORT LANGLEY PARKS &

. . . . .

> DISTANCE: 56 km (35 mi.) east of Vancouver

> ACTIVITIES: Boating, camping, cycling, dog walking, fishing, historic sites, picnicking, viewpoints, walking

> ACCESS: Take Highway 1 east to either the 200th Street or 232nd Street exit and follow the signs north to Fort Langley. If you are coming from the north side of the Fraser River, take the Golden Ears Bridge from the Lougheed Highway (Highway 7) in Pitt Meadows/ Maple Ridge. The fort is situated on Mavis Street, two blocks east of Glover Road, Fort Langley's main street.

To reach Derby Reach Regional Park from Fort Langley, head south on Glover to 96th Avenue. Turn west on 96th and follow it to where it joins McKinnon Crescent. Follow McKinnon to Allard Crescent, where you turn right to Derby Reach Park. To reach Brae Island Regional Park, head north on Glover Road to the far side of the Beford Channel bridge.

There are several approaches to Glen Valley Regional Park. You may choose to drive the 7 km (4.3 mi.) to Glen Valley from Fort Langley, or you may wish to leave your vehicle near the fort and bicycle east along 88th Avenue. The road is wide, largely untravelled and signed as part of the Langley bicycle trail network. Two-Bit Bar is located at the intersection of 88th Avenue and 272nd Street. Follow River Road east of Two-Bit Bar to reach Poplar and Duncan bars, a total distance one way of about 4 km (2.5 mi.) between the three sites.

SINCE THE demise of passenger train service decades ago it seemed that nothing stopped in Fort Langley but time. An empty CNR station stood as mute testimony, if anyone cared to notice. Even the restoration of the 19th-century Hudson's Bay

Company trading fort as a national historic site in the 1950s did little to stir excitement except during the town's annual Brigade Days festival held on the August long weekend.

Thanks to an influx of outdoor activities spurred by the creation of three regional parks, coupled with the quaint charm of the oldest European settlement in the province, that state of affairs is changing. You can walk, bike or paddle an extensive network of land and water routes that lead through town and out into the surrounding valley past a burgeoning number of wineries as well as organic farms featuring exotic produce, such as artichokes. If you're keen to camp, both Derby Reach and the recently minted Brae Island regional parks offer places to rest your head.

The handiest place to venture forth on foot or by bicycle is the fort itself. If you arrive by car, leave it here. Stroll inside its high wood walls or the Langley Centennial Museum directly across the road where memorabilia from the town's past will help cast your mind back to an era when the heritage buildings on Glover Road were new. Fronted by a spacious lawn, the sight of the colonial-style community hall and its yellow exterior brighten even the dullest day.

Before setting off, check out the interpretive map of Fort Langley posted at the 1920s train station two blocks west of the fort on Glover Road. (Engineers of all sizes will drool over the model train railroad inside.) From here, you can either follow a suggested heritage walking tour of the town—head west along the 4-km (2.5 mi.)

> FORT LANGLEY NATIONAL HISTORIC SITE

VISITING THE reconstructed Fort Langley is like stepping back inside the walls of time. From the fort's ramparts, you have a good view out over the Fraser River's Bedford Channel across to small Brae and McMillan islands, now joined as one. Much of Brae Island is a Kwantlen First Nation reserve, and the remainder is a new regional campground (visit braeisland.com for details). For information about the fort, call 604-513-4777, or visit Parks Canada's Web site at pc.gc.ca/lhn-nhs/bc/langley/index.aspx.

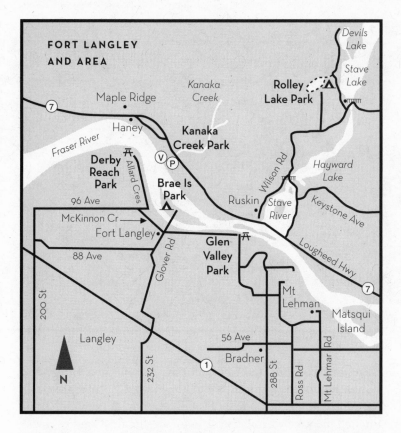

Fort-to-Fort recreation trail that begins beside the station—or head 10 km (6.2 mi.) east along River Road to Glen Valley Regional Park. Each lies within a comfortable cycling distance of the fort along roads such as 88th Avenue that are designated Langley bike routes. Don't be surprised to see a pack of colourfully clad cyclists engaged in some serious road-race training, particularly early on weekend mornings, as they scoot along the back roads around the fort, some of which are little wider than laneways.

> ### DERBY REACH REGIONAL PARK
The countryside around Fort Langley is mostly level, making for a quick 10-minute drive or an easy 30-minute bike ride between the fort and Derby Reach Park. As you approach Derby Reach's

Fort Langley National Historic Site

Edgewater Bar entrance, you will pass the Houston House and nearby Karr/Mercer historic barn. The Fort-to-Fort riverside trail's western terminus lies across the road from the farmhouse. Trails through the wooded countryside to the west of the Houston House are for walkers and horseback riders only and are well worth exploring. So is the new Golden Ears Bridge, a short bike ride west of Derby Reach. Cycling across the bridge reveals just how far transit designs have come over the past quarter-century. Cyclists and pedestrians access the Golden Ears via wide, spiraling ramps. Once on top, a panorama of the Fraser Valley opens up on both sides of the wide, muddy river. Sculpted bronze eagles appear from the tops of the bridge's stanchions as if in flight. The best part about cycling or walking the toll bridge is that passage is free.

Derby Reach is a site on the Fraser with both historic and sporting importance. Metro Vancouver owns 165 ha (407 acres) along 3 km (1.9 mi.) of the south shore of the Fraser River. The park includes Edgewater Bar, one of the best fishing bars on the river and the original location of Fort Langley, whose campsites lure anglers. Along with nearby Brae Island and Matsqui Trail regional parks (see previous chapter), Derby Beach offers overnight camping space for vans or tents. Between March and October, the 38 sites are allocated on a first-come, first-served basis. There is a fee of $19 per night, with a maximum stay of 7 nights. For information, call 604-530-4983 or visit www.metrovancouver.org/services/parks_lscr/regionalparks/Pages/DerbyReach.aspx.

Derby Reach is a great place to be whether or not the fish are biting. A hush hangs over the assembled hopefuls as long lines are strung out into the river in front of lawn chairs, and there's nothing to do except watch the Fraser roll by. Bring along rubber boots to explore the bar's mud flats. There is an open playing field with a leash-optional dog area next to the picnic area where you can toss a Frisbee or a baseball. A nature trail runs through the woods behind the reach to a marshy area. Great blue herons nest in the tall cottonwoods that line the trail. In winter, when the trees have dropped their leaves, look for their massive nests high in the branches above.

> ## GLEN VALLEY REGIONAL PARK

Glen Valley Park features three fishing bars: Two-Bit, Poplar and Duncan. Of the three, Poplar Bar is the largest and offers the most interesting options. You can fish, launch a hand-carried boat, and walk or cycle several riverside trails. Crescent Island lies a short distance offshore from Poplar Bar in the Fraser River. The island forms a natural breakwater for canoes and kayaks, away from the wake created by larger boats, which stick to the Fraser's main channel.

Spring is one of the best times of year to paddle the Fraser when water levels are at their seasonal low. Slender Crescent Island is about 2 km (1.2 mi.) long and uninhabited except by wildlife, as evidenced by flattened grass where deer have bedded down in the open fields at the island's western half. Steep embankments and bramble thickets impede visitors from scrambling up for a look around. The easiest approach is at the island's forested eastern tip where an army of deadheads stand mired in the river. The scene is unlike any found elsewhere in the Fraser and bears an eerie similarity to the curved prows of Viking ships. The Stave River enters the Fraser's north side, just east of Crescent Island in Ruskin (see chapter 22). If you are feeling really adventuresome, you can explore both waterways in the course of a day trip here.

Glen Valley is a traditional agricultural setting located between the Fraser River and a high bluff. It's quite a puff to cycle up to the small community of Bradner (see previous chapter), located on the bluff, but it does make for an interesting drive. In March and April, the fields are bright with daffodils.

> **BRAE ISLAND REGIONAL PARK**

The lower the Fraser River drops, the more sandy beach is exposed at Brae Island Regional Park. The Fraser enfolds the little island— half of which is First Nations reserve—which is linked with Fort Langley by a short bridge over tranquil Bedford Channel. Until the recent opening of the Golden Ears Bridge, a ferry linked the island with Albion on the north side of the river's main channel. These days, Brae Island has become the exclusive preserve of those who enjoy the outdoors. There's plenty to do on Brae Island, not the least of which is camping out under the stars. For day trippers, there are paddle sport and recreational program opportunities offered by the park operator, Fort Camping RV park and campground. Plenty of visitors explore the waterfront day-use area and over 2 km (1.2 miles) of wheelchair-accessible trails. For most of us, just watching the mighty Fraser River flow past will be more than enough reason to visit Brae Island in the months and years to come. For more information on camping, equipment rentals, lessons and tours, call 604-888-3678 ext. 226 or visit braeisland.com or www.metrovancouver.org/services/ parks_lscr/regionalparks/Pages/BraeIsland.aspx. *Note:* Brae Island is a leash-optional dog area.

> 33
TYNEHEAD REGIONAL PARK ♿

. . . . .

> DISTANCE: About 30 km (18.6 mi.) southeast of Vancouver, in
  Surrey

> ACTIVITIES: Birding, dog walking, nature observation, picnicking,
  walking

> ACCESS: Take Exit 53 south on 176th Street from the Trans-Canada
  Highway (Highway 1) and make the first turn west on 96th Avenue.
  From here you have a choice of two approaches. Either turn right at
  the next major intersection, 168th Street, and drive to an entrance
  at the road's north end, or continue west to the park's main entrance
  beside the Tynehead Hatchery. (See Surrey map, page 201.)

HOME TO the headwaters of the Serpentine River, Tynehead
Regional Park is a sheltering place for wildlife in the midst
of Surrey. The park also provides its human neighbours sanctuary from the same threat faced by the area's fish, game and birdlife: the overpowering forces of development. Bordered as it is by the
Trans-Canada Highway, it's a miracle that Tynehead can offer both
serenity and quietude in its 260 ha (642 acres) of grassy meadows
and second-growth cedar, hemlock, ash and maple.

If you want to delve straight into Tynehead's wild side, head to
the park's 168th Street entrance. From here, you can easily connect
with the park's main trail—the Serpentine Loop Trail—that leads to
the Serpentine Hollow Picnic Area. To reach it requires a pleasant
10-minute walk from the parking lot and information kiosk across a
meadow and past some big cedars. There's nothing to stop you from
heading off towards a quiet part of the park away from trails and roads.
Look for a sunny sheltered spot by the hedgerows if that suits your
mood. Note: A portion of the meadow is an off-leash area for dogs.

Serpentine River's headwaters

Fed by several creeks and a natural spring, the Serpentine River flows west into Mud Bay through the Surrey flood plain from its headwaters in Tynehead Park. In springtime and after rainstorms, when the river runs faster than you might expect, high water cuts into the sandy banks, regularly bringing cedar and poplar trees down across the river. These make good bridges for explorers during drier, warmer weather. Kids will enjoy spending time by the river searching for tadpoles, so bring their rubber boots and pails.

Several viewing platforms, well situated for birding, are perched above the river, as well as two small bridges that take walkers across sections. In most places, the trail is hard-packed, suitable for wheelchairs and strollers. Close to the river, the forest is predominantly second-growth cedar and mature vine maple. Thick bramble bushes, matted down by snowfalls during parts of the year, skirt the cedars' low-lying branches, and a thin, hard layer of packed snow can persist on sheltered stretches of the trail long after a storm. Dried berries from each year's abundant crop help birds in the area survive these hard times.

Near the park's southern boundary where the Serpentine flows out of the park is the Tynehead Hatchery. Run by a volunteer organization, the Serpentine Enhancement Society, this is the site of a fish release each spring as part of the salmonid enhancement program. (For information on the dates of the release, to which the public is invited, call 604-589-9127.) Come fall, you can see salmon migrating to the spawning grounds in the park. Because the Serpentine River becomes quite silty at times, a well has been drilled near the hatchery to provide a source of clean water for the fish tanks during the earliest stages of roe development.

The sound of the water in the river effectively camouflages the rumble of highway traffic. A profusion of cedar stumps throughout the park, some of them hollow, are reminders of the extensive grove that once stood here. Some stumps act as nurse logs, supporting as many as eight tall young hemlocks intent on taking their place in the sun.

Walk west of the Serpentine Loop Trail to Serpentine Hollow. Take the Trillium Trail to a viewpoint of the Butterfly Garden, which has been specifically planted to attract members of this insect order. Well-spaced cedars dot the lawn beside the garden, with several picnic tables strategically placed to catch sunlight. A viewing platform overlooks the picnic area. The trunk of a giant fir thrusts up through the middle of the platform, giving it a tree-house quality. Water music from the Serpentine's tributaries fills the air here.

34

REDWOOD AND
PEACE ARCH PARKS &

. . . . .

> DISTANCE: 35 km (20.2 mi.) south of Vancouver, in South Surrey

> ACTIVITIES: Cycling, dog walking, group functions, historic sites, paddling, picnicking, playground, tobogganing, viewpoints, walking

> ACCESS: For Redwood Park, follow Highway 99 south from Vancouver to the King George Highway (Exit 10) in Surrey. Go south on King George to 16th Avenue, then east to 176th Street, and then north to 20th Avenue and east one block to the park's main entrance. Alternatively, enter at the trailhead and small parking area on the north side of 16th Avenue just east of 177th Street.

To reach Peace Arch Park, follow Highway 99 south almost to the Canada Customs and Immigration Building, then exit onto Beach Road. Follow Beach Road a short distance towards Semiahmoo Bay, then turn south (left) off Beach to reach the park entrance.

HERE ARE two special parks in South Surrey practically within sight of each other. Redwood Park is operated by the City of Surrey, and Peace Arch Park is administered by BC Parks.

> **REDWOOD PARK**
Tucked on a hillside in South Surrey's Hazelmere Valley, this small park is a true hidden gem. Trails run through the mixed forest on a bluff overlooking lush farmland on both sides of the border; there are picnic tables and an innovative accessible play space next to the main entrance.

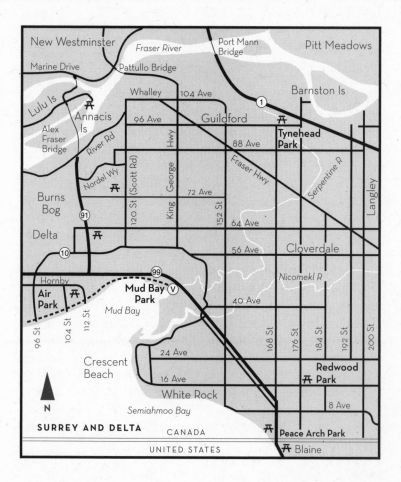

Redwood Park was the home of twin brothers, David and Peter Brown, whose family arrived in South Surrey in the late 1870s. When the twins turned 21, their father gave each 40 acres on a logged hilltop in the Hazelmere Valley where they lived until 1958. The brothers immediately set about planting exotic trees, which became as much a part of their lives as the open fields that ran along the ridge of their joint properties on North Bluff Road (now 16th Avenue). All told, they planted 32 species native to Europe, Asia and North America. The most successful of all, the tall coastal redwoods bordering the fields, tower above the rest.

The Browns' redwoods have found a home from which they can look south towards distant Humboldt County in northern California, where their cousins attain greater heights than any other tree species in the world. Four adult humans holding hands can just encircle the biggest redwood in the park. And these are only young trees—imagine how much bigger they'll be this time next century!

Over the years, the Browns had several different homes on the property, each of which was destroyed by fire. Finally, they built a tree house in the middle of the forest. This one lasted. A long ramp led up to the door of their home, which was sturdily perched a storey above the forest floor. The original was taken down in 1986, but a replica has been installed in its place and is available for use by groups. If you'd like to plan a school, Boy Scout or Girl Guide party here, call the Surrey Parks and Recreation office, 604-501-5050, to get the key. There is no charge for the use of the tree house.

Other tall evergreens add to the park's green mosaic. From November through March, when most of the deciduous trees have shed their leaves and the gnarled branches dance and sway like many-armed Shivas in the wind, Redwood Park is a surprisingly pleasant stop on a cold day, sheltering visitors from wind and rain. After a snowfall, the open ridges beside the forest will be thrilling to ride on a toboggan. Sheltered barbecues and a secluded campfire

> ## PRAYER OF THE WOODS
. . . .

YOU'LL FIND this, the Prayer of the Woods, carved on a sheltered sign at the beginning of the trail through Redwood Park, setting a tone for the rest of your visit: *I am the heat of your hearth on the cold winter nights, the friendly shade screening you from the summer sun, and my fruits are refreshing draughts quenching your thirst as you journey. I am the beam that holds your house, the board of your table, the bed on which you lie, and the timber that builds your boat. I am the handle of your hoe, the door of your homestead, the wood of your cradle, and the shell of your coffin. I am the bread of kindness and the flower of beauty. Ye who pass by, listen to my prayer. Harm me not.*

Redwood Park's tree house

area—an unusual feature in a suburban park—are among the other attractions here. *Note:* Bring your own firewood.

If you're looking to take some produce home, a good place to stop is at the Hazelmere Organic Farm, open to the public from 9 A.M. to 5 P.M. on Saturdays, on the west side of 184th Street just north of 16th Avenue beside Redwood Park.

> PEACE ARCH PARK

Imagine heading for the Canada–U.S. border without actually intending to go any farther. Peace Arch Park is ideal for strolling with the family pet past the extensive flower beds, for gathering the clan for a picnic barbecue at the well-equipped shelter on the Canadian side, or for just having your picture taken in front of the park's gazebo beside the lily pond. Step inside the gazebo and look up at the interior ceiling. The sectioned roof is constructed of wood from eight different native B.C. trees, beautifully lacquered. The patterns made by the various grains make for interesting comparisons.)

Scattered about the park are numerous picnic tables. The large picnic shelter is available for groups of 20 or more and has a kitchen equipped with hotplates and sinks. It's open from 8 A.M. to 9:45 P.M. daily. To reserve, contact the park supervisor at 604-541-1217.

Outside the shelter is a children's adventure playground. There is another playground on the American side next to o Avenue.

Once you begin to explore Peace Arch Park, you'll understand why it's a favourite photo site for wedding parties on a sunny afternoon. The lovingly tended flower beds provide a colourful backdrop. And there's a certain giddy feeling one gets in walking back and forth across the border—officially, a strip 12 m (40 ft.) wide, originally cleared in 1857—that's difficult to describe. Perhaps it's the ease with which you can wander between the two countries on foot, compared with crossing by car.

While the ambience of Peace Arch Park is a major part of its attraction, especially during months when the flowers are at their peak and a cooling breeze wafts in from Semiahmoo Bay, the centrepiece, the Peace Arch itself, is impossible to ignore. Tourists from outside North America have a special fascination with the monument when it comes to taking pictures. Yet many passersby who call Vancouver home may not be aware of the true worth and significance of the imposing white monument, the only symbol of its kind erected at any border crossing in the world.

Informative displays mounted throughout the park on both sides of the border acquaint visitors with the arch's history. British Columbia maintains 9 ha (22 acres) of park north of the 49th parallel, while Washington State takes responsibility for 7 ha (17 acres) on the southern side.

One important fact about the creation of Peace Arch Park should not be overlooked: in the depths of the 1930s economic depression, donations from schoolchildren on both sides of the border raised most of the funds required to purchase land for the park. Each year on the second Sunday in June, thousands of children and adults gather in the park for a Hands Across the Border celebration.

Use the parking lot at Peace Arch Park as your staging area whether you plan to explore on foot or by bike. Imaginative sculptures are mounted around the American picnic shelter, most concealed by the flower beds on the hill to the east of the Peace Arch and Highway 99. Be sure to find them.

RICHMOND

DELTA

POINT ROBERTS

35

SEA ISLAND AND IONA BEACH REGIONAL PARK &

. . . . .

> **DISTANCE:** 15 km (9 mi.) south of Vancouver, in Richmond

> **ACTIVITIES:** Birding, cycling, dog walking, paddling, picnicking, stargazing, viewpoints, walking

> **ACCESS:** Cross the Arthur Laing Bridge at the south end of Granville Street onto Grant McConachie Way. Turn right onto Templeton Street North and follow it across Sea Island to McDonald Beach and Iona Beach parks. Cyclists can approach Sea and Iona islands via the Templeton SkyTrain Station on the Canada Line.

> ## SEA ISLAND

During the construction of the north runway at Vancouver International Airport on Sea Island in the early 1990s, a small bay at Richmond's McDonald Beach Park was enlarged to handle the off-loading of material from barges. To make up for the loss of habitat, Transport Canada converted an old sand stockpile east of the park into marsh as part of the newly created Sea Island Conservation Area. Replanted with sedges, rushes, dune barley and snowberry bushes, it has become even more attractive as Wood's roses, Pacific crabapples, willows and black cottonwoods have taken hold.

An 11-km (6.8-mi.) dike trail runs through the conservation area beside the airport and the Fraser River along Sea Island's northern perimeter. One of the best places to begin exploring is McDonald Beach Park, a municipal landmark since the 1850s. As well as being a good place to picnic, launch a boat, buy some bait or just watch the river flow, it also provides the best place for parking. From here,

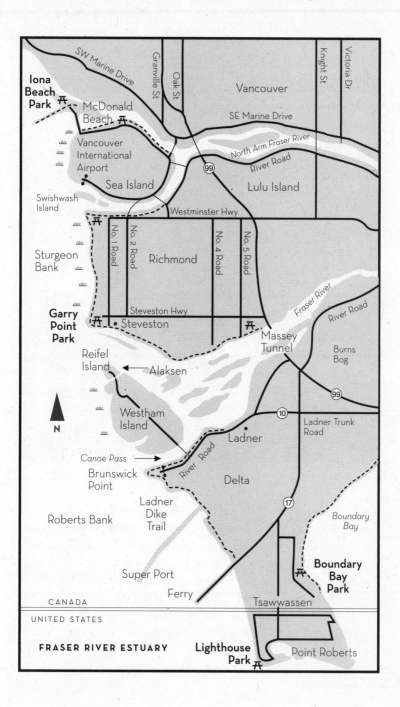

Iona Beach Park

McDonald Beach

SW Marine Drive

Granville St

Oak St

Vancouver

Knight St

Victoria Dr

SE Marine Drive

Vancouver International Airport

North Arm Fraser River

River Road

99

Sea Island

Lulu Island

Swishwash Island

Westminster Hwy

No. 1 Road

No. 2 Road

Richmond

No. 4 Road

No. 5 Road

Sturgeon Bank

Steveston Hwy

Garry Point Park

Steveston

Fraser River

River Road

Massey Tunnel

Burns Bog

Reifel Island

Alaksen

Fraser River

River Road

N

Westham Island

Ladner

99

10

Ladner Trunk Road

Canoe Pass

River Road

Brunswick Point

Delta

Roberts Bank

Ladner Dike Trail

17

Boundary Bay

Super Port

Ferry

Boundary Bay Park

CANADA

Tsawwassen

UNITED STATES

FRASER RIVER ESTUARY

Lighthouse Park

Point Roberts

207

McDonald Beach Park, Sea Island

it's your choice: cycle or walk the trail west towards Iona Beach Regional Park (about 7 km/4.3 mi. one way), or head east towards the Arthur Laing Bridge (about 4 km/2.5 mi.). This place is also a dog magnet, and the canines seem to enjoy it as much as anyone. A leash-optional grassy field on the east side of McDonald Beach Park is where many visitors with large dogs head for some ball tossing.

Views from the trail are both varied and grand. Close at hand, hefty tugboats parade along the Fraser River's North Arm like muscle cars on Kingsway. They put out a wake that you could surf on. A brow of mansions on Marine Drive dominates the ridge above

Vancouver's Southlands neighbourhood. North Shore peaks rising behind them add yet another layer. Look southeast. On a clear day, you get an impeccable view of Mount Baker profiled against the sky. To the south, alders and cottonwoods shield the airport from view for much of the distance. Late on a sunny afternoon, a lipstick sunset smears the western horizon.

> ## IONA BEACH REGIONAL PARK

Iona Island is a wild, windswept place, with a slender scissor-shaped nose jutting out into Sturgeon Bank, ending at Point No Point. It sits at the mouth of the North Arm of the Fraser River, with the Musqueam Indian Reserve across the water on one hand, and Sea Island on the other. From the entrance to Iona Beach Regional Park, you can fan out to explore the sheltered or exposed sides of the island, so evidently shaped by sediment dumped at the ocean's doorstep by the Fraser River.

As you near the regional park entrance, the road passes over a causeway built in the early part of this century to link Sea Island and Iona. McDonald Slough, on the east side of the road, is often lined with log booms. The road swings west past a sewage treatment plant to the park gates. Leave your car here if you plan to be in the park after sunset, as the gate is locked at dusk except on special occasions, such as stargazing evenings.

Iona Island is a stopover for thousands of migrating birds. Among the over 300 species that alight at Iona, more rare birds are seen here than anywhere else in the province.

During the day, birders fill their eyes with the sights of Iona's migrating flocks; stargazing visitors benefit from the increased darkness of the sky here, unhindered by the glare of city streetlights. Metro Vancouver Park's Catch a Falling Star astronomy program brings high-powered telescopes from the Southam Observatory to Iona on a seasonal basis. There are also slide shows at the interpretive centre and hot refreshments available to ward off the crisp night air. On all your trips to Iona, be sure to dress warmly, including a hat to protect your ears against the wind blowing off the Strait of Georgia.

Sea Island Conservation Area trail

You don't need binoculars to see birdlife at close range. Stalk the gently rolling reaches of the island. Find a sheltered spot beside a lagoon and watch as it comes to life, revealing itself as you wait in patient stillness. A quiet season like autumn lends itself to such unobtrusive observation.

Iona's air quality is rarely influenced by the nearby sewage-treatment plant, thanks to an outfall pipe, and the 4-km (2.5-mi.) jetty over which the pipeline runs is a hard-packed gravel walkway. The service road that parallels the pipeline doubles as a cycle path. There are two Plexiglas shelters, located at the middle and end of the jetty, that allow visitors to escape the winds off the Strait of Georgia and at the same time provide an unobstructed bird's-eye view of Sturgeon Bank. Across the strait, Vancouver Island is outlined against the western sky. Closer, the mountains on the North Shore stand out, with no office towers blocking the view. For photographers who enjoy capturing a sunrise or sunset, these shelters are ideal places to position a camera. For information on Iona Beach, call 604-432-6359 or 604-224-5739, or visit Metro Vancouver Park's Web site at www.metrovancouver.org/wervices/parks_lscr/regionalparks/Pages/IonaBeach.aspx.

36

RICHMOND DIKE TRAILS AND
HISTORIC STEVESTON &

. . . . .

> DISTANCE: 15 km (9.3 mi.) south and west of the Oak Street
Bridge, in Richmond

> ACTIVITIES: Birding, cycling, dog walking, historic sites, kite-
flying, paddling, picnicking, sightseeing, viewpoints, walking

> ACCESS: From Highway 99 South, take the Steveston Highway
West exit (#32) just before the George Massey Tunnel, and follow it
to downtown Steveston. (See map page 207.) For information about
getting to Richmond (including Steveston) by bus, call TransLink at
604-953-3333 or visit their Web site at translink.ca.

SEA ISLAND and most of Lulu Island, as well as a number of
smaller islands in the Fraser River, comprise the municipality of Richmond. There's a special spot on Lulu Island that has
drawn settlers since the turn of the 20th century—former citizens
of Finland, Japan and the sovereign nation of Newfoundland, for
instance. The first arrivals gathered on the southwestern corner of
the island at Steveston, named for a member of the Steves family,
who settled here in 1877 upon their arrival from New Brunswick.

Construction of protective dikes along the western shore of
Lulu Island was one of the first priorities for the newcomers. These
have been improved with time and now provide a level surface that
stretches for 77 km (48 mi.). Many of the old farm homes have
disappeared, but enough of the original flavour of early settlement
remains to make this westerly stretch of dike and historic Steveston
a must-see for local adventurers. It's also a jumping-off point for

exploring the whole of Richmond's western shore. Take an hour or plan an entire day to enjoy the surroundings.

> GARRY POINT PARK AND WEST DYKE TRAIL

If you drive to the western end of Steveston Highway where it meets the dike at Seventh Avenue, you'll find parking for six vehicles. In another 2 minutes, you can be at Garry Point Park, with parking for 60. Simply drive several blocks south along Seventh to reach the park. It's located two blocks west of the federal wharf, which forms the heart of historic Steveston.

Early on weekend mornings, groups of kayakers assemble at Garry Point while families on bikes head north along the West Dyke Trail and sun lovers perch on the driftwood of nearby beaches. The Canadian Coast Guard hydrofoil might skim noisily past, throwing up sea spray around its rubber skirts as it patrols the mouth of the Fraser River and around into Cannery Channel. Long-necked Steveston Island lies directly offshore, shielding from view parts of the river and the town of Ladner on the far shore (see chapter 39).

For those with rubber boots and a desire to get out onto nearby Sturgeon Bank, a hillocky trail heads west off the main trail at Garry Point and out into the marsh just north of a weathered marina's dock and boathouse. The brackish marsh renews its vegetation of cattails, bulrushes, eelgrass and sedges every spring, and the air here is filled with bird calls. Although there are picnic tables at several spots along the dike trail, out on Sturgeon Bank you'll have to make do with a piece of driftwood. You can see here what much of Lulu Island must have looked like before dikes were built to reclaim the land in the first half of this century.

A small Japanese rock garden in Garry Point Park, opened in 1988, is dedicated to the memory of the first immigrants from Japan's Wakayama Prefecture, who arrived in 1888.

The West Dyke Trail runs in an almost straight north-south line along the western perimeter of Lulu Island, a distance of 5.5 km (3.4 mi.). It's well used, especially on weekends. You can ride along at an easy pace, covering the entire distance one way in approximately 40 minutes.

Middle Arm Trail

> **MIDDLE ARM TRAIL**

As the West Dyke Trail rounds the northwestern tip of Lulu Island, it passes the parking area at the west end of River Road in the Terra Nova neighbourhood. There are picnic tables and toilets located here. The Middle Arm of the Fraser River meets the Strait of Georgia at this point. Low-lying Swishwash Island nestles offshore, with Sea Island and the airport beyond to the north. The pier at Dover Beach is an excellent spot to watch activity on the river, as across the channel jets muscle their way skyward and propeller-driven planes feather in for a landing at the seaplane dock.

The Middle Arm Trail covers an east-west route beside the Middle Arm of the Fraser from Terra Nova to the Moray Bridge, a distance of 5.5 km (3.4 mi.). Distance markers beside the trail help you monitor your progress. In spring months, the pungent green smell of willow buds and broom fills the air here. Nearby, in the shallows of the Fraser, dabbling ducks, Canada geese, herons and gulls feast on vegetation and small marine creatures.

As the dike trail continues east along the Middle Arm between the No. 2 Road and Dinsmore bridges, it passes the Richmond Olympic Oval, whose curved roof mimics the heritage hangars across the channel at YVR's south terminal. The No. 2 Road Bridge, with its circular pedestrian ramp, is the best connection to take you across to Sea Island. A dike trail continues along the banks of the Fraser on Sea Island in both directions. If you head west, you pass Vancouver airport's South Terminal and several floatplane wharves clustered around the Flying Beaver Bar and Grill and finally arrive at the gates of the Canadian Coast Guard station, a comfortable 15-minute ride from the bridge. You can picnic nearby beside a stand of cottonwoods and watch seaplanes buzz in and out on Moray Channel while jumbo jets arrive and depart.

Exploring the Middle Arm Trail on foot or by bike becomes more exciting with each passing year as more recreational facilities, such as the UBC Boathouse, and artwork are installed on the dike east of the Dinsmore Bridge.

> **STEVESTON VILLAGE**

With more than a thousand boats moored in the harbour year round, Steveston has the distinction of being the largest maritime fishing community in Canada. If there's an old folks' home for tired ships, this must be it, for collected around the harbour are all manner and size of boats that would appear to have sailed their last. How much longer many of the other, livelier-looking ones will be in service depends on the continuing strength of the commercial fishery. Down Steveston way, the fishery is definitely on the wane, but it wasn't always so.

To gain an appreciation for Steveston's fishing history, visit the restored Gulf of Georgia Cannery, which originally opened in 1894. Reopened a century later as a national historic site, it presents visitors with one of the most realistic re-creations imaginable. Although the display makes the operation of the canning line easy to understand, be sure to take in the video presentation in the Boiler House Theatre just inside the remodelled entranceway. This 20-minute introduction to the entire canning process includes archival footage from the industry's heyday.

The Gulf of Georgia Cannery National Historic Site (12138 Fourth Avenue; 604-664-9009; gulfofgeorgiacannery.com) is open daily from 10 A.M. to 5 P.M. from February to December. Admission is about $8 for adults and half that for children between the ages of 6 and 16. The exhibits at the cannery have been designed with flair and on a scale that will appeal to both young and old.

Several blocks east of the cannery at the south foot of Railway Avenue is Britannia Heritage Shipyard. A brochure outlining a self-guided tour is available at the shipyard and details much of the history of the site, as fascinating in its own right as the historic cannery. One of the best ways to be introduced to Steveston is to visit the Steveston Museum and Post Office housed in a 1905 bank (3811 Moncton Street, 604-271-6868).

The focal point of Steveston is the government wharf. Fishing boats with poetic names are tied up along rows of docks. You can even buy seafood fresh off the boat at the main dock: shrimp, squid, snapper, tuna, sole, cod and salmon are all available—in season—at good prices. For those with an immediate hunger, Pajo's floating café nearby serves up fish and chips along with a local favourite, steaming mushy peas.

If you wish to explore Steveston and the nearby dike trails by bike, rentals can be arranged at Steveston Bicycle and Kayak Shoppe (6111 London Road; 604-271-5544) and Village Bikes (3891 Moncton Street; 604-274-3865).

> SOUTH DYKE TRAIL

The South Dyke Trail begins at the south end of No. 2 Road, Richmond's original thoroughfare. Not only are aged riverboats moored here, but the history of habitation in the southwestern corner of Lulu Island—with the exception of the First Nations—is also detailed in words, drawings and archival photographs at several places along the dike. (Interpretive signs highlight places of local interest throughout the Richmond dike trail system.) On weekends, many local residents get out their bikes for rides with family and friends. Lightly travelled Dyke Road parallels the trail.

A large wharf at the foot of No. 2 Road juts out into Cannery Channel. A gangplank leads down to a small floating dock at the far end. You could launch a hand-carried boat from it and quickly paddle across to nearby Steveston Island. Tall black cottonwoods and poplars cover the slender, artificial island. Large nests can be seen in their upper branches, home to herons and eagles. Reifel Island's migratory bird sanctuary (see chapter 40) lies just across the wide South Arm of the Fraser River.

Interpretive signs on the wharf acquaint visitors with the history of London's Landing, named for the first non-Aboriginal family to settle here, in 1885. They were the first ones to dike and farm on Lulu Island. Given the growth of Richmond since then, it's fascinating to stand where the inaugural government wharf, school and post office were located. Just east of the wharf on Dyke Road is the entrance to London Heritage Farm, which was acquired by Richmond in 1974. The farm is open to visitors daily. A parking lot and a boat launch are located directly across Dyke Road.

Picnic tables and benches appear regularly along the South Dyke Trail. Watch for Mount Baker's ghostly profile to appear floating in the southern sky at the intersection of Dyke and Gilbert roads. At this point you are several kilometres east of the Steveston docks.

The dike trail leads east beside the South Arm of the Fraser River all the way to the George Massey Tunnel. You can cycle this comfortably in half an hour, ending at a small municipal park at the south end of No. 5 Road in an area called Woodwards Landing. Along the way, the trail passes a sleepy backwater known informally as Finn Slough. Ancient boathouses, riverbank shanties and float homes shelter in the lee of Gilmour Island, protected from storms and the wakes of large ocean freighters making their way to or from loading docks farther upriver. Much like Peggy's Cove in Nova Scotia, Finn Slough has been the subject of many paintings and photographs. You can drive directly to Finn Slough; turn south from Steveston Highway on No. 4 Road and continue for several minutes until the road reaches the South Dyke Trail.

37

BURNS BOG ♿

. . . . .

> DISTANCE: About 30 km (18.6 mi.) southeast of Vancouver, in
Delta

> ACTIVITIES: Cycling, dog walking, nature observation, walking

> ACCESS: To reach Delta Watershed Park, follow Highway 91 south
to 64th Avenue, then travel east on Kittson Parkway towards 120th
Street. The first of four entry points appear on your right, the best of
which is midway uphill.

There are several approaches to the Delta Nature Reserve. The
quickest route begins on River Road under the south end of the Alex
Fraser Bridge. Follow a gravel road that parallels the Burlington
Northern railway track and diminutive Cougar Creek until it passes
under the Nordel Way on-ramp. The reserve begins here. Watch for
the Machine Eating Bog Trail on the west side of the gravel road,
followed a few minutes farther south by the Interpretive Loop Trail.
Alternatively take the 72nd Avenue exit east from Highway 91, then
turn north (left) on 112th Street. Turn west (left) onto Monroe Drive
beside Sungod Arena and follow several blocks to 108th Street. A trail
leads downhill into the nature reserve from the main entrance here.

THE IMAGE of a bog doesn't resonate with the same seductive-
ness as that of an ancient rain forest, even if its stunted conifer
and sphagnum moss landscape is thousands of years old. (The
word "bog" entered the English language from the Irish Gaelic word
bogach, for wet, spongy ground. The British hold the term in such
low esteem that it doubles as slang for lavatory.) In a sudden about-
face in the 1990s, bogs went from ugly-duckling status to swan-
hood as the multifaceted role they play in world ecology took centre
stage. Bogs capture and store carbon and nitrogen emissions, they

provide habitat for unique flora and fauna, and they bestow a variety of hydrological benefits that include contributing to the health of fish stocks in adjacent river systems. The production of phytoplankton, a primary source of nutrients for fish, depends on organic iron from the lands through which rivers flow, particularly peatlands. Water in the Fraser River is not only cooled by nearby Burns Bog, but fish stocks that feed on phytoplankton are nourished by it as well.

> Burns Bog is one of the last—and by far the largest—remaining peatlands in Metro Vancouver. At 2 715 ha (6,700 acres), it's roughly half the size of nearby Richmond.

Burns bog is a damp tangle of peat, also known as sphagnum moss. The bog supports an old-growth forest of cedar, hemlock, yew and fir, some of whose perimeter trees—such as in Delta Watershed Park—are as tall as a two-storey building. At the heart of the bog, where it's most damp, these same species have a bonsai appearance, achieving heights of less than a metre. In fact, the sign of a healthy bog is very small trees. Although the forest surrounding Burns Bog as seen from the highway has a scruffy appearance, deeper inside there are stands of remarkably healthy growth.

> ## DELTA WATERSHED PARK

If you find the technically challenging trails on the North Shore too daunting, try swinging your legs or cycling along more welcoming routes, such as in Delta Watershed Park. Dog walkers and joggers will also appreciate the smooth trails that wind through the sheltering rain forest. These paths are a joy to discover, especially on a day when you just feel like moving at your own comfortable pace.

Growth here in the heavily wooded southeast corner of Burns Bog is noticeably different than the sphagnum moss and stunted spruce trees elsewhere. A ridge rises above the bog to the east of Highway 91. Beneath a leafy overstorey, you'll find an 11-km (6.6-mi.) network of both single-track mountain bike trails and smooth, dirt-surfaced service roads that double as recreational routes.

Begin on any of the park trails that spiral off from the four Kittson Way (64th Avenue) trailheads. Both the meandering Pinewood Trail

Delta Nature Reserve

and one of the best single-track trails—Gravity Bowl—run through the forest past a Boy Scout shelter with smooth granite benches and stone fireplace. The Canyon Trail snakes its way between drooping hemlocks that in many places are spaced just slightly wider than most handlebars. Constructed so that you hardly need to apply your brakes or pedal to maintain your speed, this trail is such a treat that you'll involuntarily whoop with pleasure. As soon as you finish, you'll want to double back and try it again, just for the joy of the ride.

If you're just here for a walk and to view the bog—which looks pretty firm here compared with what you see at the Delta Nature Reserve—follow the Lower Trail to its eastern terminus near the junction of Highways 91 and 99. In 30 minutes, you'll arrive at a viewpoint from where agricultural land spreads out below the park's ridge and runs south to the shore of Mud Bay. Suddenly, you are aware of what a welcome buffer the forest here provides from the intrusion of nearby highway sounds.

"Support Wildlife—Throw a Party." On National Wildlife Day in April 1994, the municipality of Delta did just that, celebrating the opening of the trails in the new Nature Reserve. The reserve had actually been in place since the early 1970s. However, it took encouragement from the Burns Bog Conservation Society to get Delta to commit to maintaining a trail network in the reserve's eastern portions.

As soon as you begin to explore here, you realize this is the real thing. Hummocks of sphagnum, which are thrust upwards as the moss absorbs and stores water, are crowned with thickets of bog laurel, Labrador tea and salmonberries. In spring, their blossoms carpet the bog in pink and white.

As you walk through the bog, the expression "Don't get bogged down" springs to mind. The rule of thumb here is if you feel yourself sinking, just walk faster. This sinking feeling defines the mystery that surrounds bogs. A prime example is the sight of a bulldozer all but swallowed now by peat. It lies beside a boardwalk along the Machine Eating Bog Trail that was blazed into the bog a decade ago by a fellow who made off with the piece of heavy equipment from a nearby construction site. For reasons unknown, he rode the behemoth into the bog, then tried to turn around when, too late, he realized he was beginning to sink in the morass. All that's left today is a small portion as a sign of the machine-eating bog.

Although Burns Bog may be a somewhat forbidding place to view from the outside, once you begin to walk the cedar bark–covered trail—whose damper sections are straddled by boardwalks—it becomes a much more inviting environment. Children will find the dwarf forest here just their size. And, although city dwellers are only visitors, they'll be interested to learn that a host of wildlife calls the bog home, including lynx, greater sandhill cranes and a resident population of Mariposa Copper butterfly.

Plan on taking several hours to enjoy your visit to Burns Bog. If you have time, follow the well-marked pedestrian walkway on Nordel Way that leads onto the Alex Fraser Bridge. From the top of the bridge, you can look south across the whole bog.

For more information, call Delta Parks, Recreation and Culture, 604-946-3300 or visit burnsbog.org.

38

DEAS ISLAND
REGIONAL PARK &

. . . . .

> **DISTANCE:** 30 km (18.6 mi.) south of Vancouver

> **ACTIVITIES:** Birding, cycling, dog walking, fishing, historic sites, nature observation, paddling, picnicking, viewpoints, walking

> **ACCESS:** Take Highway 99 south from Vancouver to the first major exit south of the George Massey Tunnel (#28) onto Highway 17 North to River Road. The park entrance is 2 km (1.2 mi.) east from this point on the north side of River Road. For bus access, call Trans-Link at 604-953-3333 or visit translink.ca.

DEAS SLOUGH is a broad, sheltered backwater that stretches for almost 3 km (1.9 mi.) between the entrance to Deas Island Regional Park and an ageing dock where a ferry once connected Delta with Richmond before the opening of the George Massey Tunnel in 1959. Towering cottonwoods and alders line the shore and frame the slough. In winter, when they've shed their leaves, their top branches weave a sinuous web of dark limbs against an enveloping backdrop of smoky grey fog.

Over the years, I've visited Deas Island often enough to have experienced all of its seasonal moods. It's a place I'm drawn back to time and again, if nothing else because of its easy access. The island is linked to the Delta mainland by a short causeway. Sturdy dikes ring much of its perimeter, particularly the north side, which faces the Fraser.

One of the best times to visit Deas Island is early in the morning on a weekend, before traffic has begun to flow on Highway 99. Although cycling (and horseback riding, too) is permitted on Deas

Island, you'll find that it's tough going in sandy sections, so be prepared to push your bike in places. Most visitors find Deas Island a good place to simply walk or paddle, not to mention exercise the dog.

As you enter the park, the boat launch and a beach on the slough are to your left. The boathouse and dock are managed by the Delta Deas Rowing Club. Racing shells are built and stored here along with a variety of other vessels. A rowing course is laid out on the surface of Deas Slough, and if you're visiting on a warm day, you can watch rowers practising as you stroll along Slough View Trail. There is a small parking lot next to the rowing facility, beside which is the trailhead for the Spirit of Delta Millennium Trail, which connects with Ladner.

You can launch a hand-carried boat from the beach and explore the slough as well as the Fraser River itself, but be careful on the river when the tide is running. One of the best times to be here is at slack tide, when the big river's South Arm is often flat calm, with the setting sun reflecting on its surface. *Note*: The park gates close at dusk; you might want to park just outside them if you're planning to be out on the slough or in the park in summer, when daylight lingers past closing time.

Deas Island was named after its first settler, John Deas, a tinsmith who built a cannery here in 1873. It thrived through good and bad times under a series of owners until World War I.

Along the banks of the slough, wild yellow irises provide an occasional colour break from the thick green reeds and eelgrass. In early summer, the air is thick with downy white fluff, drifting from tall cottonwood trees like snowflakes. Allow 30 minutes to paddle the slough one way. En route, you'll pass beneath the causeway carrying motorists to and from the tunnel.

Just past the rowing shed is the Inverholme Schoolhouse, which opened in 1909 and was moved to Deas Island in the early 1980s. It now houses the visitors' centre in an old-fashioned schoolhouse setting. The Burr family homestead, known as Burrvilla, was built in 1905 and also relocated to the park. Once typical of many residences in Delta, it is now one of the few reminders of those early Queen Anne–style houses. It is fronted by an observation tower that offers a broad, interpretive view of both wildlife

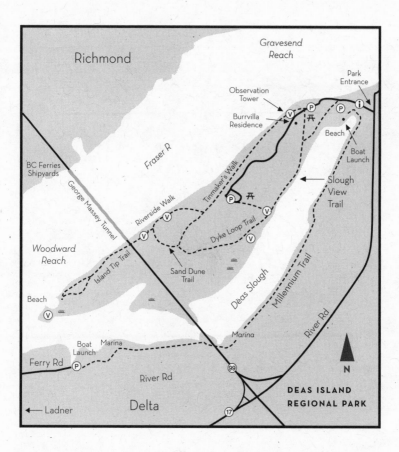

and navigational activity on the river. Next to the Burr house is the Delta Agricultural Hall, built in 1894 and moved to the park almost a century later, in 1989. Today, it's used as a park maintenance building with room for meetings and displays. The buildings stand beside wide-open Fisher's Field, with expansive views of the western sky and a covered barbecue area.

Birdsongs float through your car window as soon as you reach the western parking area. It's always a good idea to bring binoculars. Deas Island is not far from the George C. Reifel Migratory Bird Sanctuary, and there is usually an overflow crowd nesting here. Waterfowl, songbirds, shore birds, gulls and pheasants can all be seen on the island.

Riverside Walk, one of a half-dozen interconnected trails on

Deas Island Regional Park

the island, leads farther west from the western parking area. Even though the sign at the trailhead indicates the round trip takes 45 minutes, allow 2 hours if you can. You'll want to take time to sit under the shade of the cottonwood trees and observe action on the river or clamber overtop the mouth of the tunnel and watch traffic as it disappears into the round maw. (For safety, there's a fence to separate the trail from the traffic.) A plaque mounted here commemorates the tunnel's opening by Queen Elizabeth II.

In early summer sweet flower scents perfume the air. The park is lush with purple lupines, which take over from the yellow and red broom bushes lining the river. Thickets of blackberries cover parts of the island. Their white flowers put forth a rose scent in June and are transformed into lush fruit by late August.

As you near the western end of the island, look for the BC Ferries shipyards on the river's northern shore. Follow the Island Tip Trail to a cozy bay with a grey sand beach. Slightly farther west of the beach is a rocky point to which you can walk if the tide is low enough. Slip across the eelgrass to reach the most remote part of the island, just the place to leave the present behind for a moment.

> ## AROUND THE SLOUGH

There is more than one way to snoop around Deas Slough than just inside the park. As part of the "2000 Spirit of Delta" celebrations, work began on the Millennium Trail for walking and cycling that leads along a section of the south side of the slough opposite Deas Island. Completed in 2008 the trail links Deas Island with two marinas on either side of the bridge carrying traffic across the slough near the south end of the George Massey Tunnel on Highway 99. From there, a network of bike paths leads through Ladner to Brunswick Point and south from there to BC Ferries Tsawwassen jetty (see chapters 40 and 41).

One of the features that day trippers will find most appealing about this route are the two cozy pubs along the trail that provide a welcome retreat at any time of year, whether on the patios, which overlook the marinas in summer, or beside the fireplaces, which help fend off the wintry chill.

Along the way, the trail passes directly beneath the highway bridge where Delta students have installed several square-sided "peace poles" on either side of the span. Each laminated wood pole stands about 2 m (6 ft.) high and is inscribed with the words "May Peace Prevail on Earth" in a variety of languages. Over 200,000 peace poles are now positioned in public places in 180 countries. With its underlying theme of universal peace, it's heartening to read the thought that accompanies each pole: "Dedicated as monuments of peace, acting as a silent prayer and message of peace on earth."

For information on Deas Island Regional Park, visit www.metrovan couver.org/services/parks_lscr/regionalparks/pages/DeasIsland.aspx. For more information on the Peace Pole initiative, visit peacepoles. com. A Millennium Trail map is posted at www.corp.delta.bc.ca/EN/ main/residents/recreation_and_parks_services/121/trail_routes.html.

> ## 39

LADNER &

. . . . .

> DISTANCE: 30 km (18.6 mi.) south and west of Vancouver

> ACTIVITIES: Cycling, dog walking, historic sites, paddling, pic-
nicking, playground, viewpoints, walking

> ACCESS: To reach Ladner, drive Highway 99 to the south end of
the George Massey Tunnel and take the first exit (#29) onto River
Road or the next exit (#28) onto Highway 17 South, then turn right
onto Ladner Trunk Road (48th Avenue) for the short drive into town.
(See map page 207.) By taking the River Road exit, you approach
Ladner on a back road rather than through the community's newer
neighbourhoods on Ladner Trunk.

> ### RIVER ROAD

There are two intersections of note as you travel west of Highway
99 on River Road. Turning right on Ferry Road takes you out to the
marina on the south side of Deas Slough (see chapter 38), glimpsed
as you cross the slough on Highway 99. There is a public boat
launch here for quick access to the Fraser River.

A right turn off River Road at the next road west of Ferry puts you
on McNeely Way, a paved road that becomes a dirt track, leading
around the east end of Ladner Harbour and then west out towards
Ladner Harbour Park, a sandy point overlooking Ladner Reach.

As River Road enters downtown Ladner, it meets Elliott Street
near the town's other major intersection at 47A Avenue. To reach
Ladner's waterfront, turn right off River Road at Elliott, which leads
to the town dock at its intersection with Chisholm Street.

Old Ladner predates the establishment of Vancouver by almost two decades. Walk the town's core—about the size of Yaletown—and look for the imposing Leary home on Georgia Street, built in 1884. Pass the Delta Museum and Archives, housed in the restored Tudor-style former municipal hall erected in 1912. Marvel at its extensive front stairs, a signal of how high flood waters once rose here before a network of dikes brought peace of mind.

At best, Chisholm Street—Ladner's two-block-long riverfront drive—yields only half a view of the scale on which heritage businesses, like Massey's Marine Supply Store, were constructed, and it offers zero perspective on the harbour itself, which is why it pays to take to the water in order to truly appreciate structures like the Seven Seas Fish Plant whose massive wooden pilings surmount the harbour.

Of course, the height of the tide will also affect your perspective, as will the Fraser's motion, particularly if you decide to be a little more adventurous and head out of the harbour to explore nearby Ladner Marsh or any of the dozen or so islands that grip the muddy South Arm in a loose chokehold where river meets ocean.

If you don't own a kayak or a canoe, head for the little kiosk perched on the Elliott Street dock where you can arrange boat tours and paddle sport rentals with Kaymaran Adventure Tours. Racks of kayaks and canoes on a floating concrete dock moored to the pier attest to the flourishing appearance of a new breed of watercraft in Ladner. Under an arrangement with the Corporation of Delta, Kaymaran installed the dock and staircase in 2005, a move that greatly improved public access to the harbour. For hungry or thirsty paddlers, it sits in convenient proximity to two neighbouring watering holes as well—Speed's Pub and Sharkey's Seafood Bar and Grille—whose walls are adorned with vintage photographs and memorabilia from Ladner's fishing heydays when as many as 16 canneries operated locally.

The dock on Ladner's inner harbour isn't the only place to launch and explore the wildlife-rich marshes and waterways on the South Arm. A skipping stone's throw away on the north side of the harbour across from the municipal wharf sits Ladner Harbour Park, an expansive green space shaded by a towering cottonwood forest. Walking and running trails, a hard-packed beach, picnic tables and playground, plus a walkway with a raised viewing platform on the harbour, prove just as welcoming a way to experience the Fraser estuary, albeit in a more limited context. The park also provides a floating dock from which to launch, though it's more challenging to access than the one beside the Elliott Street Wharf.

No matter where you launch, there's a jigsaw puzzle of small islands to explore once you leave the harbour and enter Ladner Reach. In all likelihood, the first time you put in here you'll be content with a simple reconnaissance paddle through Ladner Marsh to test the waters. Once having reconnoitred for an hour or two, you'll better appreciate the unique lay of the landscape. Each time you return, you can sample more of the mystery. Low-slung islands blend into each other as the Fraser's South Arm spreads its silty fingers among the deposits that it's been making here over the past ten millennia since the most recent ice age.

One of the best times to adventure here is at slack high tide when with greater ease you can paddle through tall stands of reeds that ring many of the islands. The swish of the reeds as they brush your boat is a quieting sound. Relax and let the ocean cradle you as if you were one of the majestic mute swans that nest here and along with a host of wildlife call Ladner home.

For information on Kaymaran Adventure Tours, including tours and kayak, canoe and bike rentals, as well as membership in the

> ## DELTA'S DAWN

. . . .

THE FARMING community of Delta was first settled in 1868. Along with agriculture, salmon canneries were major employers. By 1899, there were 16 canneries in operation in Delta. Together with nearby Tsawwassen, Ladner grew into the commercial heart of rural Delta. Until the completion of the Massey Tunnel in 1959, residents lived in splendid isolation from Vancouver, a ferry ride to Richmond or the long drive through New Westminster the only links.

Mute swan surveys Ladner's inner harbour

Ladner Paddling Club, call 604-946-7507 or 604-946-5070, check kaymarantours.com or stop by the Elliott Street Wharf. For daily tide tables, check tides.gc.ca.

Ladner's Pioneer May Days take place in late May. For a schedule of events, visit ladnermaydays.org. Ladner Village Market Days begin in June and continue on alternate Sundays through August.

The Delta Museum and Archives, 4858 Delta Street, 604-946-9322, is open Tuesday to Saturday, 10 A.M. to 3:30 P.M.

40

WESTHAM AND REIFEL ISLANDS

. . . . .

> **DISTANCE:** 38 km (23.6 mi.) south and west of Vancouver

> **ACTIVITIES:** Birding, cycling, paddling, picnicking, walking

> **ACCESS:** Take Highway 99 south to Highway 17 South (Exit 28), just past the George Massey Tunnel, and follow the signs into Ladner. On Highway 17, there is a roadside marker announcing the turnoff to the George C. Reifel Migratory Bird Sanctuary on Ladner Trunk Road (48th Avenue). The sanctuary is located 9.6 km (6 mi.) west of Ladner on Reifel Island. To get there, once you reach the heart of Ladner, make a jog left on 47A Avenue, which leads to River Road West. Several kilometres along this diked road on the right side, past float houses and marinas, is a one-lane wooden bridge leading onto the conjoined Westham and Reifel islands.

> **WESTHAM ISLAND**

Westham Island farmers grow delicious berries as well as a variety of vegetables and herbs. June is normally the best month for picking berries, while fall is pumpkin season.

As soon as you cross the bridge onto Westham Island, you pass the local gun club's firing range on the right side of the road. You could leave your car here and cycle the level 3.2 km (2 mi.) across Westham to the George C. Reifel Migratory Bird Sanctuary entrance on Reifel Island; however, bikes are not allowed on Reifel's trails. Otherwise, drive across Westham to the gateway.

> **ALAKSEN NATIONAL WILDLIFE AREA**

By car or bike, as you reach the causeway that links Westham with Reifel Island, the road passes beside the Alaksen National Wildlife

Sandhill crane, Reifel Island

Area, operated by the Canadian Wildlife Service. Their offices are located in the former Reifel family home. Hours are from 8 A.M. to 4 P.M., Monday to Friday except holidays, when the wildlife area is closed. Although much of Alaksen is hidden from view by trees lining the road, the property is quite extensive, over 290 ha (more than 700 acres). Upon arrival, visitors must sign in on the second floor of the former country residence of Vancouver businessman George C. Reifel. Never has registering been such a pleasure. While you're there, pick up a trail map.

A modest-sized boat launch is situated on Ewen Slough. Paddle or walk out to the Fraser River and then north as the river parallels a high dike trail that runs for about 6 km (4 mi.) around Reifel Island as it spirals through the extensive mixture of agricultural lands, forests, hedgerows and old field habitat. Take 15 minutes and walk out to the mouth of the Fraser River's South Arm, where Westham and Reifel islands conjoin amid a patchwork of low-slung companions.

By boat, you enter a backwater area where towering Lombardy poplars line the riverbank. Diminutive Albion and Harlock islands, covered with bulrushes and pernicious purple loosestrife, provide a breakwater from the wakes of passing motorboats. This is a quiet, sheltered environment in which to enjoy a peaceful paddle. As you head northwest along the shoreline, you'll find that a series of sloughs make indentations into both Westham and Reifel. These are often good places in which to drift silently with your binoculars at the ready. Spectacular displays of aerial activity often occur, seemingly just for your benefit, such as when a rare golden eagle goes ballistic riding a thermal current. As you near the northeast corner of Reifel Island, you are on the opposite shore from the town of Steveston (see chapter 36), itself sheltered by the long neck of Steveston Island. This is an attractive place to be near sunset, especially at slack tide, with the lights of Steveston flickering in the distance.

> GEORGE C. REIFEL MIGRATORY BIRD SANCTUARY

Located on the western fringe of the Fraser River estuary in Delta, the George C. Reifel Migratory Bird Sanctuary is the winter home for more than 230 species. Many of these are nesting year-round residents. Others head north to their summer nesting grounds. Many migratory birds stay at Reifel through the end of March, making this the best season to visit the sanctuary.

There are several picnic tables near the entrance to the bird sanctuary, both on the banks of a pond, where mallards, coots and teals quack riotously while preening and paddling about, and inside the gate where the action is more subdued. Honking Vs of Canada geese arrive continually on the far bank to forage.

Wide trails wind for 3.5 km (2.2 mi.) through wooded and diked areas of the sanctuary, leading out to views of Roberts Bank on the western shore. Out on the marshes, you're often treated to rare sights, such as a northern harrier sitting on a distant fence with Mount Baker towering behind. There are a number of observation towers throughout the sanctuary as well as two blinds from which to stealthily observe the action in the marshes. If you're fortunate, you may even catch a glimpse of the majestic resident sandhill cranes.

A cool wind blows off the waters, so come prepared with warm clothing, a good pair of binoculars and a bird book. In case you forgot anything, there is a gift shop at the entrance to the sanctuary with a wide variety of bird-related items for sale. You can buy bags of approved bird feed for 50 cents at the entrance. *Note*: Please don't bring bread, because it provides little food value to birds. The entrance fee is $5 for adults and $3 for seniors and children under 15. A few steps past the entrance is a cozy warming hut overlooking a backwater. On cool days, a cheery fire helps take the edge off. The Reifel Migratory Bird Sanctuary was developed through the efforts of the B.C. Waterfowl Society, and it supports Canada's largest wintering population of waterfowl. Visiting hours are from 9 A.M. to 4 P.M. daily. For more information, call 604-946-6980 or visit reifelbirdsanctuary.com.

41

LADNER DIKE TRAIL &

. . . . .

> **DISTANCE:** 30 km (18.6 mi.) south and west of Vancouver

> **ACTIVITIES:** Birding, boating, cycling, dog walking, paddling, picnicking, viewpoints, walking

> **ACCESS:** Follow Highway 99 to the south end of the George Massey Tunnel and take Exit 28 onto Highway 17 South, then turn right again onto Ladner Trunk Road (48th Avenue) for the short drive into town. Ladner Trunk crosses Elliott Street (the town's main drag) and blends into 47A Avenue, which in turn joins River Road. Numerous roadside pullouts allow access to the dike trails.

WHETHER YOU explore the Fraser estuary by car, foot or bicycle, the views are tremendous: the broad expanse of the Strait of Georgia opens on the west; to the north the peaks of the Coast Mountains march along from the Sunshine Coast to the Fraser Valley. It's often sunnier out here, too, though cool winds do blow in off the open water. In exposed areas, there's little shelter from the wind except behind an accommodating piece of driftwood on the beach. Wherever you wander, the ground is level, but what's lacking in vertical challenge can be made up for in distance.

A particularly enjoyable stretch of dike trail begins in the far reaches of Delta. The ocean breeze sings a haunting song over this secluded area just west of downtown Ladner where the South Arm of the Fraser River meets the Strait of Georgia at Roberts Bank, the end of its 1 370-km (850-mi.) journey. A large dike protects the town from periodic inundation by ocean tides and river runoff. The dike trail is wide enough so that walkers, cyclists, motorized wheelchair drivers and those on horseback can share it with ease.

Brunswick Point, Ladner Dike Trail

As the Fraser sweeps past Ladner it curves around Gunn, Barber and Westham islands on the town's north side. Westham is the only one of the three that has been settled (see previous chapter). The best place to view these islands is from the pier in Wellington Point Park west of 40th Street. There is ample parking here as well as picnic tables and a public boat launch.

Nearby, Canoe Passage separates Ladner from Westham Island, providing moorage for the float houses rocking in the marinas beside the dike. Owing to the height of the dike, little of the waterway is visible from River Road as it winds westwards from downtown Ladner. In 3 km (1.9 mi.) it passes the bridge over Canoe Passage that links Ladner with Westham Island and the George C. Reifel Migratory Bird Sanctuary (see previoius chapter); 2.5 km (1.5 mi.) farther the road ends in a gated cul-de-sac. There is more roadside parking here.

From the gravel-surfaced dike trail, the mouth of Canoe Passage presents itself all at once. The channel is several hundred metres across at this point. The flat farmland of Westham Island lies demurely on the opposite shore. Aside from thick hedges of blackberry brambles and a tall stand of Lombardy poplars planted long ago, the land is wide open, with only an occasional willow for relief.

Old pilings march out into the Fraser from the river's edge like stalwart centurions, the last of a legion that once supported the Brunswick Cannery wharf, one of the Fraser River's earliest salmon canneries. The marshy ground at the point is usually wet, so if you want to explore out here, bring some rubber boots. One of the best times for this is midsummer, when much of the marsh is in bloom. Driftwood stranded above the high-tide line by winter storms provides natural bridges to clamber over. Some trunks are weathered smooth and curved just right for sitting back on while listening for bird calls. Don't forget your binoculars, or your paint box if you're so inclined. It's calm out here on a good day, and usually, there aren't more than a handful of others with whom to share the trail.

From this starting point, the trail swings south for 7 km (4.3 mi.) in a gentle curve around Roberts Bank towards the superport causeway, an easy hour's walk one way and half that on a bicycle. Viewpoints occur at regular intervals, with a bench or two set off beside the trail.

At any time of year, the view west over the Strait of Georgia is compelling, an enormous seascape of ever-changing light and dark. This is the panorama you dream of longingly when cooped up indoors. Offshore in the shallow waters of the strait, flocks of ducks and geese bob along. Depending on the direction of the wind, they take shelter on either side of the long causeway that runs out to the loading dock where ocean freighters take on coal. A hundred railway cars sit motionless in a line while the quiet drumming of a half-dozen diesel engines harnessed in tandem carries across the water towards the dike. There is a trail running along the causeway that juts out into Roberts Bank. This little diversion can easily add another half-hour of exploration time to the journey. When you look shoreward from out here, Ladner is eerily remote. Mount Baker and other peaks in the Cascade Mountains rise up to the east. Southwards, a large BC Ferries vessel heads off towards Vancouver Island. A freighter is silhouetted against the shores of the Gulf Islands, with the peaks of Vancouver Island's mountains rising above Nanaimo to the west.

Returning to Ladner after time spent out on top of the dike is like returning from a sailing trip. The water has been expansive and ever-present. Soon you are back on sheltered land with the horizon closing in on all sides, but you come away with a feeling of inner tranquillity and give silent thanks to the dike builders for allowing you to get away for a few hours.

42

BOUNDARY BAY
REGIONAL PARK &

. . . . .

> DISTANCE: 40 km (25 mi.) south of Vancouver in Tsawwassen, part of the municipality of Delta

> ACTIVITIES: Birding, boating, cycling, dog walking, nature observation, picnicking, swimming, walking, windsurfing

> ACCESS: Boundary Bay Regional Park is an easy 45-minute drive south of Vancouver. Take the Highway 17 South exit (#28) from Highway 99 towards the Tsawwassen ferry terminal, then turn south on 56th Street (Point Roberts Road), which leads into Tsawwassen. (See map page 207.) Turn left onto 12th Avenue and follow it around to Boundary Bay Road and Third Avenue, which lead south to the park entrance at Centennial Beach.

FROM OUR vantage point here in B.C.'s southwestern corner, it often appears that the farther from the city we explore, the greater are the natural rewards of the landscape. After all, B.C. has some really enormous expanses of protected land, particularly in the more remote corners of the province. Back here in the city, all that parkland looks pretty exotic.

The sheer distance between Vancouver and these remote locales contributes to their allure. If you have three days' driving time at your disposal, you might just make it as far as the jumping-off place into one of them. Then again if you have 30 minutes to spare here at home, you could be exploring the sandy shore and broad waterway of one of B.C.'s more wondrous locales, Boundary Bay. This fascinating area has few equals along the coast for size and setting, yet because of its proximity to the city, much of the bay's natural grandeur is curtained behind farmland, recent housing developments and commuter roads.

These days, not only does the bay's shoreline enjoy protection as parkland, but so too does much of the offshore area, as part of the Lower Mainland Nature Legacy Program. And what an offshore area! As much as you might enjoy exploring the sand dunes and dike trails that characterize Boundary Bay's shoreline, you'll delight in paddling the bay in calm weather, especially at high tide. Gliding across the clear waters of the shallow bay in a kayak or canoe imparts a feeling of flying above the undulating, shadowy ocean floor below.

When agitated, Boundary Bay affords both a challenge and a thrill to sailors and board riders. As waves surge in, young swimmers strive to ride slippery driftwood logs that bob in the sun-warmed water. (You can plan on enjoying a swim here well into September.) Mired high above the tide line, logs tossed up by past storms shelter picnickers when strong breezes arise. On the northern and eastern skyline, the Coast and Cascade mountain ranges converge in the far distance of the Fraser Valley. To the south, Mount Baker and its companion peaks to the west, the Sisters, shore up the sky. This is a fine spot to catch a sunset, when shafts of sunlight tint the clouds above with a palette of pastel hues. No two evenings are the same here, which is why I'm drawn back time and again.

There are a small number of parking spaces at the intersection of 12th Avenue and Boundary Bay Road. If you plan to explore the dike by bike, this is a good place to begin. A 16-km (10-mi.) dike trail runs clockwise from the park around the north end of the bay. This is a popular trail with walkers and cyclists. In fact, there is such an extensive length of level trail that the challenge will be to decide at what point you've had enough and wish to turn back. If you persist, the dike stretches to the eastern end of Mud Bay in distant Surrey. (See chapter 43 for a comprehensive description.)

For those wanting to launch a boat or board, a ramp is located at the east end of 1A Avenue, several blocks south of Centennial Beach via 67th Street. If you plan on boating, it's always a good idea to consult a tide table in advance (tides.gc.ca). When the tide goes out at Boundary Bay, it goes *way* out, revealing an expanse of firm, clean, inviting sand—great for exploring on foot but an obstacle to launching a boat.

Moon with Mount Baker, Boundary Bay Regional Park

> **CENTENNIAL BEACH**

Watch for Cammidge House at the Centennial Beach entrance to the park off Boundary Bay Road. This stately farmhouse, ringed with porches, has been a fixture here since 1907. It has been restored at the south end of the park road, where it is now used as a community meeting place. Metro Vancouver Parks is also undertaking habitat-enhancement work on the Spetifore Lands, a buffer zone between Tsawwassen and Boundary Bay, planting a variety of native and indigenous plants to benefit wildlife.

The main parking area at Centennial Beach has picnic tables beside a treed area, drinking water, changing facilities, tennis courts and washrooms. A concession stand is open during the busiest times in summer. From here, a network of short walking trails fans out to the north, perfect for wildlife viewing. Even on a crowded weekend, Centennial Beach always has room to spare, especially if you avoid the immediate area of the parking lot. The beach runs north for more than 2 km (1.2 mi.), so stretch out.

Be careful of incoming tides when walking out into the bay. If you're here for a picnic, try putting up a marker, such as an umbrella or piece of driftwood, to act as a beacon by which to fix your position on the beach. Otherwise, from a distance out in the bay you may find that you have only a vague idea of where you left your picnic basket.

The ocean drains out of the bay past Point Roberts to the southwest, with Crescent Beach and White Rock to the east. From a vantage point on the dunes, it's possible to get one of the best views of Mount Baker in the entire Lower Mainland. On a hot day, when the ocean rises over the sand floor heated by the sun's rays, Boundary Bay is as warm as bath water; in very cold weather, the shallow bay can freeze solid.

The intertidal plants and animals of the salt marsh attract several species of hawks and owls. Boundary Bay, especially at the foot of 64th and 72nd streets, is a well-known place to spot snowy owls in winter. To be silently overflown by a white-faced pair is a mind-altering experience.

For more information on wildlife viewing programs and other nature activities offered at Boundary Bay Regional Park, call 604-432-6359. For general information on the park, call 604-224-5739 or visit www.metrovancouver.org/services/parks_lscr/regionalparks/Pages/BoundaryBay.aspx.

> **HEADS UP**
. . . .

TWO ELEVATED, wheelchair-accessible viewing platforms are located along the 1-km (0.6-mi.) 12th Avenue Dyke Trail, which connects Centennial Beach and the 12th Avenue entrance to the park. During seasonal migrations, thousands of waterfowl stop at Boundary Bay. Black brant are especially noted for their spring stopovers—20,000 to 30,000 visit during April. The best viewing is at high tide, when the incoming water forces the ducks who have been out feeding on the sand flats to move closer to shore. Here, they mingle with gulls, terns and herons.

> ## 43

MUD BAY &

. . . . .

> **DISTANCE:** 22 km (13.7 mi.) southeast of Vancouver, on the Delta–Surrey border

> **ACTIVITIES:** Birding, cycling, dog walking, nature observation, picnicking, viewpoints, walking

> **ACCESS:** If you take the Highway 10 exit (#20) off Highway 99, you'll be within a mile of Mud Bay. The only alternative is to take the Highway 17 South exit (#28) and then turn east onto the Ladner Trunk Road (Highway 10 under another name). Cross south onto Hornby Drive at the first set of stoplights. There is an RCMP detachment at this intersection. Take the first right turn off Hornby onto 96th Street and drive to the south end. There is parking on the dike and beside the road. At this point, you're no longer on Mud Bay, having come out onto much-larger Boundary Bay. As if to make the distinction clear, beyond is the Boundary Bay Airport, much grander in turn than the nearer Delta Air Park. Another approach is to stay on Hornby to 104th Street, following the signs to the Delta Air Park. You might find that parking is limited here, especially on busy weekends. Nonetheless, if you are travelling with small children, this might be the better approach, for it's closer to the features they'll likely find most intriguing at Mud Bay, such as the antiquated airplane fuselage that graces the entrance to the air park.

Mud Bay Park is located on the northeastern corner of Mud Bay near the Surrey–Delta border. Take exit 10 from Highway 99 and follow King George Highway (Highway 99A) north 4 km (2.5 mi.) to the Colebrook Road exit. Turn left on Colebrook; in 4 km (2.5 mi.), turn left on 127A Street. Follow unpaved Railway Road a short distance to the park.

Note: In deference to overwintering waterfowl, the Mud Bay dike is closed to dogs, bikes and horses from October 15 to April 15.

Mud Bay Park

T HE JUNIOR member of a triad of bays, Mud Bay is a broad, shallow expanse of gumbo on the border where Delta and South Surrey meet. Boundary and Semiahmoo bays are its senior partners. You pass beside Mud Bay when you drive along Highway 99 between Ladner and Crescent Beach.

Much of the time Mud Bay looks as if someone has pulled the plug and forgotten to clean the tub. Two rivers, the Serpentine and the Nicomekl, empty into the bay's eastern end. They bring silt from runoff and from headwaters many miles inland (see chapter 33). This is the dumping ground for all that mud, deposited year after year. The Boundary Bay Regional Trail, which includes the East Delta Dike Trail, winds around both Mud and Boundary bays, skirting the mud flats that once extended much farther inland. You can put in a full day of cycling, making the 33-km (20.4-mi.) round trip between the Surrey–Delta border and Boundary Bay Regional Park in Tsawwassen (see previous chapter).

Early in the last century, crude dikes were built around the shorelines of Mud and Boundary bays to hold back the ocean. They have been improved considerably in the years since then. Greenhouse gardeners and turf farmers are still the main occupants of the land behind the dikes. A few cows, sheep and horses are pastured around the old Delta homesteads scattered along the roads leading down to the bays. Urban sprawl is eating up many of the fields closer to Tsawwassen, but down around Mud Bay, agriculture still holds sway.

When hard-packed, dike trails are wonderfully level surfaces to roll along on a bicycle or motorized wheelchair, and the East Delta Dike Trail on the north side of Mud Bay is no exception. The dike is wide enough for everyone to share. Hawks, eagles and owls patrol the fields on one side, while on the other, shorebirds in the thousands flock back and forth. Dunlin and sanderling, overwintering members of the sandpiper family whose combined numbers here peak in the tens of thousands, are particularly active. Their ability to instantly change direction in midflight is a survival technique against raptors. To onlookers, they present an ever-changing pattern in white and black: one moment they are a white cloud, the next they blend invisibly with the dark background of the ocean.

As you progress along the dike eastwards from 96th Street, you pass the historic Delta Heritage Air Park out of which the Boundary Bay Flying Club operates (www3.telus.net/airpark). Over 50 light planes of various vintages are parked and hangered here. If the wind is blowing cool off the bay, you might wish to visit the club's small coffee shop next to the runway for a quick warmup. Best time to be here to see both vintage aircraft and automobiles is early July at the annual Fly-In.

Mud Bay comes into its own as the dike leads towards the foot of 112th Street. The dike's surface becomes increasingly rough east of here as it curves inland past a point of marshland that juts out into the bay, then parallels the bay once more. Here and there are the shells of old boats, mired in the mud. Highway 99 edges closer to the trail until only a small fence separates the two. The trail swings away from the highway after 10 minutes of this and joins Surrey's Mud Bay Park beside the Burlington Northern railway line. A long wooden bridge carries the track across Mud Bay. If you've come by bike, it will take you an hour of steady riding to return to 96th Street.

Find a seat on the driftwood "furniture" here and take time to admire the light show over the bay. The mud is speckled with small ponds of water that reflect the colour of the sky; sunlight striking the surface of the ponds turns them a silvery-blue colour. One of the best times of the day for making this journey is late afternoon, when, even on overcast days, the bay lights up with a brilliance all its own. At dim times of year, hints of seasonal affective disorder will immediately be expunged from your mind, replaced by waves of empathy for the birdlife dabbling in the salt marshes beside the 3.8 km (2.3 mi.) of wheelchair-accessible trails that lead through the open park and ring the shoreline. How do they survive winter? According to ornithologists, the concentration of saltwater marshes around Mud, and its larger companion, Boundary Bay, forms the basis of a rich food chain. The two bays are unique in this regard. Together they boast the largest eel grass beds in Canada and provide an organic richness that's complemented by nutrients washed into the bays by the Serpentine and Nicomekl rivers, as well as those from the Fraser River's plume. Unlike most bays along the coast that have sandy bottoms, Mud Bay's surface is, well, mucky. Shorebirds such as dunlin, which arrive in November from their summer breeding grounds on the northern tundra, feast on crustaceans there at low tide. At high tide, flocks of as many as 50,000 of these medium-sized sandpipers group up close to Mud Bay Park's trails in an effort to avoid predation from resident falcons and eagles. If you're hoping to see overwintering shorebirds like dunlins, grebes and loons, time a visit to coincide with high tide. Take along a bird guide and binoculars.

Of the many spottings that have occurred here, few match the discovery of 600 ancient murrelets counted in deep waters off Boundary Bay and the Gulf Islands. Until recently, scientists thought their habitat was only in the Queen Charlotte Islands. For reasons not well understood by scientists, this is part of a general trend of breeding birds heading farther south than previously seen. Or north, as in the case of a tropical kingbird. How this tyrant flycatcher wound up at Mud Bay when its breeding range is typically between Arizona and Argentina is as much a mystery as finding your way in Surrey. There's no need to hide out here—Colebrook is already hidden. This may be one of the least-known and seldom-visited corners of Metro Vancouver. Which perhaps explains why Surrey preserved the soggy habitat as much for the benefit of wildlife as for exercise-seeking urbanites. Over the past decade, Surrey City Council's priority has been to create more waterfront parks.

44

POINT ROBERTS &

. . . . .

> DISTANCE: 50 km (31 mi.) south of Vancouver

> ACTIVITIES: Birding, boating, camping, cycling, dog walking, historic site, nature observation, paddling, picnicking, swimming, viewpoints, walking

> ACCESS: Take Highway 99 south through the George Massey Tunnel to the Highway 17 South exit (#28). (See map page 207.) Turn south off Highway 17 South to Tsawwassen on Point Roberts Road (56th Street) and follow it to the Canada–U.S. border. You can leave your car on Wallace Avenue on the Canadian side and cycle or walk from here. By car, head south on Tyee Drive, then west on Marine Drive to reach Lighthouse Marine Park. *Note:* Bring passports or enhanced driver's licences and vaccination papers for your pet.

HOWDY, NEIGHBOUR. The famous borderline that demarcates this tiny American enclave from adjoining Tsawwassen is celebrated by a stone marker laid in 1861 under the terms of the Treaty of Washington. To search out the monument, turn right onto Roosevelt Way immediately after crossing the border. Make your way the short distance to the western end of the road before it veers sharply south onto Marine Drive. Far below, the waters of the Strait of Georgia lap the beach, and the jetties of the Tsawwassen ferry causeway and the Roberts Bank coal facility jut into view.

Don't bother trying to make your way down the slippery slope here. Instead, continue farther south along Marine to much more hospitable approaches to the sea at Lighthouse Marine Park.

> **LIGHTHOUSE MARINE PARK**
Land's end. There's a special allure in those words. They hook the imagination and draw the curious to the shoreline. By implication,

Sunsweep sculpture, Lighthouse Marine Park

this is where one slips off the mooring lines that ground us. Even if we don't physically ship out to sea, in our minds at least, we sail off across the earth's watery surface.

Such is the mood at Lighthouse Marine Park. Stand on the pebble-strewn beach at the southwestern tip of the Lower Mainland. Spread out before you are three broad straits: Haro, Georgia and Juan de Fuca. This is a dramatic point of convergence. An ever-shifting line formed by a rip tide dances off towards the horizon. Shipping lanes merge in the distance. Perspective plays tricks on your eyes. Freighters appear, then are seemingly swallowed whole behind distant islands in the San Juan and Gulf Islands chains. A mist renders them dull-coloured, mere outlines in the haze. So vast and complex is this panorama that, at best, one can only form a sketchy notion of the power of nature's forces at play here.

Lighthouse is a treasured part of the Whatcom County parks system. Marooned from the rest of Washington State by a political twist of fate, it and the rest of Point Roberts are frequented almost entirely by Canadians. Since its inception in 1973, Lighthouse Marine Park has grown beyond being a simple beach destination. A network of boardwalks and trails now runs through the windswept dunes. Constant breezes gust in off the straits. Stunted pines with a bonsai appearance and wild rose bushes thick with fragrant pink and white blossoms help anchor the dunes. Slope-roofed shelters supported by sturdy log posts provide picnickers with welcome relief. The wind only loses its edge in summer. A dip in the ocean demonstrates how chilly these waters are year round.

Set back off the beach on the west side of the park is a tusk-shaped slab of polished black granite. Known as the *Sunsweep* sculpture, this small installation is one of three such markers placed along the Canada–U.S. border in the 1980s as part of an international art project. Roosevelt Campobello Park in New Brunswick bookends the imaginary path between them. (See fdr.net/did-you-know for details.) Inscribed on the base of the Boundary Bluff marker are these words:

Aligned to the north star, solstices and equinoxes, portrays the path of the sun from east to west. Designed by David Barr in 1985 and given to the people of this community as a symbol of international friendship.

During shipment, the tusk broke in two, but willing hands glued it back together, and it stands solidly in place once more, facing Vancouver Island in the western distance and Mount Baker rising above the waters of Semiahmoo Bay in the east. Two enormous anchors have been moved into position around the sculpture. They lend an air of rusty grandeur to the site.

Here at land's end, winds and countervailing currents swirl against each other, encouraging the water into playful surf. Between swells, kayakers nimbly launch out into the strait. For their

The three resident killer whale pods that frequent these waters have been busy, according to the Washington State-based Center for Whale Research. They now boast a total population of 87.

efforts, they are rewarded with views of the North Shore mountains that are otherwise, on the beach, concealed from sight by the dunes. Occasionally, an unwary paddler will be unceremoniously upended by the choppy motion of the waves. A modest breakwater of wooden pilings valiantly but vainly tries to hold back the surf rolling towards the lighthouse (which, in this case, is less of a house and more of a metal scaffolding).

Perched inland a short distance from the beach, a three-storey observation tower rises above a small orca interpretive centre. Profiles of three pods of killer whales—denoted as J, K and L pods—that frequent the waters off the point are presented on murals. The distinctive dorsal fin markings of some of the older pod members are displayed in a photographic exhibit inside the centre. Using these as clues, visitors fortunate enough to sight the whales can positively identify individual animals.

June to October is the best time to come whale watching here, when all three pods pass near the park, usually daily. It often takes them as long as an hour to journey past. Attractions for them include coho, chinook and pink salmon (also called humpy by the Americans) and rock fish that school up in the nutrient-rich waters off the point. It's worth overnighting in the adjacent campground to increase your chances of seeing the whales. The orcas forage for food, slap their flukes and occasionally surface for some spy hopping, leaping skywards for a look-see of their own. A Vancouver-based organization, Lifeforce Foundation, is often present during these times. Members not only provide helpful insight on the behaviour and personality of individual killer whales, but they also update information in the interpretive centre. (Call 604-649-5258, or visit lifeforce foundation.org for information on the Lifeforce Foundation. For the latest sightings, visit orcanetwork.org/sightings/map.html#map.)

Sightings of jaegers, turkey vultures and hot-ticket items such as albino barn swallows also send birders winging to the park.

In summer, a small parking fee is charged to those who arrive by car, with extra charges if you use the boat launch or wish to stay overnight. For information on Lighthouse Marine Park, check out whatcomcounty.us/parks/lighthouse/lighthouse.jsp or call 1-360-945-4911.

SQUAMISH

WHISTLER

45

PORTEAU COVE
PROVINCIAL PARK &

. . . . .

> **DISTANCE:** 43 km (26.7 mi.) north of Vancouver

> **ACTIVITIES:** Boating, camping, dog walking, diving, paddling, picnicking, swimming

> **ACCESS:** Off Highway 99 North, 22 km (13.7 mi.) north of Horseshoe Bay.

FOR ALL of its beauty, Howe Sound provides few points of public access along its rugged shoreline. In most places the mountains plunge sharply into the waters of the deep fiord—Canada's most southerly—forcing the railroad and the highway close together, with scant room left over for visitors to spread a picnic blanket, let alone set up a tent. One of the few places where these things *are* possible is the provincial park at Porteau Cove.

From Highway 99, Porteau Cove's beach and BC Ferries' emerging ferry pier are what first catch the eye. As you turn into the park, information signs, directed at divers, detail the location of several marine vessels scuttled offshore specifically for underwater exploration. The first of these boats was sunk in 1981 when the park was opened. Marine life is attracted to such wrecks, making a dive even more exciting. Watching divers hardly qualifies as a spectator sport. That said, there is something rather entertaining in seeing a group of neoprene-clad people entering or emerging from the cold waters of the sound while you enjoy your picnic at one of the numerous tables spread around the broad, driftwood-littered beaches on both sides of the pier. Small floats positioned offshore help divers orient

Porteau Cove Provincial Park

themselves. Divers affix a flag to the top of these if they are diving below, warning boaters to stay well away.

If you are visiting Porteau Cove for the day, use the large parking area beside the pier. The wheelchair-accessible walkways are a wonderful place to take a break from highway traffic and enjoy the spectacular views of Howe Sound, with Anvil Island's telltale profile to the southwest and the peaks of the Tantalus Range rising in the northwest. The gravel beach slopes gently into the sound. On days when the tide is low and the sun high, the gravel heats up and warms the incoming waters, making swimming here a pleasure. *Note*: Dogs are not allowed on the beach.

The welcoming boat launch at Porteau Cove is the only public one accessible from Highway 99 between Horseshoe Bay and

Squamish. There are often times when Howe Sound is flat calm, a perfect invitation to enjoy a paddle; however, always be aware that strong winds can rise quickly. By sticking close to shore, you can safely enjoy views of the Howe Sound Crest and Britannia ranges that are not otherwise revealed from land. If you paddle north to Furry Creek, look for pictographs painted on the rock face on the north side of the small bay just past the creek's entrance into Howe Sound. Note: Do not attempt a paddle crossing to Anvil Island without wearing a wet suit.

Since Porteau Cove is the only provincial park on the sound accessible by car, the 44 vehicle and 16 walk-in sites are in constant use. Even if you are visiting just for the day, have a look at Porteau's camping facilities with an eye to making plans for a future visit. If you head here with the intention of staying overnight in summer, arrive early and have a contingency plan in case all the spaces have been taken. You can also reserve a campsite here by calling 604-689-9025 or visiting discovercamping.ca.

In the early 1900s, a small settlement sprang up beside Porteau Cove's sheltered bay, brought there by the Deeks Sand and Gravel Company. The Squamish Nation now has title to this land and a 1,400-unit housing development is planned.

The drive-in sites go quickly throughout the summer and on Friday and Saturday nights from May to October, but there is usually a good chance of getting one of the walk-in sites even if you arrive late, except in the months of June to August. A user fee is collected year round: from $16 to $30 for drive-in sites and $10 for walk-ins.

As soon as you enter the campground, bear right to check out the oceanfront sites. In the middle of the campground is a washroom facility complete with showers. The walk-in sites are located at the far end of the campground road. From the walk-in parking lot to the sites is only a short distance, easily covered in several minutes. An amphitheatre is located between the drive-in and walk-in campsites. Interpretive displays are presented here at one of the most scenic locations in the park on summer evenings. Because there is so little level land, most sites are relatively closely spaced compared with other provincial parks. Campsite 44, at the westernmost end of the road next to the walk-in parking, is one of the few that have some breathing room. It sits in the shelter of the Sitka spruce forest and commands an attractive view of the sound. The only drawback is its proximity to the railroad tracks. Visitors can count on several trains passing by at all hours of the day and night.

Discreetly tucked in behind the walk-in sites is the cove itself. There is an open lawn beside the cove, and a small bridge spans the narrow backwater. Take a walk to the viewpoint on the trail that leads west from the walk-in sites and up onto the forested bluff. Stunted shore pines—a coastal variety of lodgepole pine—and stately Sitka spruce provide shelter on the point, from where you can look down on the cove or out across the waters of the sound. This is a quiet place in which to enjoy the surroundings, especially in the early or late hours of the day, or to stop for an off-season breather from the highway.

New to the park are the two Olympic Legacy log cabins, both fully serviced and fully furnished with all the amenities of home. Cabins rent from $139 per night in the low season to $219 per night in the high season with a three-night minimum. Rates are based on four people and include complimentary parking for one vehicle during the stay. Reservations are required and can be made by telephone at 604-986-9371 or by email at info@seatoskyparks.com.

46

SQUAMISH &

. . . . .

> DISTANCE: 60 km (37.2 mi.) north of Vancouver

> ACTIVITIES: Birding, camping, dog walking, hiking, kiteboarding, mountain biking, mountaineering, nature observation, paddling, picnicking, viewpoints, walking, windsurfing

> ACCESS: Squamish is located about 40 km (24.8 mi.) north of Horseshoe Bay on Highway 99.

The well-marked entrance to Shannon Falls Provincial Park is located on the east side of Highway 99, 7 km (4.3 mi.) north of Britannia Beach. The Shannon Falls parking lot is usually full by noon on weekends from May through September. There are two large picnic areas suited to families and groups who like room to stretch out and play.

There are two approaches to Stawamus Chief Provincial Park. One trail starts from Shannon Falls Park. Markers indicate the way. Alternatively, you can drive to the base of the Chief via the designated turnoff at the viewing area on Highway 99 just north of Shannon Falls. Follow the road that leads up the embankment in the middle of the viewpoint and leads south to the provincial campsites and trailhead parking lot.

To reach the Squamish estuary, turn west from Highway 99 into Squamish at the second set of traffic lights, where an Esso station is the anchor tenant, and drive south along Cleveland Avenue, the town's main drag, to Vancouver Street, then right to Second Avenue. Park and follow signs from there.

To reach Squamish Spit, turn west from Highway 99 at the third set of traffic lights onto Industrial Way, then turn north on Queensway, which feeds into Government Road. The gravel road to the spit starts off Government Road's west side. It is 4.3 km (2.7 mi.) from

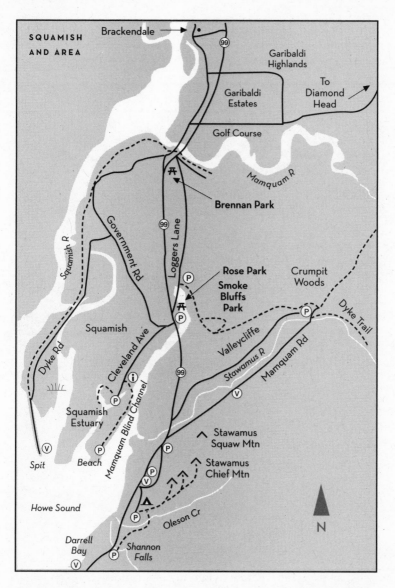

SQUAMISH
AND AREA

Brackendale

99

Garibaldi
Highlands

To
Diamond
Head

Garibaldi
Estates

Golf Course

Mamquam R

Brennan Park

Squamish R

Government Rd

99

Loggers Lane

P

Rose Park

Smoke
Bluffs
Park

Crumpit
Woods

P

P

Dyke Trail

Squamish

Valleycliffe

Stawamus R

Mamquam Rd

Dyke Rd

Cleveland Ave

i

P

99

V

Squamish
Estuary

Mamquam Blind Channel

Stawamus
Squaw Mtn

V

Spit

P

Beach

P

P

V

Stawamus
Chief Mtn

Howe Sound

P

Oleson Cr

N

Darrell
Bay

P

Shannon
Falls

V

the turnoff to the end of the spit. Just before the road climbs up on the dike, turn left onto a service road and follow it south to the very end.

Alice Lake Provincial Park is located 12 km (7.4 mi.) north of downtown Squamish just east of Highway 99. Signs near the park

Squamish Spit

entry direct visitors to Alice Lake's day-use facilities and campsites (see map page 266). For more information, visit www.env.gov.bc.ca/ bcparks/explore/parkpgs/alicelk.html.

The strikingly designed Squamish Adventure Centre on Highway 99 just north of Loggers Lane is the best place to find out about events and services in the area. Contact them at 1-604-815-5084.

WELCOME TO the outdoor recreation capital of Canada. That may seem like a tall claim, but a quick scan of the recreational opportunities in Squamish—or Squish, as it's affectionately known—quickly substantiates it. Yet despite the town's veneer of newness, this diversity is no overnight sensation. For more than a century, day trippers have been exploring the mountains and lakes that surround this easy-going community of 16,000 at the head of Howe Sound.

Squamish's skyline is defined by the arresting features of Stawamus Chief Mountain. Rock climbing on the Stawamus Chief, a freestanding granite monolith that rises beside Highway 99 at the town's southern entrance, caught national attention in 1961 when Jim Baldwin and Ed Cooper made the first successful ascent while crowds of more than 10,000 looked on. Climbers such as Baldwin and Cooper put Squamish on the map—and more than a few magazine covers—as the town began to quietly cement its mountaineering reputation. And success bred success. In the 1970s, and again in the 2000s, when first windsurfing and, more recently, kiteboarding took off, a new kind of recreational tourist blew into town. There may not be much surf where the Squamish River meets Howe Sound along the town's northern perimeter, but this junction features one of the most challenging and easily accessible stretches of windsurfing- and kiteboard-friendly water found anywhere on the North American west coast.

Another technologically innovative piece of sports gear, the mountain bike, arrived on the local scene in the 1980s. Today, thanks to the trail-building efforts of volunteer groups such as the Squamish Off-Road Cycling Association, there are over 150 trails on offer, enough to rival the number of climbing routes posted on the Chief. This is definitely a year-round destination, with a sea-level location that guarantees its low-elevation trails remain snow-free most of the year.

Thanks to fall and winter salmon runs, Squamish has also established itself as *the* place to view bald eagles by the hundreds, either while rafting on the Squamish and the Cheakamus Rivers or simply cycling or walking the dike trails, particularly in the Brackendale neighbourhood. For families, this is by far the most popular tour offered at the Squamish Adventure Centre, the best source for details on all things Squishy.

With the legacy of the Whistler Olympic Park (www.whistler olympicpark.com), the municipality has also begun to position itself as a snowshoeing and Nordic skiing destination. Aside from the well-known trails at Diamond Head in Garibaldi Park (see chapter 47), Squamish is taking advantage of the Olympic cross-country facilities in the Callaghan Valley, a 30-minute drive north.

> ## SHANNON FALLS AND
> ## STAWAMUS CHIEF PROVINCIAL PARKS

Out-of-province licence plates adorn the cars parked at the base of the Stawamus Chief, attesting to Squamish's decades-old drawing power among the international climbing community. Even a casual passerby would find it hard to ignore the mountain's lumpy magnificence.

At the same time as the granite features of the Stawamus Chief catch your eye, Shannon Falls, B.C.'s third-highest waterfall, presents itself for admiration. Linked by a 1.6-km-long (1-mi.-long) trail, these two natural wonders provide plenty of rewards for those in search of adventure. Shannon Falls' white veil of water drops 335 m (1,100 ft.) from a ridge above Highway 99 to a creekbed below then empties into nearby Howe Sound. One of the thrills of visiting a waterfall is getting as close to the base as possible, not just to feel the earth tremble beneath your feet but also to witness the prismatic effect of rainbows when spray is backlit by sunlight. At Shannon Falls, clouds of fine mist hang in the air as polished cliff shelves shred Shannon Creek into plumes of tumbling whitewater. Two separate trails, one of which is wheelchair accessible, lead uphill to viewing platforms adjacent the tumult. The majority of visitors follow the lower path, which winds through a sheltering forest beside the clear, winding creek. Just before this hardpacked route reaches the main viewpoint, watch for a staircase on the left. Several minutes' climb will bring you to a

Almost a century ago, Shannon Falls drove a wooden waterwheel to provide energy to a nearby sawmill. A replica of the large wheel is mounted beside the creek.

less-frequented spot closer to a boulder field across which water from the falls percolates as the creek's tranquil nature is restored before flowing into nearby Howe Sound. A rough trail leads even closer to the base from the observation platform. Owing to the slipperiness of the rocks, this approach is hazardous, particularly when the volume of water in Shannon Creek, fed by both rain and snowmelt from peaks on Goat Ridge unseen above, is at its seasonal peak. Be content to savour the double-whammy jolt of the falls coupled with a close-up view of adjacent Stawamus Chief Mountain.

The first half of the well-maintained trail that links Shannon Falls and Stawamus Chief parks is over level ground through an alder forest. Plan on 15 minutes to cover the route. At the base of the mountain, the trail begins to climb beside the smooth granite rock face, which is covered in places by green lichen. You might have to clamber over the occasional blowdown blocking the trail just before the small bridge over Olesen Creek, which gurgles down through a cleft in the mountainside. The Stawamus Chief Mountain Trail begins across the creek, slightly above its trailhead in the 62-site provincial campground (15 vehicle and 47 walk-in sites; self-registration fee is $9 per site per night) where out-of-town climbers are typically ensconced.

Stawamus Chief Mountain has three summits, each one progressively higher and separated by deep clefts. At the outset, a common trail leads upwards towards all three; then it divides into two separate routes. At this junction, the majority of hikers, particularly those with children, head for the South (or First) Summit, a 7-km (4.3-mi.) round trip, where the handrails are smooth and well oiled from constant use.

Wood and stone stairs lead upwards beside Olesen Creek. There is little shade on much of the trail, so pack plenty of fluids for the higher sections of the climb beyond the creek.

You'll find numerous benefits—such as some modest rock climbing and a great view of a notch on the Chief's north face—if you choose the slightly more challenging route to the Centre (Second) and North (Third) Summits, an 11-km (6.8-mi) round trip. In fact, one of the most pleasant options, particularly if you have an extra hour's time, is to follow the loop that links both.

No matter which summit you choose, be prepared for an

unrelenting regime of up, up and up (and the resultant knee-knackering corollary of down, down and down). Take the time to enjoy your surroundings beneath tall stands of ramrod-straight Douglas-fir, which provide shade as welcome as the steady breeze that funnels round the mountain off Howe Sound.

Even if you never intend to scale its walls, be sure to explore the base of the sheer west face known as the Apron below the mountain's second summit. The best place to begin is the well-marked climbers' access parking lot beside Highway 99 just north of the Chief's more prominent viewing zone. Follow a welcoming trail that leads a short distance up through the forest. An easy stint of free climbing deposits you on a ledge from where most climbers begin to rope up. Even if you go no higher, you can now claim to have climbed on the Chief. Enjoy an unobstructed view of the town spread below.

Rock climbing's popularity around Squamish is not limited to the Chief. Close by to the north is Smoke Bluffs Park, a small ridge easily reached from its trailhead beside the Squamish Adventure Centre. Because of the ridge's southern exposure, the granite walls dry quickly in the morning sun. A walking trail leads up to the base of the ridge from a parking lot on Loggers Lane. Small groups of climbers practise on the smooth walls here. Although this isn't a spectator sport, they won't mind you watching if you are quiet; safe climbing requires great concentration.

> **RAPTOR ROYALTY**

BRACKENDALE EAGLES Provincial Park is the bald eagle-spotting nexus of North America. From mid-November to mid-February, you may see 30 eagles or more at any one time along the Squamish River dike trail. A wheelchair ramp leads up onto the dike where benches fashioned from driftwood provide good perches for enjoying grand views of the river, valleys and mountains. Information kiosks, including a Sko-mish First Nations display, detail the natural history of eagles. To reach the park, follow Government Road 7 km (4.3 mi) north of downtown Squamish, or just west of Highway 99 on Depot Road where a large sign of an eagle is posted.

> SQUAMISH ESTUARY

When your aim is to get outdoors, downtown Squamish might seem like an odd starting point. However, walking the town's waterfront estuary trails makes perfect sense if you like to explore the borderline where river banks fall away at the ocean's doorstep. A grass-covered trail leads away from new residential waterfront developments past the channelled waterways of the estuary, home to a large population of migratory waterfowl during spring and fall as well as an overwintering population of geese and raptors. Out here the uncluttered views really open up. The smooth granite walls of the Stawamus loom large. White stalks of pearly everlasting rival Shannon Falls' snowy tress, which can be seen cascading down the slopes to the south of the Chief. Spires of solitary, stunted Sitka spruce anchor the estuary's perimeter. Depending on the season, be sure to wear waterproof footwear. A stop at the Howe Sound Inn and Brewing Company near the trailhead makes a fitting end to a journey here.

> SQUAMISH SPIT

The Squamish Spit is a long finger of dike at the mouth of the Squamish River where it flows into Howe Sound. The spit helps keep the harbour free of silt so that large freighters can tie up nearby to take on loads of lumber. On busy summer weekends, there can be more than a hundred cars parked here. At the very end of the spit are the windsurf and kiteboard launch areas. The views from the spit are spectacular, the best in the area: Shannon Falls, the Stawamus Chief, Sky Pilot Mountain and Goat Ridge, Mamquam Mountain, Atwell Peak and Mount Garibaldi all stand out in one great panorama.

Year round, a strong wind known as a "squamish" blows each afternoon across Howe Sound with such force that unwary windsurfers in the waters off the Squamish Spit often can't right themselves if they get dunked. Fortunately, there is an emergency rescue service on standby.

The spit is administered by the Squamish Windsports Society. Launch fees are currently $15 per day. For information on daily wind conditions, dial the society's Wind Talker phone line in Squamish, 1-604-892-2235, or visit www.squamishwindsports.com.

Alice Lake is the largest of four tightly knit lakes nestled in the woods below Alice Ridge. Camping with all the amenities of home—at least electrical hook-ups, hot showers and indoor plumbing—is a big attraction here. An overnight fee is charged from May to October: $30 for one of the 108 vehicle campsites—two of which are wheelchair accessible—and $19 for one of 12 walk-/bike-in sites. Reservations made well in advance are strongly recommended; call 604-689-9025 or visit www.discovercamping.ca. Two group campsites are available; call 604-986-9371 to reserve. All campground trails and the Lake Trail around Alice Lake, as well as picnic tables, are wheelchair accessible. *Note:* Dogs are restricted to the campground and are not allowed in the day-use, beach, and picnic areas.

Of the four lakes in the park, Alice is the one most suitable for paddling. (Motorized boats are not permitted on any of the lakes.) There are launch sites at each end of the lake beside the picnic areas. Rows of tables ring the shore, each with its own barbecue. The setting, with its manicured tranquillity, is quite pleasant. There is a pier to fish from at the south end. Lakeshore Walk links the two picnic areas, shaded by cedar groves that thrive on the moisture provided by the lake. The view from Alice Lake's north end is one of the best in the park, short of climbing nearby DeBeck's Hill.

The most popular trail in the park links Alice with its three smaller companion lakes. Budget 2 to 4 hours to complete the loop. All of the trails are well marked, with both directions and distances indicated to Stump, Fawn, Edith and Alice lakes. This is a good trail for cycling as well as walking, though it is restricted to pedestrians in summer.

Stump Lake's name conjures up images of decrepitude, so it's a pleasant surprise to discover that the only stumps in sight stand beside the trail, not in the lake itself. The smooth trail divides as it rounds the small lake. On one side, it's quite level; on the other, it climbs the hillside. Looking down, you may see anglers casting for rainbow, cutthroat and brook trout. Unlike at Alice, there are no lawns or beaches here or at either of the other two lakes.

From Stump Lake's north end, the trail winds close beside the Cheekye River for a time, then begins to climb gently towards Fawn

Lake. The forest floor is thick with ferns; beside the trail, delicate wildflowers such as white trilliums and dusty-rose bleeding hearts appear in clusters. Beneath several large old-growth cedars is an especially pretty viewpoint overlooking the river. (If you are walking with young children, this may be as far as you care to go on the Four Lakes Loop Trail. Instead of retracing your steps, you can take a short connector to an old logging road that leads back to Alice Lake.)

Fawn Lake is smaller and shallower, and its shoreline is not as accessible as those of Stump and Alice. It's possible to swim from the banks of a small clearing. This is exactly what many cyclists do after the long ride uphill on the old road.

A former logging road and the Four Lakes Loop Trail merge for the short 10- to 15-minute walk between Fawn and Edith, most of whose waterfront is not within the park boundary. (The old logging road doubles as a mountain bike trail called Tracks from Hell, leading south from Edith Lake to the Garibaldi Highlands neighbourhood. The shorter Mike's Loop Trail begins here as well.) There are some steep stretches as the Four Lakes Loop Trail from Edith to Alice keeps company with a small creek. Simple wooden bridges span the creek in several places.

If you like views, try tackling DeBeck's Hill, an option that presents itself at Alice Lake's south end. During some seasons, you may find yourself fending off the persistent bugs, but the cool breeze that usually blows across the top of DeBeck's Hill will dissipate the insects as quickly as the panoramic views appear. You'll get the complete picture of local geography from up here. If you're exploring by bike and consider DeBeck's Hill too challenging, head south to Garibaldi Highlands along Jack's Trail, which begins at the bottom of the hill.

47

DIAMOND HEAD

Garibaldi Park

· · · · ·

> **DISTANCE:** 74 km (46 mi.) north of Vancouver near Squamish

> **ACTIVITIES:** Camping, hiking, mountain biking, picnicking, snow sports, viewpoints

> **ACCESS:** From Highway 99 in Squamish's Garibaldi Highlands neighbourhood, take the Diamond Head (Garibaldi Provincial Park) turnoff east and follow Mamquam Road 16 km (10 mi.) to the trailhead parking lot. Parking and camping fees must be paid at the parking lot prior to entering the park—cash only; no credit cards. *Note:* Dogs are not allowed in Garibaldi Park.

DIAMOND HEAD is a fortresslike ridge that rises above the Squamish Valley in Garibaldi Provincial Park. It makes a bold statement about the elevation of the Coast Mountain peaks here, which tower from 1 980 m (6,500 ft.) to well over 2 440 m (8,000 ft.) You'll be surprised at how quickly you can get a close look at these peaks.

There is a large map of the Diamond Head region at the trailhead. From the parking lot to the subalpine region is an 11-km (6.8-mi.) hike along an old road. Because the grade is gentle for most of the road, you should be able to reach the Elfin Lakes—a fine viewing spot—in 2 hours if you are reasonably fit. The map at the trailhead gives a longer estimate of 4 hours. You can also journey into this region of Garibaldi Park by mountain bike.

Profound silence envelops Diamond Head. Few birds sing, no dogs bark. Visitors cross into this zone of tranquillity almost as soon

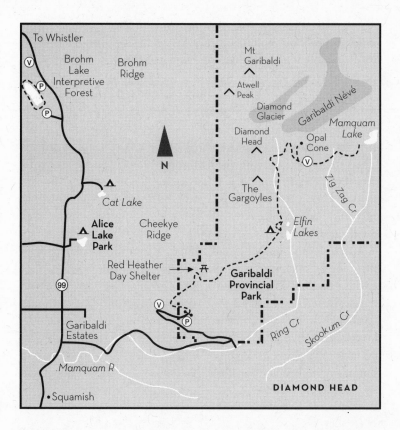

To Whistler

Brohm Lake Interpretive Forest

Brohm Ridge

Mt Garibaldi

Atwell Peak

Diamond Glacier

Garibaldi Névé

Mamquam Lake

Diamond Head

Opal Cone

Cat Lake

The Gargoyles

Zig Zag Cr

Alice Lake Park

Cheekye Ridge

Elfin Lakes

Red Heather Day Shelter

Garibaldi Provincial Park

99

Garibaldi Estates

Ring Cr

Skookum Cr

Mamquam R

Squamish

DIAMOND HEAD

as they embark on the old road along which supplies and Diamond Head Lodge guests were once transported. If you are on foot, allow 75 minutes to reach Red Heather Meadows. BC Parks maintains a day shelter here, complete with kitchen facilities. In winter, skiers and snowshoers will find the small cabin's wood-fired stove especially welcoming. An elevated pit toilet, fronted by a steep staircase, hints at the depth of snow in winter. It also adds new starch to the term "throne room." *Note*: Bicycles are not permitted beyond this point.

The Elfin Lakes are 90 minutes up the road from here on Paul Ridge. All sense of time redefines itself en route. Much like the altered state induced by stargazing, one's mind is drawn into another world where the rhythms of change occur on a vastly amplified scale.

Crevasse-laced glaciers that took millennia to form speak of a time frame that eclipses mortal comparisons.

A loyal following of day trippers and campers trek year round to Diamond Head. With the demise of the lodge, BC Parks opened a campground nearby. A stone's throw away stands the cozy alpine-gothic Elfin Lodge, a two-storey, 34-bunk shelter, complete with kitchen facilities at a cost of $10 each per night, $25 per family. From this vantage point, lava beds on the south flank of a stubby feature called the Opal Cone are visible through binoculars, at least on a clear day. Clouds frequently cluster around the tips of the dominant peaks, Mount Garibaldi to the north and Mamquam Mountain to the east. It's also cooler at this elevation than in the Squamish Valley, visible far below.

A narrow trail leads beyond Elfin Lakes to the Opal Cone, an intriguingly shaped granite plug formed when the spew of molten lava hardened. The cone is neither conical nor opalescent in appearance. It squats like a green-grey molar at the foot of Mount Garibaldi's south tower, dagger-nosed Atwell Peak, surrounded by a battleship-grey moonscape scoured clean by the retreating Garibaldi and Lava glaciers. As topsoil will be scarce for a while, vegetation has yet to become established here. The few traces of flora that

> ## DIAMOND HEAD LODGE

THE SCALE of the mountains in the Pacific ranges that transect Garibaldi Park is truly astonishing. It's easy to see what drew a trio of entrepreneurs to hew a log chalet here. Diamond Head Lodge welcomed guests from the mid-1940s to the early 1970s. Although reduced in size and sagging at the corners, the lodge is still standing. Given the volumes of snow recorded locally in past winters, it's a wonder the building hasn't fallen in on itself. Sheets of plywood cover the windows. Saggy soffits outline the roof like lipstick applied by a dipsomaniac. Nestled in a meadow beside the twin Elfin Lakes, with peaks surrounding it on all sides, the old lodge still enjoys one of the best prospects in Garibaldi Park.

Looking deep into Garibaldi Park from Paul Ridge

do cling to the sides of the cone flourish somewhat mysteriously. At this elevation, above 1 400 m (4,593 ft.), growth is very slow. Core samples taken from stunted groves of cypress on nearby Paul Ridge indicate the trees are many hundreds of years old, qualifying them for the vaunted forest appellation of "ancient."

If the lava is rather bland in appearance, it only serves to heighten the intensity of hues in the broader panorama. Frost triggers dramatic displays of fall colour in these alpine meadows. Pumpkin-yellow and orange leaves blaze on black huckleberry and oval-leafed blueberry bushes, augmented by an understorey of white partridge-foot and pink-tipped Pacific mountain-heather. Even if you're not up for going much farther than Diamond Head, at least explore the first stretch of the Opal Cone Trail as it leads to the rough bridge across Ring Creek. The aptly named Gargoyles, then the Dalton Dome, Atwell Peak and Mount Garibaldi's snow-capped summit present themselves as a reward for your effort. Some of the richest fall colours carpet the gulleys that plunge beside the trail.

Spend a night here. The view from the campground is superb. Immersed in the silence of the surroundings, revel in the view of the Tantalus Range to the west when first lit by the early-morning light. At that magic hour, you'd think that the sun was pouring forth lava like primordial plasma, the cosmic soup from which matter evolved.

48

GARIBALDI LAKE
AND BLACK TUSK

Garibaldi Park

. . . . .

> DISTANCE: 99 km (61.5 mi.) north of Vancouver

> ACTIVITIES: Camping, fishing, hiking, paddling, picnicking, snow sports, swimming, viewpoints

> ACCESS: The turnoff to Black Tusk and Garibaldi Lake is just south of Daisy Lake, 19 km (11.8 mi.) south of Whistler. Watch for the BC Parks signs on Highway 99. This paved road runs 2.5 km (1.6 mi.) east to a large parking lot beside Rubble Creek. A 9-km (5.6-mi.) trail to Garibaldi Lake begins here. There are campgrounds beside the lake and in nearby Taylor Meadows, 7.5 km (4.7 mi.) from the parking area. Along the way, the elevation gain is 810 m (2,660 ft.) to the lake, slightly more to the meadows. *Note:* Dogs are not allowed in Garibaldi Park.

THE TRAIL to Garibaldi Lake and the Black Tusk offers so many choices for adventure that you could easily revisit the area for years before exhausting the possibilities. If you can arrange to go on a weekday, you will have the area more to yourself. On weekends, the trail back to the parking lot at the end of the day can be as congested as the highway—just be patient and revel in your new memories.

The popularity of the Garibaldi Lake and Black Tusk trails makes for a full parking lot on weekends between May and October. Vandalism here is an unfortunate problem, so leave nothing of value in your car if you're planning to be away for long. Consult the information

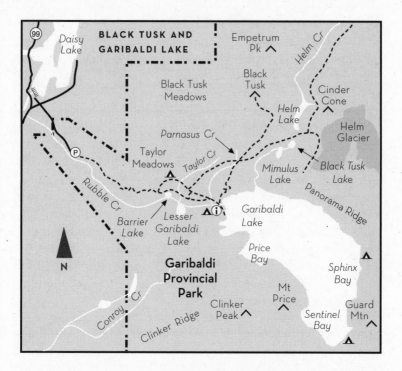

kiosk at the trailhead for a detailed map of Garibaldi Park, or visit www.env.gov.bc.ca/bcparks/explore/parkpgs/garibaldi.html.

> ## THE APPROACH

Care to take a hike in the footsteps of pioneers? Follow the trail to Garibaldi Lake and the Black Tusk and you'll be doing just that. A decade or more before the creation of Garibaldi Provincial Park in the 1920s, climbers from Vancouver's fledgling B.C. Mountaineering Club were already clearing a route to the turquoise-hued lake and somber volcanic pillar, one of the most iconic natural features in the Sea-to-Sky corridor. With the exception of Stawamus Chief Mountain, no other rock formation in the surrounding fortress of coastal peaks is so readily identifiable in a region that's a living lesson in geological history.

During the ascent to the lake, one of the most arresting sights is the Barrier. In the mid-1800s, a large portion of its red rock face calved off. Remnants of the avalanche are easily spotted along the banks of aptly named Rubble Creek, which vents from the base of the Barrier, and in the debris fan on both sides of the Cheakamus River. For the best perspective, pause at the 6-km (3.6-mile) viewpoint. Rocks dislodged from the sheer wall continually tumble down into Rubble's percolating whitewater below.

The Garibaldi Lake Trail is surprisingly smooth and welcoming, unlike other rocks-and-roots routes, such as the Helm Creek Trail, an alternative approach to the lake from the Whistler side of the lake. Thanks to crews of hydrologists dispatched to the lake in the 1930s to investigate the energy-generating potential of the region, accompanied by wagonloads of summer hikers, today's trail covers much the same gently switchbacked path. Just as then, hikers are well advised to carry emergency supplies, including toilet paper, to cope with ever-changing conditions in the backcountry. BC Parks still provides outhouses at Garibaldi Lake, but the ministry's current budget allots no funds for tissue.

> ## GARIBALDI LAKE

Depending on what time of year you visit, water may or may not be flowing out of nearby Barrier Lake. The outflow occurs only in late summer when water levels are at their highest. Year round, the waters from Barrier, Garibaldi and Lesser Garibaldi lakes percolate

> ## THE BARRIER

EVEN IF you don't intend to walk the trail, you should at least drive the short distance in from Highway 99 to the parking lot to enjoy the wide-open view of the Barrier. The broad wall of red volcanic rock is especially appealing when lit by the setting summer sun. It's a unique formation in this region, the result of a flow of molten lava coming face to face with a glacier that once occupied what is now Rubble Creek. The ice cooled and hardened the lava, forming the thick rock face that holds back the waters of Garibaldi Lake, a basin that filled as the surrounding glaciers melted and retreated.

down through a layer of scoria—porous volcanic rock—venting into Rubble Creek through a series of springs at the base of the Barrier.

The best time to enjoy the visual delight of the three lakes is in August and September when the water is at its highest level and at its most intense blue. Their luxurious colouring is a result of sunlight reflecting off the very fine sediment in the water. Earlier in the summer, the particles washing into the lakes from winter snowmelt are larger, resulting in pallid, cloudier shades.

Just around the corner from the "6 km" viewpoint, the scene is even more astonishingly beautiful. Barrier Lake lies spread like a table before you. Fish jump in full profile. Without turning your head, you can see white water entering and leaving the small lake at each end. If you look back along the trail, you'll see Cloudburst Mountain framed by the notch at the lake's west end. You'll have a bounce in your step as you walk around Barrier Lake to Lesser Garibaldi Lake because it feels so good to be here. Near the bridge over Taylor Creek, whose waters feed into Lesser Garibaldi, there is an approach to lakeside that anglers will find helpful. The trail rings the lake on the hillside above but offers little other access.

Past the lake, the trail enters the forest once more, dividing again just before the "8 km" sign. The trail to the left is one of several that lead to the Taylor Meadows campground. You are now cloistered among the evergreens, 15 minutes from Garibaldi Lake. This is to prepare you for the screamingly grand views that await at the big lake. From the bridge over Parnasus Creek, you may see other hikers taking in the view from a bridge over the outflow creek from Garibaldi Lake, framed in a cleft of red volcanic rock and evergreens with the white of the glaciers behind them. By this time, you may be wondering whether your nervous system can handle the volume of visual stimuli being fed to your brain.

Cross the bridge and walk (or wade) around to the Garibaldi Lake campground, which overflows on weekends between May and October with outdoor buffs drawn from the Lower Mainland, Europe and Australasia. There are 50 campsites scattered on the hillside above the lake. Some of them have wooden platforms on which to pitch a tent, helpful when the ground is wet. You are allowed a stay of up to 14 days and at present, the fee per night is $10. There are four covered shelters for day use, with picnic tables situated both inside and in front of them.

Just offshore are the Battleship Islands, a string of small, rocky outcroppings. There are several benches along the lakeside trail and on the largest island. A sign on the lakeside trail lets you know that you've reached the "9 km, Elev. 1470 m" mark. When lake levels are at their highest, sections of the boardwalk leading out to the islands double as rafts from which you can swim, fish or just stretch out and relax.

> ## BLACK TUSK

Black Tusk is the magnet that has been attracting attention since the first mountaineers arrived to explore it in 1912. To reach this arresting pinnacle, follow the trail from Garibaldi Lake as it climbs through the forest above the lake, meeting up with the trail from Taylor Meadows after a 30-minute walk. Along the way, it passes a series of small ponds dotting the mountainside. The views from the open meadows around these ponds change constantly as you gain altitude. Below you, Garibaldi Lake unfolds, revealing the full extent of its long, broad contour.

At this point, you have a choice of several trails: you may climb to the Black Tusk, 3 km (1.9 mi.) above, or head to Helm Lake and Panorama Ridge, closer by. The Helm Lake Trail leads north to Cheakamus Lake, 14 km (8.7 mi.) distant, through a distinctly volcanic zone. Even if you are not prepared to go the distance, you can still visit the area a little over a mile away around the lake and glacier. From Panorama Ridge, 3 km (1.9 mi.) farther along, you get unlimited views around Garibaldi Lake, with features that were hidden at lower altitudes now revealed in detail. To the south, the peaks of Mount Garibaldi rise higher than all others.

The trail to the Tusk begins to climb steadily towards a nearby ridge. Little streams constantly parallel or cross the trail. Even if you find the hike strenuous, it's worth going at least a short distance up the trail to get a view of Garibaldi Lake. In midsummer, the meadows on all sides bloom with blue lupine, red heather, Indian paintbrush and yellow cinquefoil.

If you persist, in an hour you will reach the ridge. Now nothing stands in the way of views of the Black Tusk's south face. The last

Black Tusk from Whistler Mountain

of the alpine firs fade away, and a barren expanse of degenerating granite takes over. A dusty trail leads across the flats and up to the Tusk, whose peak is still another hour away. The going isn't easy, and it's not for novices. It's prudent to wear a helmet when making the final ascent, as the terrain is unstable. On top your reward is being able to see every place from which you've ever viewed the Tusk, and then some.

> 49

CHEAKAMUS LAKE

Garibaldi Park

· · · · ·

> DISTANCE: 123 km (76 mi.) north of Vancouver in Garibaldi Park

> ACTIVITIES: Camping, cross-country skiing, fishing, hiking, mountain biking, paddling, picnicking, snowshoeing, viewpoints, walking

> ACCESS: To make your way to the Cheakamus Lake trailhead parking lot, follow Cheakamus Lake Road, which begins across from Whistler's Function Junction industrial neighbourhood, 45 km (27.9 mi.) north of Squamish. The trailhead lies some 8 km (5 mi.) east of Highway 99 along this well-marked road. *Note:* Dogs are not allowed in Garibaldi Park.

GLACIER-FED CHEAKAMUS LAKE lies within the shadow of Whistler Mountain (1 220 m/4,000 ft.) to the north. In winter, the big lake freezes solid, and getting to the trailhead in Garibaldi Provincial Park, let alone the lake, is a challenge. In summer, this is one of the most rewarding destinations in Whistler.

The trail to Cheakamus Lake does not rank as a true hike; most of its 3.5-km (2.2-mi.) distance is over level terrain. Its length, however, qualifies it as an energetic walk, jog or cucle. This is one of only two trails in Garibaldi Park open to mountain bikers. The route to the lake takes slightly more than 1 hour on foot and from there, it's another hour along the shore to the trail's terminus at the mouth of Singing Creek. Campsites are located at the near end of the lake—he outflow point for the Cheakamus River—and at the end of the trail. Park rangers patrol the trail during the busy season, answering questions and checking to make sure there are no dogs.

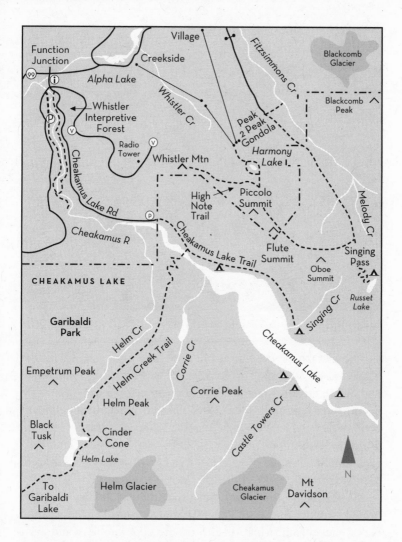

A rich, resinous smell of balsam hangs in the air at this entrance to Garibaldi Park. Visitors must bend down to clear the low-hanging boughs of a sturdy western red cedar as they enter the dimly lit grove. During one especially snowy winter in the late 1990s, one of the mature amabilis firs near the park boundary snapped, and it now bars the route as effectively as a wall. It's a bit of a scramble to get around it, particularly if you're cycling or portaging a canoe or a kayak.

Old-growth forest along Cheakamus Lake Trail

The first part of the trail is hilly and hugs a steep embankment above noisy Cheakamus River below. The trail is well established and slightly spongy underfoot. Walkers can set their own pace. Kids can run on ahead and still be seen and heard among the tall trees. A cool wind often blows down off the glaciated peaks, and the sunlight is diffused as it filters through the large overhead branches. Dress accordingly. Moss grows in a dozen shades of green on all sides of the tree trunks.

A bridge spans the Cheakamus River near its outflow from the lake. The wood-and-steel structure provides hikers access to the Helm Creek Trail, which begins on the opposite bank and eventually leads to Garibaldi Lake. The Helm Creek Trail, an all-day 12-km (7.5-mi.) excursion to a small lake on the slope high above Cheakamus Lake, is suitable for summer and early fall hiking.

As the trail nears Cheakamus Lake, it brings you closer to the emerald-coloured Cheakamus River, which broadens and becomes even noisier where it leaves the lake. Soon after you sight the lake, several rough campsites appear. Just beyond the first campsites is a cathedral-like grove of trees that for many visitors will crown the journey. The scale of the rain forest at Cheakamus is imposing. There is a hush here found only at exalted elevations.

> ## SINGING CREEK

Trees shelter two-thirds of the trail to Singing Creek's 3.5-km (2-mi.) distance, but the woods occasionally open up into thickets of black-berry and alder where small creeks flow down from the ridge of Whistler Mountain. In places, the trail rises above the lake. Here, semi-arid banks of sand and stone sprout clumps of alpine flowers, small but brilliantly coloured patches of orange paintbrush, wild tiger lily, white valerian and blue lupine that climb up the hillside in summer.

In late spring, the ground is still damp in many places and the ground cover is just beginning to show itself. Lush ferns thickly carpet the slopes above the lake, vividly green in the forest twilight. At several places along the way to Singing Creek, rockslides have cut paths down from the southern ridge of Whistler Mountain. In places, the trail is so overgrown with nettles that you will want to be wearing long pants for protection. The nettles also hold the dew or raindrops; brushing past them can quickly soak a pair of jeans.

The farther along the trail you go, the more the views to the east and west open up. Brandywine Mountain is northwest in the distance, the Overlord group (hidden by forest for the most part) behind you to the east, the McBride Range to the southeast. Whis-tler Mountain is to the north and west, very evident as a long ridge above the trail. The Cheakamus Glacier covers the near side of the mountains at the southwestern end of the lake. A cool wind is always blowing down off the slopes.

Sounds of rushing water in Singing Creek and wind in the tree boughs harmonize with the deep bass notes emanating from Castle Towers Creek on the far shore. Several good campsites are cleared here beside a small beach. There are few access points to the lake, so the one at Singing Creek is a welcome opening. Families of mer-ganser ducks share the lakeside with visitors. Because Cheakamus Lake is fed by numerous creeks that originate in the surrounding glaciers and snow fields, the water is chilly year round. Don't expect to do more than give your feet a refreshing soak to revitalize them for the return trip.

50

BROHM LAKE, WHISTLER
AND SHADOW LAKE
INTERPRETIVE FORESTS

. . . . .

> DISTANCE: 78 to 140 km (48 to 87 mi.) north of Vancouver

> ACTIVITIES: Cycling, dog walking, nature observation, picnicking, swimming, viewpoints, walking

> ACCESS: The Brohm Lake Interpretive Forest is located 14 km (8.7 mi.) north of downtown Squamish on the west side of Highway 99. The Whistler Interpretive Forest lies beside Cheakamus Lake Road east of Highway 99 at Whistler's Function Junction intersection, 44 km (27.3 mi.) north of Squamish. The road is initially paved, then turns to gravel. A detailed map is displayed at the blue information kiosk on the north side of the Cheakamus Lake Road, near the intersection with Highway 99.

Shadow Lake Interpretive Forest lies 10 km (6.2 mi.) north of Whistler beside the BC Rail Green River Crossing. To reach the lookout, turn west off Highway 99 onto the Soo River Forest Road just south of the BC Rail crossing. Alternatively, trails to the lake and lookout lead off from the crossing, where there is ample parking.

> **BROHM LAKE INTERPRETIVE FOREST**
Many travellers have stopped at Brohm Lake to swim and on occasion walk the rough trail that encircles it. They may be surprised to discover an extensive network of trails running through the forest to the south and west of the lake as well. One of the reasons these

MacLaurin's Crossing, Whistler Interpretive Forest

trails often escape notice is that their best approach is from a gated entrance 1 km (0.6 mi.) south of the lake rather than from the main paved parking area. The trailhead is marked with a large brown Forest Service sign and trail map.

You'll enjoy a walk through the woods here even if you haven't brought a mountain bike. There's probably more ground to cover on foot than you can explore in one visit, which makes the Brohm Lake Interpretive Forest an ideal destination for repeat visits. Although the lake itself is the main magnet, particularly for families in summer, the more remote forest trails have a quiet charm of their own. The sounds of the highway quickly fade away as you begin walking. At several places, the trail divides, offering visitors a choice of

Brohm Lake Interpretive Forest

directions. For example, the High Trail leads north to Brohm Lake, while the Cheakamus Loop Trail leads west onto a ridge.

Within an hour's walk from the parking lot, starting on Alder Trail and then branching onto the Cheakamus Loop trails, you're rewarded with two viewpoints that look across Paradise Valley to the glacier-clad Tantalus Range. Staircases assist visitors up the steepest stretches. Here, next to a covered lookout shelter, is one of the best picnic spots. The Cheakamus River flows past far below, and the Squamish waterfront is visible in the distance. All of the peaks in the Tantalus Range—including Mount Tantalus itself—stand revealed in their glory.

> **WHISTLER INTERPRETIVE FOREST**

Whistler forester Don MacLaurin spearheaded the Whistler Interpretive Forest's development. It's a joint project of the B.C. Ministry of Forests and the Resort Municipality of Whistler as well as other players from both government and industry. Various aspects of a managed second-growth forest are explained at pullouts along the logging roads that run through the forest on both the east and west sides of the Cheakamus River.

The Whistler Interpretive Forest's major recreational feature is the extensive network of narrow trails, especially suited to mountain biking, that crisscross both the Eastside Main and Westside Main roads. The trails have garnered a reputation as some of the best-built and, therefore, most enjoyable rides in Whistler. In addition, there are signs that indicate time, distance and elevation gain for biking.

Several kilometrres upstream from the entrance to the forest, the MacLaurin's Crossing suspension bridge links the trails on both sides of the Cheakamus. Paired with a BC Parks bridge farther upstream in Garibaldi Park near Cheakamus Lake (see previous chapter), the two invite adventuring along both sides of the river.

A good place to begin is the Riverside Trail, which runs along the east side of the Cheakamus. It's easy to find and, aside from several short, steep stretches, suited to all ability levels, whether you're exploring on foot or by bike.

> ## SHADOW LAKE INTERPRETIVE FOREST

An easier approach to water can be found at Shadow Lake. As Highway 99 leads north of Whistler towards Pemberton, it passes through the Shadow Lake Interpretive Forest. Signs point to a sheltered wooden lookout above the lake. Diminutive Shadow Lake lies nestled below beside the Soo River. A series of loop trails runs through the forest and to the viewpoint.

Unlike the hard-packed trails beside the Cheakamus River, these ones are softened by a thick covering of leaves and evergreen needles. Although they don't run for nearly the distance of those in the Brohm Lake or Whistler interpretive forests, the route around Shadow Lake offers enhanced rewards. For one thing, the views of surrounding peaks, including Wedge Mountain and the sunbaked bluffs above the Soo River, are superior. Lush displays of wildflowers, such as Pacific bleeding heart and trailing yellow violet, carpet the forest floor in a wetland zone between the lake and the river. Follow the section of trail that leads through a stand of old-growth fir and cedar out onto a sandbank where tall black cottonwood trees tower above the Soo. This is a sunny spot to enjoy a picnic.

51

WHISTLER RESORT PARKS &

. . . . .

> **DISTANCE:** 115 km (71.4 mi.) north of Vancouver

> **ACTIVITIES:** Cycling, dog walking, in-line skating, nature obser-
vation, paddling, picnicking, playgrounds, skateboarding, snow
sports, swimming, viewpoints, walking

> **ACCESS:** Follow Highway 99 north to Whistler, a 2-hour drive.

> **VALLEY TRAIL**

If there's one facet of Whistler that garners as much praise from visitors as do the mountains, it's the Valley Trail. Whistler's neighbourhoods are knit together by an extensive network of pathways that
together comprise this 35-km (22-mi.) trail system. For recreational-
ists and commuters alike, when it comes to getting around Whistler,
the Valley Trail functions as an alternative to busy Highway 99.

Almost entirely paved, the Valley Trail passes beside seven parks,
five lakes, a river and several creeks. In summer, it's a cycling and
in-line skate path as well as a walkway; in winter, it's primarily a
cross-country ski trail, though with a good pair of snow boots you
can tramp along quite comfortably. Whistler Village sits at its hub.
The beauty of the Valley Trail is that you can get onto it easily from
almost anywhere in Whistler. Each year it gets longer, keeping pace
with the resort's growth. It's difficult to say where the trail begins
and ends; most of it forms a loop.

Before you start out on the Valley Trail, decide whether you are
going to do the entire loop or make one of the parks or lakes your
destination. On foot, it takes 3 to 4 hours to complete the loop; by
bike, half that or less.

Whistler Village

> ## WHISTLER'S MUNICIPAL PARKS

As befits a town that annually welcomes millions of visitors, a neck-lace of parks adorns Whistler Valley. Many of these are located beside lakes where you'll find picnic tables, beaches, boat rentals and splendid viewpoints. Several of the parks, such as Alpha Lake and Meadow, feature play areas specifically designed for younger children. Two adjacent parks, Fitzsimmons and Rebagliati are dedi-cated to skateboarding and dirt-jump riding, respectively.

As Highway 99 winds between Creekside and Whistler Village, a distance of about 4 km (2.5 mi.), it passes Wayside and Lakeside parks. Both are situated on the west side of the highway, and their entrances are well marked. Lakeside Park is an open area on the

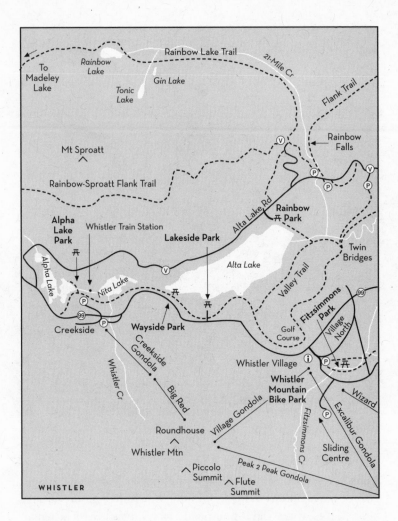

southeast side of Alta Lake. A lawn runs down to the beach, where there are six well-spaced picnic tables, most with their own barbecues, and two L-shaped docks. There is no lifeguard, and dogs are not allowed on the beach. In summer, you may rent boats and windsurfers here; guided tours of the lake and the colourfully named River of Golden Dreams nearby (see below) can also be arranged.

Wayside Park is smaller than Lakeside. Four picnic tables, each with its own barbecue, sit on a sloped hillside overlooking the south

The map contains the following labels:

To Madeley Lake
Rainbow Lake
Rainbow Lake Trail
21-Mile Cr
Gin Lake
Tonic Lake
Flank Trail
Mt Sproatt
Rainbow Falls
Rainbow-Sproatt Flank Trail
Alta Lake Rd
Rainbow Park
Alpha Lake Park
Whistler Train Station
Lakeside Park
Twin Bridges
Alpha Lake
Alta Lake
Nita Lake
Valley Trail
Fitzsimmons Park
Creekside
Wayside Park
Golf Course
Village North
Creekside Gondola
Whistler Village
Whistler Mountain Bike Park
Wizard
Whistler Cr
Big Red
Village Gondola
Fitzsimmons Cr
Excalibur Gondola
Roundhouse
Whistler Mtn
Sliding Centre
Piccolo Summit
Peak 2 Peak Gondola
Flute Summit
WHISTLER

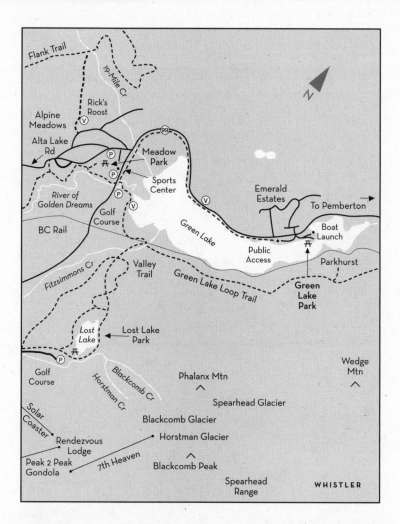

Flank Trail

19 Mile Cr

Rick's
Roost

Alpine
Meadows Ⓥ

Alta Lake
Rd

99

Ⓟ

Meadow
Park

Sports
Center

Ⓟ

Ⓟ

River of
Golden Dreams

Golf
Course Ⓥ

BC Rail

Green Lake

Emerald
Estates

To Pemberton

Boat
Launch

Public
Access

Parkhurst

Fitzsimmons Cr

Valley
Trail

Green Lake Loop Trail

Green
Lake
Park

Lost
Lake

Lost Lake
Park

Ⓟ

Golf
Course

Blackcomb Cr

Horstman Cr

Phalanx Mtn
⌃

Spearhead Glacier

Wedge
Mtn
⌃

Solar
Coaster

Blackcomb Glacier

Horstman Glacier

Rendezvous
Lodge

Peak 2 Peak
Gondola

7th Heaven

Blackcomb Peak
⌃

Spearhead
Range

WHISTLER

N

end of Alta Lake. There is a modest beach with an open lawn above for sunbathing. A dock is moored just far enough offshore to make swimmers appreciate reaching it after a plunge into the cold waters of Alta Lake.

Two of the largest parks, Rainbow and Meadow, are located on the west side of the valley. To reach them by car, travel along Alta Lake Road from its intersection with Highway 99 either across from the Bayshores neighbourhood in south Whistler or from the Alpine

Lost Lake Park, Whistler

Meadows neighbourhood north of the village. Rainbow Park, at the northwest end of Alta Lake, stands on the site of Whistler's first lodge, which was built here in 1914. This location still commands the finest viewpoint in the valley, hands down. A sandy beach, a grassy playing field, an array of picnic tables, two floating docks and a quaint collection of heritage log cabins make this a spot where you can easily spend an entire summer's day enjoying Whistler.

Meadow Park, in Whistler's Alpine Meadows neighbourhood, is linked to Rainbow Park by both the Valley Trail and the River of Golden Dreams, which flows north between Alta and Green lakes. Meadow has many of the same amenities as Rainbow, with the additional treat of a children's water park, but is often far less crowded. The municipal swimming pool and enclosed ice rink are situated nearby. The only drawback to swimming outdoors at Meadow Park is that there is no beach. Bathers here simply dive into the River of Golden Dreams and haul out onto the riverbank. Because the water is cold and deep, this is not a suitable place for young children to swim.

Lost Lake hasn't gone missing in years. Still, it is the most remote of Whistler's parks. Tucked on the benchland beside the Chateau Whistler golf course, it is most easily approached via the section of the Valley Trail that begins at the well-marked Lost Lake parking lot on Blackcomb Way, across from the municipal offices. Near its outset, the trail passes beside the Fitzsimmons skatepark. Farther along, a bridge crosses Fitzsimmons Creek and passes the log cabin that in winter houses the cross-country ticket office and concession stand

> **THE INSIDE TRACK**
· · · · · · · · ·

BOTH BACKROADS ADVENTURE TOURS (1-604-932-3111; backroads whistler.com) and Whistler Eco Tours (1-604-935-4400; whistler ecotours.com) offer guided and indepen-dent canoe and kayak trips on the River of Golden Dreams with the option of a pedal ride back.

and in summer is a hub for cycling. Free maps of the Lost Lake trail system are available from Cross Country Connection (1-604-905-0071; crosscountryconnection.ca) where you can also rent bikes in summer, as well as get repairs and advice. A detailed bike trail map for Whistler is published by TerraPro and is available from most bike shops and book stores in Whistler. Another good source is the Resort Municipality of Whistler's Web site. Visit www.whistler.ca and click on the bike icon.

A network of gravel and paved trails trace the slopes around Lost Lake. Take your pick, depending on your fitness and skill level. This applies equally to those exploring in summer on foot or by bicycle and those adventuring in winter on cross-country skis or snowshoes. Not all the trails lead directly to Lost Lake—stay right at all points for the quickest approach to the beach. Centennial, Old Mill Road and Panorama are the major trails, but a warren of narrower tracks also crosshatches this area, including a forest nature walk and the multi-use Tin Pants Trail, a family favourite.

A sandy beach and grassy picnic area are located at Lost Lake's south end. From here, a trail circles the lake. A floating dock juts out from the shoreline at the lake's midpoint; an access trail branches off the main loop to reach it. This more remote location offers bathers a quieter environment from which to enjoy splendid views of Blackcomb. Discreet clothing-optional sunbathing has been a hallmark of this part of the lake since Whistler's hippie days.

From June through September, Whistler Transit operates a free shuttle bus service from Gondola Transit Exchange (stop #3) and the Blackcomb Park and Ride Lot to Lost Lake. *Note:* There is no parking at Lost Lake.

> ## RIVER OF GOLDEN DREAMS

Whistler is located at the summit of a pass. Balanced here on the fulcrum between north and south is Alta Lake, which, until the 1960s, was the name by which the town of Whistler was known. Alta Lake drains into Nita Lake from its south end and into Green Lake from its north. The storybook-titled River of Golden Dreams (more properly named Alta Creek) links Alta with Green Lake and provides paddlers with a perspective on the valley that can only be appreciated from a canoe or kayak. All signs of habitation vanish behind riverbanks thick with low-lying willows. The river's channel is hidden by tall stands of reeds but is not difficult to locate. If you have your own canoe or kayak, the beach at nearby Rainbow Park is the most convenient place to put in. If you're renting, launch at Lakeside or Wayside Park (see above).

Just east of the Valley Trail bridge across the river that provides access to and from Rainbow Park, paddlers will encounter a small concrete weir. This is the only man-made obstacle on the River of Golden Dreams. A portage is required, albeit only a few steps. River shoes come in handy. Beyond here, the river's course is squeezed between railway tracks on the west and high banks on the east. At low-water times, it may be necessary to help your canoe or kayak across short sections of the creekbed along this stretch.

Once the river begins to oxbow its way towards Green Lake, the best views of the trip begin to open up before you. Yellow finches swoop past, and muskrats swim in and out of their riverbank burrows. Allow an easy hour to make the journey from Alta Lake to the well-marked pullout beside a bridge that carries Highway 99 traffic.

If the river current allows (remembering that you must paddle against it to return to the pullout), complete the journey to Green Lake. Fine examples of stately Sitka spruce and black cottonwood trees line the riverbank along this final stage of the journey. A telephone is mounted at the parking lot next to the pullout. Call a taxi—numbers are posted by the phone—to arrange transport back to Rainbow Park, or make other plans, such as leaving bikes at the pullout so that you can ride back to Rainbow Park on the Valley Trail to retrieve your vehicle—and then your boat. Although this might seem complicated, it's actually quite straightforward. Return transportation for those who rent canoes or kayaks on Alta Lake is prearranged.

52

SEA TO SKY TRAIL

. . . . .

> DISTANCE: Between 76 km (47 mi.) and 118 km (73 mi.) north of Vancouver

> ACTIVITIES: Cross-country skiing, dog walking, hiking, mountain biking, picnicking, snowshoeing, viewpoints, walking

> ACCESS: Paradise Valley Road begins 4 km (2.5-mi.) west of Highway 99 via the Squamish Valley Road, 12 km (7.4 mi.) north of downtown Squamish. Paved for much of its 11-km (6.8-mi.) length, Paradise Valley Road links with the Sea to Sky Trail, which leads 5 km (3.1 mi.) through the Cheakamus Canyon to Highway 99.

Brandywine Falls Provincial Park lies 107 km (66.5 mi.) north of Vancouver, 11 km (6.8 mi.) south of Whistler. Cal-Cheak Forest Service Recreation Site lies 4.3 km (2.7 mi) north of Brandywine Falls Park. A "Whistler Bungee" sign marks the turn. The Cheakamus Crossing trailhead lies on the east side of Highway 99 opposite Whistler's Function Junction neighbourhood. Turn east at the stop lights, bear right across the Cheakamus River, and park beside the Jane Lakes/Sea to Sky trail marker.

THE SEA TO SKY Trail project is nothing if not ambitious. Modelled after similar point-to-point trails, such as the Trans Canada Trail, with which it is allied, the 180-km (112-mi.) non-motorized, multi-use route is a bold endeavour that's dear to my heart. I've been tracking its progress for two decades, from when the first section opened in the early 1990s to the most recent advances post–2010 Winter Olympics. When finished, the trail will link Horseshoe Bay with Lillooet. For the moment, managers with the Squamish-Lillooet Regional District—the government body responsible for

Cheakamus Canyon

Brandywine Falls

coordinating construction—are focusing their efforts on complet-
ing the links between Squamish and Whistler. A detailed description of the route would fill a book, but here are two of my favourite
sections. For an overview of the project thus far, watch the video at
www.seatoskytrail.ca, where updates and information are also posted.

> **CHEAKAMUS CANYON**

From Paradise to Starvation sounds like a pot-boiler of a journey. It
certainly was when construction of the Pacific Great Eastern Railway began almost a century ago north of Squamish. Even today,
there's a wild flourish of adventure to be had while retracing the
well-worn route that leads through the Cheakamus Canyon from
Paradise Valley to Starvation Lake. This 5-km (3.1-mi.) section serves
as one of the most scenic links in the Sea to Sky Trail. (For those
with a yen to experience the narrowest confines of the Cheakamus
Canyon from the comfort of a front-row seat, Rocky Mountaineer's
tourist train that runs daily on its "Sea to Sky Climb" route between

North Vancouver and Whistler during the summer is the ultimate way to go.)

No matter which manner you choose to explore the canyon, the experience will leave you breathless, particularly between May and early July while the spring runoff in the Cheakamus River is in full bore. The river is fed by snowmelt that collects in Cheakamus Lake in Garibaldi Provincial Park (see chapter 49) and is further abetted by numerous creeks and rivers as it races to meet the ocean at Squamish. Where the sheer walls of the canyon channel the clear green-hued water into a white froth, the river roars.

The current pathway through the canyon is a remnant of the road built in 1913 to facilitate construction of the railway. Should you wish to visit the Cheakamus Canyon on foot or by mountain bike, keep several factors in mind. With the exception of toddlers toted on their parents' backs, children will not find this portion of the Sea to Sky Trail friendly, particularly from the north end of Paradise Valley, where a short, steep stretch leads uphill atop granite boulders shaped like giant molars. From there, allow 30 minutes to reach gem-like Starvation Lake set on a secluded plateau between Highway 99 and the canyon. If this is as far as you wish to go, follow a rough road just south of the lake downhill to the train tracks. From that viewpoint, water in the Cheakamus can be witnessed repeatedly transforming between tranquillity and turbulence where the river falls through a series of short drops and swirls among boulders.

. As the Sea to Sky Trail climbs steadily uphill beyond the lake, the most dramatic scenery occurs within a 30-minute hike, including one stunning clearing where the massive Tantalus Range peaks display their best faces. Further on lies a bolted cliff crossing, definitely not for the squeamish but sturdy enough to support a steady stream of hundreds of cyclists in the Cheakamus Challenge mountain bike race held each September. Beyond there, the trail rises and curves as views open of the canyon's north end and Highway 99. This is a good point to turn back. Beyond, the trail climbs and falls until it reaches the highway with not much to recommend along the way, particularly on foot. Enjoy the views on the way south, which somehow always look remarkably different from the way they did on your way into the canyon.

One of the trail's most superbly built sections links Brandywine Falls Provincial Park with Whistler's Cheakamus Crossing neighbourhood, a distance of 11 km (6.8 mi.), where it then connects with the Valley Trail, Whistler's paved 35-km (20.2-mi.) portion of the Sea to Sky Trail (see previous chapter). If you're travelling by car, I suggest parking at either Brandywine Falls Provincial Park or the Cal-Cheak Forest Service Recreation Site, rather than beginning in Whistler. Take time to view the falls or cross a suspension bridge above spirited Callaghan Creek—the sight of water in motion is impelling.

If you begin at Brandywine Falls, cross the wooden bridge over Brandywine Creek. The well-marked, 4-km (2.5-mi.) trail leads north through open pine forest and passes a necklace of pocket lakes. By bike, this is a scenic cruiser route. Carefully cross the railway tracks at the whistle stop of McGuire. The Cal-Cheak Forest Service Recreation Site lies a short distance farther north via a bouncy suspension bridge. In winter, snowshoers and cross-country skiers alike will also enjoy this approach. The trail's one challenging section appears at the beginning, where it climbs steadily for a short distance above Brandywine Creek before levelling off and following a BC Hydro right-of-way. Be cautious when making the descent down this steep, slippery section on your return to Brandywine, particularly on skis. Trail markers placed high up on the trunks of trees help snow trekkers find their way. In winter, when parking at Brandywine Falls or Cal-Cheak may be limited by snow, a better approach to link up with this section of trail would be to drive east of Highway 99 at the Brandywine Forest Service Road turnoff, about 3.5 km (2.2 mi.) north of Brandywine Falls Park.

The Resort Municipality of Whistler's trail-building crew saved their best efforts for the 7-km (4.3-mi.) connection between Cal-Cheak and Whistler. Contoured with the terrain, the 1.5-m-wide (4.9 ft.) crushed-gravel route is a flagship trail and makes for a rollicking ramble as it winds back and forth through the woods, past rivers, lakes and crumbling basalt rock formations. It's the opposite-end bracket of the Whistler Mountain Bike Park, which likes to think of itself as the biggest, gnarliest, baddest park in the world. The Sea to Sky Trail is a constant reminder that time spent enjoying the outdoors will not be deducted from our lives.

INDEX

· · · · ·